Reading Essays

Reading Essays

An Invitation

G. Douglas Atkins

The University of Georgia Press *Athens & London*

© 2008 by the University of Georgia Press
Athens, Georgia 30602
All rights reserved
Set in 11/14 Adobe Garamond by BookComp
Printed and bound by Thomson-Shore
The paper in this book meets the guidelines for
permanence and durability of the Committee on
Production Guidelines for Book Longevity of the
Council on Library Resources.

Printed in the United States of America
12   11   10   09   08   C   5   4   3   2   1
12   11   10   09   08   P   5   4   3   2   1

Library of Congress Cataloging-in-Publication Data
Atkins, G. Douglas (George Douglas), 1943–
Reading essays : an invitation / G. Douglas Atkins.
        p. cm.
Includes bibliographical references and index.
ISBN-13: 978-0-8203-2826-3 (hardcover : alk. paper)
ISBN-10: 0-8203-2826-x (hardcover : alk. paper)
ISBN-13: 978-0-8203-3030-3 (pbk. : alk. paper)
ISBN-10: 0-8203-3030-2 (pbk. : alk. paper)
1. College readers.   2. English language—Rhetoric.
3. Report writing.   I. Title.
PE1417.A77 2008
808'.0427—dc22   2007027795

British Library Cataloging-in-Publication Data available

for Rebecca

CONTENTS

PREFACE

FOR MORE THAN FIFTY YEARS, poetry, fiction, and drama have been read closely. And although the age of literary exegesis seems to have passed, the resulting industry established strong factories that have not and probably will not collapse but have, instead, morphed into new cubicles of analysis. The heyday of so-called critical readings was also, as it happens, the lowest point in the essay's four-hundred-year history. Joseph Wood Krutch declared "No Essays, Please" in 1951 just as the exegetical industry was approaching its most productive period with its most impressive and lasting contributions to our understanding of the major genres, the works comprising them, and the incumbent questions of how to read. The essay seemed not to need close attention, analysis, or helpful commentary.

In the past twenty years, roughly, the essay has shown its resiliency and asserted its birthright and in the process has made clear how premature were the cries of its imminent demise. In fact the essay is now in the midst of something of a renaissance, writers and readers alike turning to it for the opportunities and rewards often and lamentably unavailable in poetry, fiction, and drama. Arguably, the form has never been so popular—so important, indeed, that ours has been termed "the age of the essay." Hyperbole aside, college and university curricula and the textbooks that support them, as well as academic journals, have begun to accept, or declare, the essay—or at least "nonfiction"—as the "fourth genre." (I dislike both "nonfiction"—for its invidiousness—and "creative nonfiction"—for, among other faults, its inelegance.)

Nothing has yet emerged to parallel such determinative texts as the now-legendary *Understanding Poetry* and *Understanding Fiction*, nor have teachers and commentators yet been swift to offer "readings" of individual essays, thus to assist students and faculty alike in the burgeoning courses in the essay. In the following pages, I am unabashedly old-fashioned, although decades of work in theory stand behind these efforts, both in returning to the traditional, personal, and familiar essay and in offering sustained *readings* of over two dozen instances of the essayist's art—the *impure art*.

The essay's inherent value and importance lie not least in its focus on and identification with the particular, the local, and the rooted—old-fashioned values perhaps, but also perennial ones now beginning to appear revitalized. In other words, the essay's domain is the familiar (as well as the personal, in some way), and significantly the familiar is one of the two major sorts of essay, the other being the personal. What may not be so well recognized is that this attention and dedication to the particular, the local, and the rooted—in short, the familiar—constitutes but half the story. Equally important is the essay's own rooting, at the same time, in meaning, the timeless, the universal. When, in a quite different context, the American poet and critic Allen Tate referred to "local universality," he pointed to the pattern whereby and wherein the universal emerges in, through, and by means of the local. Hilaire Belloc's magnificent essay "The Mowing of a Field" is a strikingly successful instance of this pattern, which T. S. Eliot identifies in his essay-poem *Four Quartets* as Incarnation: "The hint half guessed, the gift half understood." Another way of putting the matter: the revealed universal *estranges the familiar*, which is otherness embodied.

The essay is unique as a literary form. Like Roland Barthes, I do not think it a genre (rather, he said, it is a-generic), nor do I consider it quite literature. It is "almost literature" and "almost philosophy," a little of both, although not quite either—not a thoroughgoing thing. More: the essay hangs *between*—between literature and philosophy, creation and fact, fiction and nonfiction, process and product—born of tension, then, and with tension as perhaps its essential characteristic.

Because it has been so little considered, we do not know how to read well this in-between thing. A tradition accompanies the reading of poetry, fiction, and drama, but the essay has none—yet. It presents particular challenges and offers particular rewards, and I hope to make some of those clear in the chapters that follow. I begin with a comment or two on reading in general and the essay in particular, and later I return to the entailed issues in "A Note on Writing the Essay," which offers some introductory advice on writing the essay. I am stiff-necked in believing that reading and writing the essay go together, that, indeed, they should be—and are—inseparable.

The readings I offer—by no means intended to be exemplary—amount to a sort of informal history of the essay in English, and I have arranged them here in more or less chronological order, although with the more recent instances of the form, I have been less concerned with dates of composition or publication and more interested in thematic likeness and difference, more interested in groupings that will spark comparison and analysis. The reader may, then, wish to begin with the more recent essays, turning to historical considerations and the first instances of the form—Dryden, Swift, Pope, Johnson—as she or he becomes interested in the art of, say, E. B. White, Richard Selzer, James Baldwin, Annie Dillard, or Nancy Mairs. (Montaigne and Bacon, the first essayists, I treat in a sort of second introductory or background chapter, and in so doing I do not so much offer readings as illustrate beginnings by means of these essayists and their crucial *essais*.) Because I did not intend a historical survey, I have committed major omissions: Addison, for one, essayist of the famous *Tatler* and *Spectator* papers in the early eighteenth century, although I take him up briefly in "A Note on Writing the Essay." Frankly, I chose essayists that I like especially and examples of their work that I have tried and tested in the university classroom, with both graduates and undergraduates, over the past twenty years or so. Something remains to be gained by reading through these chapters in the order I have chosen; all that I can vouchsafe, though, is that that order is not arbitrary, while admitting that it is also not necessary. There may be no "thesis," or progress, but at the same time there is more than simple addition. Like so much else with the essay, the order depends on both the object and the subject. I take some comfort in believing that if I have not chosen your favorite or two or three, you will, after reading these readings, return there with renewed appreciation and deeper understanding, able, in any case, to apply whatever discoveries you have made here to other instances of this venerable and "glorious" form (*Antioch Review*).

The readings herein engage in a conversation with one another—to say so, however, does not excuse an occasional repetition. Some readings are more technical than others, having to do with the essay itself: its form, its history, its meaning and significance. I am, in other words, concerned with context as well as text. I have sought not to enforce any commonalty of theme, focus, or even length. I have, however, been concerned to treat, in the main, essays that are themselves shortish: Thoreau's "Walking" is the longest here considered at some thirty pages; Bacon's, at the other extreme, is little more than a single page. Most of the essays read are readily available, although widely scattered. I could wish for an accompanying "reader" of the essays I have chosen, a single source to which the reader might turn.

Throughout I have, perforce, kept the "common reader" in mind, for the *amateur*, the layperson, is the one for whom essayists characteristically write. Still, I have sought to maintain a high "level of discourse," and indeed much that emerges from the assembled readings of essays is new. Both the teacher and the student, then, could be well served by these *essais*, an impure combination of the introductory and, I reckon, the revelatory. Although I envision these readings as a possible supplement in introductory and advanced courses in composition and in the essay, the latter an increasingly but belatedly popular and prominent feature of college and university curricula, I have written not just for a college audience; I hope very much that the "common reader" still exists and will find much of interest and value here.

My efforts, these *essais*, thus reflect in all sorts of ways the impurity of the form they are meant to celebrate.

ACKNOWLEDGMENTS

I OWE MOST, NATURALLY, to the "glorious" form that is my subject, and to their makers, the remarkable artists who have crafted essays with love since Montaigne showed them how, over four hundred years ago. At the same time, I wish to acknowledge the hundreds of students, graduate and undergraduate, to whom I have introduced the essay during the past twenty years—students nearly all of whom felt invited in and accepted that invitation. In particular I should like to express my gratitude to students who have taught me much and to critics, writers, and friends from whom I have taken more than is conscionable; these include, but are not limited to, Lydia Fakundiny, Scott Russell Sanders, Lynn Worsham, Jasper Neel, Geoffrey Hartman, Tod Marshall, Randy D. Gordon, Andrew C. West, Simone Sessolo, Nedra Rogers, Samuel Alexandr Schneider, Cara McConnell, Dan Martin, Steven Faulkner, Melissa Bagley, Carol Estes, James Farnen, Kirsten Bosnak, Annie McEnroe, Jackie McClenny, Jen Humphrey, and Chris Arthur. I cannot but single out the extraordinary help Lydia Fakundiny provided as "first reader" for the University of Georgia Press (I feel like Eliot acknowledging his debt to Pound, without, of course, imagining myself on either of their levels). Also, Nicholas Taylor, for his copyediting, and Jennifer Reichlin. And once more, Nancy Grayson, associate director and editor-in-chief of the press, was exemplary—supportive, encouraging, critical—in handling this project, from an inchoate notion to a proposal to this book. None of these persons, or any others, bears any responsibilities for errors, omissions, or remaining awkwardnesses. I thank the University of Kansas for a sabbatical leave, during which a good deal of the writing was done. Long-standing debts of a different sort remain to my daughter, Leslie Atkins Durham, and to my son, Christopher Douglas Atkins. In recognition and with gratitude and love, I dedicate this *essai* to my wife, Rebecca, who incarnates invitation and welcome.

A NOTE ON TEXTS

FOR THE SAKE OF CONVENIENCE, I have read a number of the essays here in Lydia Fakundiny's *The Art of the Essay* and Phillip Lopate's *The Art of the Personal Essay*, both available and accessible. Other texts I have read in first editions, wherever possible. Full documentation appears in my list of works cited. Given the nature of this *essai*, I have sought to keep scholarly apparatus to an unobtrusive minimum; I have accordingly used in-text, parenthetical documentation, and that as sparingly as possible, and have forsworn an index.

Reading Essays

Then I dare; I will also essay to be.
— Ralph Waldo Emerson, journal

Essaying to Be

On Reading (and Writing) Essays

MICHEL DE MONTAIGNE, reputed father of the essay, wrote at the end of the sixteenth century: "To compose our character is our duty, not to compose books, and to win, not battles and provinces, but order and tranquillity in our conduct. Our great and glorious masterpiece is to live appropriately" ("Of Experience," 3:13; 851). In this supreme venture, the trial, the effort, the *essai*, is enabled by, as it is embodied in, the form to which he gave a name: "The doing, the writing itself, is both a path *to* knowing and a path *of* knowing; as I write, I am 'forming my life,'" and *that*, he concluded, "is the greatest task of all" ("Of the Resemblance of Children to Fathers," 2:37; 596; and Fakundiny, *The Art of the Essay* 678). "Self-fashioning" some have called this process, especially as the Renaissance engaged in it. Writing early in the seventeenth century, perhaps the second to do so in English, the young Sir William Cornwallis offered his essays as "an apprenticeship in self-knowledge" (Fakundiny, *The Art of the Essay* 13). Mine, wrote Montaigne in "Of Practice," "is not my teaching, but my study; it is not a lesson for others, but for me" (2:6; 272). What I write, added he, "is not my deeds . . . ; it is myself, it is my essence" (274). And yet in this essay, an apologia for the form he was virtually creating out of whole cloth, Montaigne acknowledges the usefulness of the *essays* for others. He even calls "the other sciences . . . incomparably less useful" (273), reflecting tension, which comes as close as any term to defining this elusive, protean, venerable, and, according to the *Antioch Review*, "glorious" thing.

The essay has not always and everywhere focused on the self and its explorations—"home-cosmography," I have called it elsewhere, borrowing from the seventeenth-century poet Sir William Habington, cited by Thoreau in *Walden*. Perhaps the greatest of twentieth-century American essayists, E. B. White, acknowledged—with some apparent mischievousness—that "some people find the essay the last resort of the egoist, a much too self-conscious and self-serving form for their taste"; "only a person who is congenitally self-centered has the effrontery and the stamina to write essays," he also wrote (viii). Another successful essayist, Phillip Lopate, has more recently admitted that a "stench of ego" accompanies the essay, marking its very being (xxxii). But not long after Montaigne penned his *essays*, first as brief excursions in 1580 and then as developed representations of his "cogitations" over the following two decades, the estimable English scientist, philosopher, and political figure Sir Francis Bacon wrote *The Essayes or Counsels, Civill and Morall*, the very title of which dramatizes a significant difference from Montaigne, whose term he nevertheless borrowed. They appeared first in 1597 as twelve pithy, often gnomic pronouncements on familiar topics. Bacon kept revising them over the next couple of decades, expanding them just as Montaigne did his. Bacon embraced the didacticism that Montaigne disavowed, drawing on his considerable experience and worldly wisdom for advice and instructing his readers on topics not unlike those that Montaigne treated with totally different motives and in very different tones. Bacon's influence continues today, often in *familiar* essays, whereas Montaigne's enjoys greater popularity as *personal* essays. The difference is neither precious nor sophistical, although it is subtle. Although the personal and the familiar are the two main sorts of essays, essays are, truth to tell, often both familiar and personal, the difference at least nowadays residing mainly in the degree to which a particular instance emphasizes the tiny prepositions that we find in Montaigne and Bacon alike: "on" and "of." If the essay tips toward being *about* a topic—books, say, or solitude—it may be termed "familiar," whereas if it focuses a bit less on the general or universal and more on the character of "the speaking voice," it is likely a "personal" essay. An attempt to distinguish between these sibling subforms reveals the delicacy due in any attempt to describe the essay—I know of hardly anyone reckless enough to attempt to *define* it.

Tension attends the form, marking it in several ways. T. S. Eliot, no mean essayist himself, once said that the middle way is the most difficult to tread and maintain, and the essay is a *via media* creature. That said, I must immediately add that, while balance and poise characterize many if not most essays—Montaigne espoused the "*ondoyant et divers*" that he found in Seneca—the essay shows very little interest in compromise as such. Ideas as such do not so much interest the essay, in which attitude matters much more; and attitude has to do with living, thus with ideas mainly as they are *incarnated*. When I describe the essay as embracing tension, I mean to say that it exists *in-between*.

We may recognize familiar attempts to describe the essay that are themselves marked by such—often unwitting—acknowledgment of this tension, this in-betweenness. Thus we speak of, and often endorse, "process" while having to admit that the essay rejects licentiousness, that it differs radically from mere self-expression, and that, despite its peripatetic proclivities, it reveals artful form. (Struggling with this tension, I have once or twice presumed that an essayist begins without end and design, which he or she discovers *in the writing*, and proceeds to revise from the point of that discovery—a wholly inadequate surmise, this abortive effort evincing the essay's resistance to being pinned down, this "greased pig" [Hoagland 691].) As I indicated above, the essay is "about" something other than and outside the self, which remains the crucible in which experience is tried and tested, and which is thus also (sometimes) its subject. A form of what we niggardly refer to as nonfiction, the essay traffics in fact and tells the truth, yet it seems to feel free to enliven, to shape, to embellish, to make use as necessary of elements of the imaginative and the fictive—thus its inclusion in that rather unfortunate current designation "creative nonfiction." It is, we might say, a product of both nature and culture, whether or not the desperate term "formless form" is quite deserved. Among the many dualisms that the essay inhabits, perhaps bridges, none is more important, I reckon, than that of literature/philosophy.

Montaigne, we feel safe in declaring, is one of the literary masters, yet many philosophers welcome him into their circle, sometimes calling his *Essais* "personal philosophy." It is better to assign his magnificent creations to an in-between spot, what I call a site, for his essays, and those that have followed in his wake, exist somewhere between literature and philosophy: they represent experience while reflecting on it, weighing and evaluating it, attempting to draw out its meaning. (So easy is it to have the former and lack the capacity for the latter, for as T. S. Eliot writes in *The Dry Salvages*, the third of *Four Quartets*, a poem that I believe is also an essay: "We had the experience but missed the meaning, / And approach to the meaning restores the experience / In a different form . . .".) A creature of experience that is (unlike most memoirs) not *merely* the representation or dramatization of that experience nor (unlike most philosophy) the representation of meaning alone, shorn of experience, the essay also reveals its basic indirectness in that it approaches meaning only in, through, and by means of experience, a pattern or structure that defines Incarnation. The situation that I describe creates enormous and largely unexplored opportunities, as well as difficulties, frustrations, and challenges.

First of all, we should estrange the familiar by recognizing that the essay is less an object or a genre than, as I mentioned in passing, a site or locus: "The form is an activity not a fixture" (West 41). The essay thus clears a space, creating opportunity, not least for the self of the writer. To recognize that the essay is a site, rather than an object, not only allows us to approach closer to its heart, but it also renders unmistakable the essay's *inviting* nature. Commentators have often remarked on the form's openness and inclusive ways, but the essay does more: it "admits others." That is, "obfuscating its borders," the essay "opens space for more than just the authorial self, for both writer *and* reader rampage in the text, wrestle to control that which can be found there. The self sacrifices control for the gift of being; the self compromises, acquiesces to the call of the world, of both objects and strangers" (West 42). I once described the essay, borrowing from Cynthia Ozick, as "envisioning the stranger's heart." In part because it pretends to no special authority and forgoes the temptation to "know it all," the essay allows the reader space, space already created for an-other via its penchant for quoting. Thoreau, I think, is the exception that proves the rule. Whether we refer to his essay "Walking" or the collection of essays published as *Walden*, we are not invited in or welcomed but instead made to feel inferior and inadequate, unable, for example, to devote "at least" four hours a day to walking (preferably alone). Prior to averring that "I will not through humility become the devil's attorney" (304), Thoreau writes of *us* that "it is very evident what mean and sneaking lives many of you live" (262). Thoreau reveals what an undergraduate recently labeled a "purity perplex," so insistent is he on rooting out the animal in us. Thoreau is not, like the essayistic character, one among ordinary men and women—a point he literalizes in his famous flight to Walden Pond (although even here tension exists, because he builds but two miles from town and stays for but two years). Instead of showing sympathy for our plight, Thoreau hammers us with his injunctions, his sounds as shrill as those of his reviled "iron horse": portentous, demoralizing, unsettling, and disruptive of nature. For essays that invite and welcome, see E. B. White's, with their characteristic self-deprecation; or, to be specific, see Hilaire Belloc's "The Mowing of a Field," where the essayist literalizes invitation by taking in the swarthy Celt, the stranger not envisioned but actually welcomed and given employ.

Because it is a site rather than an object, the essay also presents hitherto unrealized and untapped opportunities and resources for college and university curricula, particularly in literature and writing. Its basic inviting nature plays here, too. These opportunities revolve around precisely its not being a "verbal icon" or "well-wrought urn" or otherwise sacred object before which the student, especially the beginning student, must cower and even genuflect—and certainly never expect or hope to emulate. Because it is not quite (although very nearly) literature, students rightly feel that they can work on it—and even make one of their own! Because it is not attached to any aura of perfection, of symbolic and thematic depth, of arcane allusiveness, students are not afraid to approach it—to *read* it, to *enjoy* it. Then perhaps they will find themselves moving, thanks to its indirectness and "sneakiness," in, through, and by means of that pleasure to meaning incarnate. It is a marvelous, subtle, beguiling, and wondrous kind of writing.

The essay is also a peaceable form, the "opposite" of "that awful object, 'the article'" (Gass 25). Democratic, respectful and inviting of others, the essay differs, and acquires distinction, by eschewing the militaristic language and strategies of much—indeed, most—academic writing, which desires to overcome opponents, master texts, and, above all, *to win* (see my debate some years ago in *The Scriblerian* with a willful scholar fortuitously named Winn).

Ideally writing and reading essays will occur together, as finally inseparable: parts of one whole. They are relations. Although I offer some concentrated remarks on writing in the last essay of this book, I wish to say a word or two here about writing, partly in order that we not separate the two acts.

Writing is always and undeniably better when you feel the need to write, not when you are forced to do so, for instance as part of a course requirement. You write better, too, when you write about what you want to write about, rather than something—again—you are forced to write about. The personal and the familiar essay do not give themselves to specific, dictated assignments. Thus I ask my students only (!) to attempt essays on a subject or topic of their own choosing, one that is important to them, one that they want or perhaps feel the need to respond to; their only guidelines are what they have seen in their readings of other essays and learned in our comparative discussions. Arriving at a topic is often the most difficult part of essay writing, and so I encourage students to think of what first comes to mind, thence to "take a line out for a walk," allowing themselves to enter into the will of the writing.

Essay writing works, in part, because it is more likely to be an effort that interests and, preferably, matters to students. It is at the same time something they feel they can do—everyone has had experiences, even if they have not often mined them for their meaning and significance. Not everyone has read Philip Massinger or *Moby Dick* or *Paradise Lost* or *My Antonia*, nor, I dare say, does everyone need to. As Montaigne puts it, writing about essays as he pens them, the essay derives from such experiences as we have all had, even if young in years: "have you not lived? That is not only the fundamental but the most illustrious of your occupations. . . . Have you been able to think out and manage your own life?" (3:13; 850). Therein lies plenty of material ready for the harvesting.

It is notoriously hard for the layperson, the amateur, the common reader (if such exists) to develop the skills or acquire the background required to understand Pound's *Cantos* or Joyce's *Ulysses* or Spenser's *The Faerie Queene*; it is much less hard, and much more rewarding because more practical, to read one's own experience and do the kind of writing that that breeds. The essay offers sufficient challenges, for it is precisely addressed to the layperson, amateur, common reader whose name today is Student.

For a number of reasons, then, essays afford college and university curricula remarkable and unique opportunities. You cannot separate reading essays from writing them, writing them from reading them—nor essays from life. Nor can the teacher of essays be just a creative writer or a critic (even less a scholar). He or she must be at least both. As one of my graduate students, Kirsten Bosnak, an amateur of the form herself, recently put it, the essay—as well as teaching inspired by and indebted to it—at once requires and promotes both "academic rigor" and "creative freedom."

And now as to reading essays: You do not plumb the depths of "Death of a Pig" or "Shooting an Elephant" for symbols or worry about allegory. You need not worry about Christ figures in "The Courage of Turtles" or probe for hidden meanings in "A Piece of Chalk." Essays may be indirect, but you need not dissect them; indeed you may be better off not doing so. Essays are not superficial, however, nor are their meanings simply available to the merest, disinterested consumer. In essays, you attend to the literal; if an essence, that is, a deeper meaning, a spirit, is to be found, it will be only in, through, and by means of the letter. Quotations abound in essays, and they are often not numbered, footnoted, and scrupulously identified, for you need mainly to enjoy them as partners in a conversation underway, too familiar to require documentation. Tone matters in essays, as it does in ordinary conversation; reading it correctly is, though, a matter of attention and mental acuity rather than of engagement with arcane lore. Least of all must you become, or pretend to be, an adept, part of a clique or cult in possession of sacred knowledge or privileged tools. "Professional" readers care little for essays because they do not draw out erudition and critical and theoretical sophistication or reward abstruse lucubrations; such readers have, therefore, tended to dismiss essays as unworthy. Essays invite you to work on them, not so much in the sense that you must do so in order to understand them, but in the sense that they clear a place for you to stand and to bring your everyday tools of observation and attention to bear. Little wonder that during the heyday of academic close reading, often called New Criticism, the essay's death knell was heard—indeed, in 1951, with some irony, Joseph Wood Krutch proclaimed its demise in "No Essays, Please!," endorsing in the process the definite, professional, academic "article," the essay's opposite. The very different appeal of essays cements their importance for curricula, embodying diversity as they do.

I have suggested that essays typically lack the depth as well as some of the literary devices, strategies, and aims that we normally associate with worthwhile creations of imaginative power. This by no means deplorable situation arises in part from the essay's skeptical attitude toward disembodied ideas; it trades, rather, in sensuous apprehension, although its focus is often, as Edward Hoagland effectively puts it, "what I think, what I am." Notoriously wary of systems, essays found themselves in ordinary, common, and familiar notions and activities. The essay is democratic in this sense, too. The senses rightly matter, and the essay appeals to the senses. In essays, experience is a more reliable guide to living than the intellect. Reason has produced countless disasters—see Swift in *A Tale of a Tub* and *Gulliver's Travels* and, not so differently, Edmund Burke on the French Revolution. Still, it would be wrong to link the essay with cultural or political conservatism, despite an obvious relation. Better, perhaps, to think of essays as *pre-servative*, for they keep notions and ways alive, preventing their spoiling and turning rancid and indigestible. Better, too, to think not of tightly reasoned arguments, where logic dictates, but of Wordsworth's "short essays," as he called the poems in the revolutionary *Lyrical Ballads*, inaugurating Romanticism. He, too, preserves, "preservative" not conservative, offering these works in opposition to "the gross and violent stimulants" that were at the time, he felt, poisoning and deadening the sensibility, which he and his coauthor, Coleridge, sought to refine.

At the same time, essays exhibit layers of treatment and a richness of texture that charms, endears, and proves telling and significant. The best essays, I am tempted to say along with William Kittredge, start with one notion and pick up other lines of thought and feeling as they proceed, ending with a convergence of layers. Rather than depth, then, there are layers, and the layers bear some responsibility for the importance of *relations* in essays. Meaning does not exist or come into being by itself but rather by means of relation; as Eliot writes, "two things are measured by each other" (*Selected Essays* 15), and the essay consistently weighs, takes the measure of, relates.

Made of layers, essays function laterally more than vertically, eschewing depth in favor of relations. You do not "dig" into "The Mowing of a Field" but rather lay it out, putting beside the denunciation of Prometheanism both the account of the buying of a pig and that of the selling of land. Depth makes for not relation but hierarchy, and although essays take a stand and stand for something, usually quite specific and characteristically local and particular, they, like Wordsworth's *Lyrical Ballads*, function democratically. "Lateral" also defines the essay's particular way of engaging by quoting other essays, creating a sort of intertextuality. A community of essays appears, perhaps a tradition, and the reader's pleasure grows as he or she realizes this relationship.

In a well-known passage in *ABC of Reading*, Ezra Pound writes that "literature is language charged with meaning, . . . great literature . . . simply language charged with meaning to the utmost possible degree" (28). No one, I think, will claim that essays—other than the most extraordinary—meet the latter definition, and perhaps only a few would agree that essays satisfy the former. Again exceptions exist—for instance Gretel Ehrlich's "The Smooth Skull of Winter," Bernard Cooper's essays, Chris Arthur's; still, except in essays composed in verse, the charge is local rather than consistent and pervasive. Language matters in essays, sentences more, and I have in mind not just Bacon's apothegms but also Edward Hoagland's finely chiseled sentences and Cynthia Ozick's "comely and muscular" ones in, say, "The Seam of the Snail." Still more important is the perception that an essayist renders, along with the dramatization of the way his or her mind works.

Whereas literature challenges, essays tend to affirm. Essays do not necessarily support the status quo; on the contrary, they are quite often critical (see, for instance, Hilaire Belloc's "The Mowing of a Field"). Literature challenges the reader by means of its imaginative richness and technical sophistication—the ways in which its language is charged with meaning—but it also frequently challenges our assumptions, questions our understanding, and even undermines cherished values. Joseph Epstein, former editor of *The American Scholar* and an important essayist himself, claims that affirmation is the one value "the great essayists" hold in common, and I once irked Joyce Carol Oates by asserting that essays *smile*. What I had said was that an "earned" smile, akin to the poet Keats's affirmations in the face of life's horrors, creases the essayist's face. Essayists are by no means blind to pain and suffering, terror and meanness, and they certainly do not shrink from their recognition—no tweedy, pipe-puffing, sherry-sipping Edwardian, pre-1917, penning delicate belles lettres, the caricature that may have prevailed until recently (according to Graham Good). Essayists do not, however, dwell on such things; James Baldwin, for one, resists the lure of his own father's consuming bitterness, arriving at the essay's characteristic capacity for sympathetic involvement (also brilliantly displayed in Zora Neale Hurston's "How It Feels to Be Colored Me"). Perhaps essays do challenge, but if so, it is by means of a founding affirmativeness; certainly essays preserve perspectives, positions, and values threatened for extinction or, less dramatically, second-class citizenship.

Still they do not demand so much of the reader as does poetry, or often fiction—and that makes them all the more relevant, I suggest, for today's curricula. *Essays are readable*; often they do not require interpretation, or what John Dryden reviles as "expounding." They are clear enough, plain enough, the literal sufficient and not secondary and subordinate to some "spirit" that transcends it. They precisely infuse the familiar with interest, power, relevance, and significance, thus revealing the extraordinary capacities of the ordinary (but see Cynthia Ozick's "stiff-necked" Jewish opposition in "The Riddle of the Ordinary"). In essays the writer has mined and assayed his or her own experience for meaning, which is then offered up to the reader; in literature, oppositely, the reader bears responsibility for extracting meaning from events represented.

Sharing the essay, even proselytizing for it, does not equate with popularizing, least of all with the "vulgarisation" that C. H. Sisson once claimed that David Hume had inherited from "the egregious Addison" (35). Accommodation there may be, however, and I must now pause to consider the implications of putting forward the essay as a way of addressing today's students and their declining capacities for reading. We are in nothing short of a crisis, at least in this country: an alarming, frightful, deplorable number of us cannot read well enough to understand a newspaper column, and often will not try. Many more of us do not consider these incapacities cause for alarm. The essay, I argue, is well suited to address such current needs, being neither quite literature nor quite philosophy (but very nearly both).

So saying is not to represent the essay as a sop to the partially literate, with whom, in any case, I sympathize: I know the debilitations, shame, and sense of failure associated with being unable to read, for my late father, an honest man and brilliant automobile mechanic, could neither read nor write, having never gotten beyond first grade. (My mother, bless her heart, could do both, though not well, having managed to finish ninth grade.)

Difficulties in reading *well* I also know and sympathize with, having taught both graduates and undergraduates for four decades and having witnessed, close-up, the accelerating disparity between technical know-how and the ability to read with understanding and insight—that is, sympathetically, imaginatively, and critically. To this situation, the essay brings hope as well as promise.

Beyond what I have already suggested, the reasons are several. For one important thing, the essay begins with the way things actually are, and accepts the current educational situation, without, of course, yielding to it. It does not blithely assume, as some textbooks do, that college and university freshmen, or even English majors, already know how to read responsibly and well. It does not pretend that this sorry situation will go away—or that there are more important things to teach and do. Instead it starts from the reality we are given and then asks, "Now that this is so, what do we do?" Its focus is, in other words, responsibly on response.

As I have been claiming, the essay's manner is indirect, sneaky. E. B. White, for one, can be read, as my students always take great delight in maintaining, just for the story, for the humor, for the pleasure—which is, in fact, quite a lot. The essay typically does not *require* that you go further, certainly not to dig deeply. But you can, although you best be wary, for the essay honors no dissection or symbol mongering. Once you begin to read White, though, or Cynthia Ozick, or Richard Selzer, you notice more and more: *utile* in, through, and by means of *dulce*.

Something else: the reader always retains responsibility, bearing a considerable burden. The essay is, though, often interested in lightening that burden. E. B. White said it well, as usual, writing of his Cornell teacher Will Strunk, who evidently indulged "vulgarisation": everywhere in the original *Elements of Style* you find "evidences of the author's deep sympathy for the reader. Will felt that the reader was in serious trouble most of the time, a man floundering in a swamp, and that it was the duty of anyone attempting to write English to drain this swamp quickly and get his man up on dry ground, or at least throw him a rope" (261).

Let me try now to be more specific about reading essays. I begin, as you might, with *the essayistic character*. We often refer, in un-deconstructed fashion, to the voice we (imagine we) hear speaking in essays. There is, in fact, for most readers of essays—Chesterton's, say, or White's—a palpable sense of *a particular person, with a distinctive voice.* It is that, in any case, that attracts—and charms, sometimes beguiles, but always matters. Annie Dillard once opined that if you do not like the voice you hear speaking in an essay, you will likely stop reading. In this she is right, as about almost everything else. The nineteenth-century essayist Alexander Smith posited *mood* as the heart of the form, preferring as a Romantic the lyrical; clearly, though, that is but one aspect or mode of voice.

This matter of voice looms with particular significance in Jonathan Swift's famous satire "A Modest Proposal," frequently anthologized as an essay. It is not. I include it here in order to help us see what an essay is—by means of realizing what it is not. Biographical knowledge allows us to realize, before beginning to read, that the author, an Anglican churchman, would not himself advocate, as his speaker does, cannibalism of young children as a solution to Ireland's extreme woes. Without such knowledge, the reader may be taken in, although doubts surely begin as early as the fourth paragraph when the speaker refers to children "dropped" from their "dam." Evidence mounts that the speaker is untrustworthy, his tone roughly scientific, putatively objective, almost clinical, certainly unemotional—a frightening precursor of distanced, merely rational analysis. A thesis appears in an italicized paragraph, offered by the insouciant speaker as unworkable because impractical. By this point the jig is up, and we know, or should, that the gap could hardly be greater between author and speaker, a fictional creation just like Lemuel Gulliver. What "A Modest Proposal" contributes to understanding the essay is this: in this form we can expect the voice we hear to be the author's. Essays allow for, indeed thrive on, the inclusion of fictional elements, but voice is not one of them. Veer a bit from autobiographical truthfulness, and the essayist encounters trouble—as Sam Pickering did in modifying himself in his early essay on box turtles.

If character or voice is the first thing to attend to in learning to read and appreciate essays, the second is structure. This is a delicate matter. Essays ramble, or saunter, as Thoreau suggests, in no particular hurry to get anywhere in particular, interested in the journey rather than its end. *That,* it seems to me, is another unfortunate instance of oppositional thinking such as has governed our take on essays. The truth is, the essay is both process and product. To call it, as Walter Pater did, setting off a slew of followers, "formless form" does not help particularly, mainly evincing the desperate lengths to which critics will go in an effort to pin this thing down. The end does matter, as Edward Hoagland says, for there is a point somewhere—"which is its real center, even if the point couldn't be uttered in fewer words than the essayist has used" (691). The journey matters as well, perhaps equally and no more. The point is, I reckon, that you reach the end by means of the journey, but "end," as T. S. Eliot reminds us, is not the equivalent of conclusion; it is also purpose, and purpose, or end, may well emerge in the course of the journey, rather than simply at its terminus. I return to these matters in the last essay in this book.

Essayistic form sometimes beguiles, even befuddles. Take White's afore-mentioned essay on his teacher Will Strunk, also published as introduction to *The Elements of Style*. The first couple of pages treat living in an apart-ment without air conditioning in New York City, the focus on Strunk emerging only later. Extra white space also divides "The Ring of Time": first, observations on a circus rehearsal in Florida, then analysis of the South and the then-urgent matter of integration. Of course White brilliantly links these layers, his "point" being time's refusal to stay still. In perhaps his best-known essay yet, "Under the Influence," Scott Russell Sanders organizes *in chunks*. Indeed the essay is no great friend of linearity, as its proclivity for rambling and sauntering suggests, nor of logic. It is not, however, antilog-ical or alogical. A *particular* logic obtains, as in Sanders, but do not count out "association," as in William Hazlitt's "On Going a Journey," a near allegory of essaying. The essay's structure, we may be forced to conclude, is imaginative and evocative, which may present more problems for writing than for reading.

Essays are best approached, and best appreciated, not singly but in rela-tion to one another, comparatively, as part of a community and a tradition. Essays' fondness for quotation, as I have noted, suggests a certain commu-nal nature. The more you read, the better prepared you are—and the less likely to be betrayed. I think we can do better, though, than merely rec-ognize one when we see it, not being able to say exactly what it is. Essays point, in my estimation, to the parts/whole matter, and indeed they both invoke and exploit this age-old question. You best appreciate a particular essay when you place it in relation to other instances of its kind, like and different. You best understand a particular essay when you place its parts side by side, considering their relation to each other and to the whole. Such divisions as I noted above in essays point to this requirement. The essay, in short, necessitates *lateral reading.*

It often proves helpful to think of form as "purposive movement," an important notion I take from Walter A. Davis. "Put in the simplest and most exacting terms," he writes in *The Act of Interpretation,* the task

> is to apprehend the purposive principle immanent in the structure of a literary work which determines the mutual interfunctioning of its component parts.
>
> . . . Function, structure, and purpose, in that order, become the primary categories of interpretation: for parts function only by serving a purpose and structure is the process through which purpose is actualized . . .
>
> . . . Purpose coincides with structure because it gives birth to it. It is the most concrete category in criticism because its embodiment is constant and comprehensive: the purpose that shapes a work of art is realized by no more and no less than that entire work of art. (2–3)

While sometimes helpful — for example, in reading Dryden's *Religio Laici* — this sense of "purposive movement" flounders with a work like *Four Quartets,* which deconstructs precisely this notion of time and is, differently, structured around sudden and unexpected eruptions of the timeless. Eliot's pattern is that of Incarnation, whereas Davis's is "half" that truth in its apparent commitment to immanence.

Ultimately more helpful, perhaps especially in reading essays, is a no doubt surprising source. I refer to Eliot's classic essay on the seventeenth-century Anglican Divine Lancelot Andrewes, originally the lead essay in a 1928 volume with the title *For Lancelot Andrewes: Essays on Style and Order.* After some remarks on Andrewes's way of writing, Eliot offers wholly apposite comments on the divine's prose that suggest a theory of reading. He proceeds via a comparison of Andrewes and John Donne.

> When Andrewes begins his sermon, from beginning to end you are sure that he is wholly in his subject, unaware of anything else, that his emotion grows as he penetrates more deeply into his subject, that he is finally "alone with the Alone," with the mystery which he is seeking to grasp more and more firmly. . . . Andrewes's emotion is purely contemplative;

it is not personal, it is wholly evoked by the object of contemplation, to which it is adequate; his emotions wholly contained in and explained by its object. But with Donne there is always the something else. . . . Donne is a "personality" in a sense in which Andrewes is not: his sermons, one feels, are a "means of self-expression." He is constantly finding an object which shall be adequate to his feelings; Andrewes is wholly absorbed in the object and therefore responds with the adequate emotion. (*Selected Essays* 351)

I extrapolate from Eliot's admirable criticism a crucial difference between two ways of responding to a text: one derives from the needs—and will—of the respondent (writer or reader), reflects his or her personality, and uses the text in a manner that subordinates it to *self*-expression; the other, that of Andrewes, and Eliot, submits to the will of the text, expresses not the personality of the respondent but instead seeks to let the object speak itself, and so is contemplative rather than reflective.

One way to get "inside" a manageably short form like the essay effectively short-circuits the power of personality and the will to self-expression. Let me explain, briefly, describing my own procedure in the readings that follow. I offer these remarks, I hope it goes without saying, in the spirit of the essay itself: they are not intended as either prescriptive or exemplary, but rather as suggestive.

Bringing together reading and writing may well be the key. I get to know an essay, which I have gone through several times, by following the instruction offered by an excellent undergraduate teacher of mine. At Wofford College in the early 1960s in the classes of Vincent E. Miller, we learned to read, and we did so by writing "papers" on what we read. A breakthrough for me came with the assignment one Wednesday (I think it was) to write a ten-page paper for the next class, two days later, on Basho's most famous haiku. Initially flummoxed, I eventually found that I had surprisingly little trouble making so much commentary on the seventeen-syllable poem. What the assignment forced—what it required—was immersion in the poem, and contemplation such as Eliot describes.

Even now, close to half a century later, I am not sure that the submission-immersion-contemplation that assignment required is possible apart from writing. The *putting in other words* is necessary, for you do not understand precisely until you translate—no wonder that (Dr. Miller's friend) Pound taught that translation is a crucial form of criticism, about which more directly below. And writing requires not just precision but also fidelity and responsibility to the calling text—as nothing else does so intensely: you have to get it down right, which is another matter of ethics.

Intent on both the text and your own re-presentation of what it says, you inevitably find yourself recalling other parts of the whole as well as relating—comparing—other texts, reading laterally. The reader is something other than a machine, in other words, different from the voice we hear in "A Modest Proposal"; he or she is, or should be, also a sentient, involved, and engaged participant, who, for all his submitting to textual will, cannot efface himself—nor should he or she try. This situation makes not for relativism but rather for perspective, for angle of vision: what I see is also what you see, albeit in a somewhat different light, as it were. Most important, I am not reflecting on what I have read, but instead observing what I am in the process of reading. This "present" act helps mitigate, or even at best to obviate, the natural readerly willfulness that reflection unfortunately entails.

In a very real sense, you are writing and reading together, the writing helping you to clarify, to see, *to understand.* And at the same time, the reading impels your writing; more, you are writing *as you read.* There is the necessary slowing down, the scrupulous attention to the object as well as to your re-presentation of it, your putting in other words.

As I was finishing the readings here, I chanced upon an essay by the unduly neglected American poet and critic Allen Tate, himself, incidentally, coeditor of a 1938 volume, *America Through the Essay.* Here, in the foreword to *The Hero with the Private Parts: Essays by Andrew Lytle,* an essay later reprinted as "The Local Universality of Andrew Lytle," Tate describes his fellow Agrarian's way of reading, which in important ways closely resembles my words just above. Tate begins by recalling R. P. Blackmur's acute description—which I have incorporated in my discussion of Dryden—of "the formal discourse of an amateur," which he misremembers as "the passionate discourse of an amateur," meaning, Tate surmises, "the man *devoted* to the object of his attention . . . the man whose developing awareness and possession of the imaginative object becomes in the end self-knowledge" (xiv). Following this insight, Tate devotes a paragraph to his friend Lytle's procedures, which resonate with Montaigne's own description and defense of his *essaying.* Along the way Tate makes the case for what I am calling *writing as reading*:

Lytle's passionate discourse as an amateur is, first, before it gets on the page, a way of talking to himself about what he has found in other novelists who have been useful to him; but once he starts writing out what he has found useful he begins to impart it to the general reader who is standing over his shoulder. But I am not sure that he ever has, in his essays, the general reader before him as a person to whom he feels responsible; and this is as it should be. The kind of high programmatic criticism that we find in these essays is "creative" . . . in a formal sense similar to that which we find in his best fiction. . . . *For reading is translation.* The essays are close translations of works which Lytle has read, reread, read once again, so that his last reading assumes so complete a mastery of the text that he no longer needs to refer to it. This sentence is his modest declaration of purpose for his critical writing: "It is part of the author's discipline to read well, *and to read well you must write it down.*" The deceptive simplicity of this statement need not mislead us into supposing that writing it down means making casual notes for his own future use. Writing it down here means a formal effort of the imagination which places the writer inside the consciousness of Stephen Crane, Flaubert, Faulkner, Tolstoy. (xiv–xv; italics added)

Lytle's quoted words, by the way, come from his preface to *The Hero with the Private Parts*. Regrettably he does not expand on them beyond writing, immediately after my second italicization above, "It is the only way to explore and develop the first glimmer of meaning which by refraction [not *reflection*, note] flashes out of the abyss, that matrix of all knowledge. Words beget words and the meaning is there" (xx). Reading and writing emerge, then, as two parts—two halves—of one whole: each is one-half the truth, the understanding. Writing, we may conclude, is reading embodied.

[O]f all authors Montaigne is one of the least destructible. You could as well dissipate a fog by flinging hand-grenades into it. For Montaigne is a fog, a gas, a fluid, insidious element. He does not reason, he insinuates, charms, and influences; or if he reasons, you must be prepared for his having some other design upon you than to convince you by his argument. It is hardly too much to say that Montaigne is the most essential author to know if we would understand the course of French thought during the last three hundred years.

—T. S. Eliot, "The *Pensées* of Pascal"

The Advent of Personality and the
Beginning of the Essay

Montaigne and Bacon

IT ALL STARTED WITH MONTAIGNE, although a broken lineage may be traced back to his beloved Seneca, as well as perhaps to Plutarch, and even to Plato. The essay as we know it takes its origin and its texture, if not entirely its direction, from Michel de Montaigne's publication of *Essais* in 1580. Montaigne penned his "attempts" or "trials"—the respected Hungarian theorist Georg Lukacs described the chosen term *essays* as an "arrogant courtesy"—in seclusion from the horrible scenes then transpiring in his great country. The first edition of *Essais* consisted of books I and II, that of 1588 adding the third and final one. Not until the first posthumous edition, seven years later, did the *Essais* attain completion: 107 essays of varying length, most of the titles of which begin with the tiny but pregnant preposition "of." Appropriately enough, these essays are as self-conscious as their author, and also self-referential. As he states in the long "Of Vanity," in the third book: "My book is always one. Except that at each new edition, so that the buyer may not come off completely empty-handed, I allow myself to add, since it is only an ill-fitted patchwork, some extra ornaments" (9; 736). Prominent, in fact, are qualities crucial to the form as it developed over the next four centuries: from that certain beguiling self-effacement to the representation of the essay as a quilt, patched together and consisting of diverse pieces, remnants, perhaps, saved from the trash bin—a nonorganic and impure creation, thus a thing redolent with tension.

Because many of his fellows were then engaged in mapping the physical world, Michel de Montaigne turned inward, his writing in every sense an exercise in "home-cosmography." The essay is very much a child of the Renaissance, as well as a product of the "self-fashioning" that Stephen Greenblatt some time ago revealed as characteristic of the time. The self-reflexiveness then being invented both called attention to, as it helped to create, *personality*, and meant that the new form would find itself often talking about itself (earning Swift's rebuke, in *A Tale of a Tub*, for being writing "upon *Nothing*"). Ever since, you find essayist after essayist writing essays about the essay. Montaigne was the first, the "second" English essayist, Sir William Cornwallis, the second, and neither Cynthia Ozick nor Scott Russell Sanders nor Sam Pickering will be the last.

If, as Harold Bloom has recently claimed, Shakespeare in *Hamlet* virtually created "our" sense of human being, Montaigne may well be responsible for the Bard's representation of the introspective and skeptical young Dane. What Montaigne bequeathed may have come, to Shakespeare, largely via Seneca. At least T. S. Eliot suggests so in an important essay prefaced to a then-new edition of the Latin poet's tragedies. Referring to some of Shakespeare's own "great tragedies," one observes, says Eliot, "a new attitude":

> It is not the attitude of Seneca, but is derived from Seneca; it is slightly
> different from anything that can be found in French tragedy, in Corneille
> or in Racine; it is modern, and it culminates, if there is ever any culmi-
> nation, in the attitude of Nietzsche. I cannot say that it is Shakespeare's
> "philosophy." Yet many people have lived by it. . . . It is the attitude of
> self-dramatization assumed by some of Shakespeare's heroes at moments of
> tragic intensity. (*Selected Essays* 129)

With reference to *Othello*, a passage from which he quotes to illustrate the point, Eliot pinpoints the nature of this "new" attitude. What he is intent to show is that Othello

> is *cheering himself up*. He is endeavouring to escape reality . . . and is thinking about himself. Humility is the most difficult of all virtues to achieve; nothing dies harder than the desire to think well of oneself. Othello succeeds in turning himself into a pathetic figure, by adopting an *aesthetic* rather than a moral attitude, dramatizing himself against his environment. He takes in the spectator, but the human motive is primarily to take in himself. I do not believe that any writer has ever exposed this *bovarysme*, the human will to see things as they are not, more clearly than Shakespeare. (130)

In Elizabethan England—and, although Eliot does not say so, the Renaissance in Europe as well—conditions were ripe for this major shift in the way human beings looked at themselves, indeed in promoting self-examination, for it was, Eliot writes,

> a period of dissolution and chaos; and in such a period any emotional attitude which seems to give a man something firm, even if it be only the attitude of "I am myself alone," is eagerly taken up. I hardly need . . . to point out how readily, in a period like the Elizabethan, the Senecan attitude of Pride, the Montaigne attitude of Scepticism, and the Machiavelli attitude of Cynicism, arrived at a kind of fusion in the Elizabethan individualism. (132)

Eliot's essay bears importance on several accounts and several levels. For us, here, that resides primarily in what he avers about the nature of this "individualism," significantly affected and influenced by Montaigne:

> What influence the work of Seneca and Machiavelli and Montaigne seems to me to exert in common on that time, and most conspicuously through Shakespeare, is an influence toward a kind of self-consciousness that is new; the self-consciousness and self-dramatization of the Shakespearian hero, of whom Hamlet is only one. It seems to mark a stage, even if not a very agreeable one, in human history, or progress, or deterioration, or change. (139–40)

"Taken up into Christianity," continues Eliot, Roman stoicism was just this "development in self-consciousness," and "it broke loose again in the dissolution of the Renaissance. Nietzsche, as I suggested, is a late variant: his attitude is a kind of stoicism turned upside-down: for there is not much difference between identifying oneself with the Universe and identifying the Universe with oneself" (140).

Now, what Eliot seeks, and tries to embody, in poetry — and I would say, also in the essay — is precisely what Montaigne does not. "Great literature is," claims the modern poet-philosopher, "the transformation of a personality into a personal work of art" (*Selected Essays* 217). It is the integrity of the work of art that matters, not, as in Romanticism, the personality of the poet, individual and dramatized: "it is not," writes Eliot in "Tradition and the Individual Talent," "the 'greatness,' the intensity, of the emotions, the components, but the intensity of the artistic process, the pressure, so to speak, under which the fusion takes place, that counts" (*Selected Essays* 19). Any philosophy treated is *re-presented*, any ideas or thoughts, reflections; they exist, in the work of art, "not as matter for argument, but as matter for inspection" (*The Sacred Wood* 147). In short, for Eliot, poetry is not an expression of personality: it is "not a turning loose of emotion, but an escape from emotion; it is not the expression of personality but an escape from personality" (*Selected Essays* 21). In fact, "the progress of an artist is a continual self-sacrifice, a continual extinction of personality" (17). The poets who followed the "Metaphysicals," in the wake of the "dissociation of sensibility," sometime around the mid-seventeenth century in England, turned precisely toward reflection, a defining character of the new form Montaigne had created a few decades earlier. That turn reached its apogee, of course, in Romanticism; Wordsworth, probably the most reflective poet in the language, called his and Coleridge's revolutionary "lyrical ballads" by the term "short essays."

Montaigne engages in little other than self-reflection: "What I chiefly portray," he writes in "Of Practice," "is my cogitations," and they reflect, in turn "myself, . . . my essence." He thus focuses on the opposite of what Eliot insists upon: "It is not my deeds that I write down," but his thinking, "a shapeless subject that does not lend itself to expression in actions" (2:6; 274). Born of and with these reflections is the self-consciousness that naturally proceeds to self-dramatization and so the creation and expression of *personality.* Whom do we know so well, other than ourselves, as Michel de Montaigne?

As Graham Good wrote some time ago in his important book *The Observing Self: Rediscovering the Essay,* in the case of Montaigne "the essays develop with his personality" (27). In fact his "book was 'consubstantial' with himself." In other words, "the book and the self continue to influence each other and reflect each other, with the book finally becoming the 'portrait' . . . of its author" (27).

"Of Practice" is especially revealing. It begins with the general, or the universal, with reflection authoritatively delivered. Then the essay takes a decisive turn. Now, that is, Montaigne recounts a climactic experience, one in which he came perilously close to dying; as such it proved immensely valuable. "During our third civil war, or the second (I do not quite remember which)," he begins with beguiling casualness, "I went riding one day about a league from my house, which is situated at the very hub of all the turmoil of the civil wars of France"—a site, in other words, that represents both inside and outside. That momentous day, at any rate, on his return from riding, upon a horse "not very strong," Montaigne suffered a collision: for one of his men, "in order to show his daring and get ahead of his companions, spurred his horse at full speed up the path behind me, came down like a colossus on the little man and little horse, and hit us like a thunderbolt with all his strength and weight, sending us both head over heels." Montaigne's companions feared him dead. After "more than full two hours" he fortunately began to revive, "to move and breathe; for so great an abundance of blood had fallen into my stomach that nature had to revive its forces to discharge it" (268–69).

Montaigne then begins to zero in on what he was thinking and doing as he hovered somewhere between life and death. As he represents those awful moments, he does so with the help of quotations from revered Latin authors: Tasso, Lucretius, Ovid, and Virgil. As William H. Gass observed some time ago, quoting enjoys favored status in essays, serving, not as in the essay's "opposite, that awful object 'the article,'" for needed support and proof, but for pleasure and company (25). Montaigne thus bequeaths something important in quoting. As Gass puts it, "the essay is born of books"; it is often, in fact, "the words of others which . . . bring the essay into being" (26). As a result, "You can be assured you are reading an excellent essay when you find yourself relishing the quotations as much as the text that contains them. . . . The apt quotation is one of the essayist's greatest gifts . . ." (28). By means of judicious quoting, the essay "confirms the continuity, the contemporaneity, the reality of writing": "Virginia Woolf writes of Addison by writing of Macaulay writing of Addison, of whom Pope and Johnson and Thackeray have also written. On and On" (27).

After scrupulously examining his thoughts that fateful day, Montaigne takes another, decisive, and final turn. "Of Practice" becomes, in the event, nothing less than an apologia for essay writing, Montaigne the first in a distinguished tradition of essayists writing about the form they have come to cherish and to believe in, trying hard to say what this thing is, why it is important, how it achieves its effects, thus justifying writing so much about oneself. It amounts, too, to a justification of the page's creation of personality.

Of the dozens, if not hundreds, of subsequent attempts to rationalize and justify the essay, none is more enlightening than Montaigne's own. The account is pleasurably brief and well written, interesting and indeed moving. There is a capaciousness to these three pages or so, an honesty, a candor such as E. B. White described as the essay's "basic ingredient" (viii).

Just how Montaigne got to this point, to this matter, will not be readily apparent to the casual or first-time reader of the essay. Nothing quite prepares us for this last turn. The explanation resides solely in self-consciousness. "Of Practice" itself now turns inward, reflecting on itself: What have I been doing? What *am* I doing? How can I justify it? What good is served? The directness and the candor engage, as well as the assurance that derives from Montaigne's acknowledgment of the relation between his opening theme(s) and the story he has related of his own near-tragic accident:

> This account of so trivial an event would be rather pointless, were it not for the instruction that I have derived from it for myself; for in truth, in order to get used to the idea of death, I find there is nothing like coming close to it. Now as Pliny says, each man is a good education to himself, provided he has the capacity to spy on himself from close up. What I write here is not my teaching, but my study; it is not a lesson for others, but for me. (272)

A bold declaration, indeed, this is contextualized, and its boldness striated, by the classical allusion, and yet the case is clear: Montaigne is writing about himself—and to a far greater detail and intensity than Thoreau does when he appears to invoke Montaigne at the beginning of his essays known as *Walden*, having learned the lesson well and accepted the bequest ("In most books, the *I*, or first person, is omitted; in this it will be retained. . . . We commonly do not remember that it is, after all, always the first person that is speaking. I should not talk so much about myself if there were anybody else whom I knew as well") (259).

Montaigne is well aware of tension, which he is in fact in the process of establishing: "And yet it should not be held against me if I publish what I write." Indeed he now suggests that there may well be "a lesson for others" in what he writes, his "study" having the effect of "teaching" (272). This has always been, incidentally, the self-conscious dilemma that essayists struggle with: Scott Russell Sanders summarizes that effort in "The Singular First Person," *and* incarnates the other-ness that post-Montaignian essayists have generally and typically claimed for themselves, when he avers, "I choose to write about my experience not because it is mine, but because it seems to me a door through which others might pass" (*Secrets of the Universe* 198).

Montaigne is aware as well that this *essai* writing is "new and extraordinary amusement," in fact "a thorny undertaking, and more so than it seems, to follow a movement so wandering as that of our mind, to penetrate the opaque depths of its innermost folds, to pick out and immobilize the innumerable flutterings that agitate it" (273). A better description of the work of the essayist is hard to find, this internal journeying that attains virtually mythic status analogous to the geographical journeys of older heroes like Odysseus and Aeneas, this newfangled effort at "home-cosmography."

Montaigne follows here with another autobiographical representation, an illustration of the point, in other words, derived from his own experience—the "wandering" way of the form to which he knows he is giving birth.

> It is many years now that I have had only myself as object of my thoughts, that I have been examining and studying only myself; and if I study anything else, it is in order promptly to apply it to myself, or rather within myself. And it does not seem to me that I am making a mistake if—as is done in the other sciences, which are incomparably less useful—I impart what I have learned in this one, though I am hardly satisfied with the progress I have made in it. There is no description equal in difficulty, or certainly in usefulness, to the description of oneself. Even so one must

spruce up, even so one must present oneself in an orderly arrangement, if one would go out in public. Now, I am constantly adorning myself, for I am constantly describing myself. (273)

An admirable enough effort; you almost pass over, so charming is Montaigne, his assertion that *essaying* is a "science" and that it is uncommonly "useful." Eliot was right about this essayist's wiles.

To the general issue of writing about oneself, Montaigne now turns, abetted by a quotation from Horace. In defense, Montaigne asks, "What does Socrates treat of more fully than himself?" The following sentences I find powerful and moving—and highly suggestive. Still speaking of Socrates, he asks, beginning,

> To what does he lead his disciples' conversation more often than to talk about themselves, not about the lesson of their book, but about the essence and movement of their soul? We speak our thoughts religiously to God, and to our confessor, as our neighbors do to the whole people. But, someone will answer, we speak only our self-accusations. Then we speak everything: for our very virtue is faulty and fit for repentance.

Abruptly, I would say, Montaigne now returns to the direct description of what he is doing: "My trade and my art is living" (273–74). This is a somewhat different tack, linking essaying to living and so associating his writing with such "practice" as he has been reflecting upon and advocating throughout.

Following references to Cicero and Hortensius, further enriching his text and continuing the contextualizing, Montaigne moves into a useful distinction between recording one's actions and representing one's thoughts, the latter the province of this new form, the essay. Clearly Montaigne is shifting attention, offering a new kind of writing where the focus is the internal rather than the external, an art, if you will, of the subject and the subjective. The real is, in any case, within. Perhaps, he surmises, those who forbid him to speak about his "living" mean that

> I should testify about myself by works and deeds, not by bare words.
> What I chiefly portray is my cogitations, a shapeless subject that does not lend itself to expression in actions. It is all I can do to couch my thoughts in this airy medium of words. Some of the wisest and most devout men have lived avoiding all noticeable actions. My actions would tell more

about fortune than about me. They bear witness to their own part, not to mine, unless it be by conjecture and without certainty: they are samples which display only details. I expose myself entire: my portrait is a cadaver on which the veins, the muscles, and the tendons appear at a glance, each part in its place. One part of what I am was produced by a cough, another by a pallor or a palpitation of the heart—in any case dubiously. It is not my deeds that I write down; it is myself, it is my essence. (274)

With these last words, Montaigne shows the capacity for memorable phrasing and sentence making that will come to characterize the essay and in some writers, like Bacon, to make for epigrams and sententiae of lasting interest and value.

Reflection dominates in the remainder of this essay, Montaigne having tipped his hand that he is moving toward the general and universal, the precise movement that characterizes the essay as form. The manner is undogmatic, the tone balanced; and the argument is moral, Montaigne finishing on the note that comes to mark the essay—Bacon came to exploit this aspect, this tendency, most fully. As elsewhere, Montaigne proceeds in, through, and by means of the self that he knows.

> I hold that a man should be cautious in making an estimate of himself, and equally conscientious in testifying about himself—whether he rates himself high or low makes no difference. If I seemed to myself good and wise or nearly so, I would shout it out at the top of my voice. To say less of yourself than is true is stupidity, not modesty. To pay yourself less than you are worth is cowardice and pusillanimity, according to Aristotle. No virtue is helped by falsehood, and truth is never subject to error. To say more of yourself than is true is not always presumption; it too is often stupidity. To be immoderately pleased with what you are, to fall therefore into an undiscerning self-love, is in my opinion the substance of this vice. The supreme remedy to cure it is to do just the opposite of what those people prescribe who, by prohibiting talking about oneself, even more strongly prohibit thinking about oneself. The pride lies in the thought; the tongue can have only a very slight share in it.

Montaigne is here confronting, willy-nilly, an arch-enemy of essaying, and that is simplistic and reductive thinking, which results in what Eliot calls the "thoroughgoing" and what others see as imbalance. Montaigne calls it excess: it seems, he writes, that to such persons as he has been referring to, to be occupied with oneself means to be pleased with oneself, that to frequent and associate with oneself means to cherish oneself too much. That may be. But this excess arises only in those who touch themselves no more than superficially; who observe themselves only after taking care of their business; who call it daydreaming and idleness to be concerned with oneself, and making castles in Spain to furnish and build oneself; who think themselves something alien and foreign to themselves. (274)

If Montaigne appears a Modern—and he does, and is—he ends "Of Practice" sounding properly respectful of his predecessors. Honesty is simply key in this advocated process of self-exploration and self-examination that marks the essay as a new form. In the essay's penultimate paragraph, Montaigne hits all the right notes, it seems—a balanced perspective from which Thoreau might have learned. As much as candor and honesty, the humility that Montaigne incarnates here will figure henceforth as perhaps the essay's preeminent virtue.

If anyone gets intoxicated with his knowledge when he looks beneath him, let him turn his eyes upward toward past ages, and he will lower his horns, finding there so many thousands of minds that trample him underfoot. If he gets into some flattering presumption about his valor, let him remember the lives of the two Scipios, so many armies, so many nations, all of whom leave him so far behind them. No particular quality will make a man proud who balances it against the many weaknesses and imperfections that are also in him, and, in the end, against the nullity of man's estate. (275)

These sentences—these thoughts—do more than charm and engage the reader. In presenting Montaigne as modest—and no doubt "*ondoyant et divers*"—they also point to the *character* of the essayist: he embodies and incarnates values the reader cannot fail to respect and admire.

The voice works, I am tempted to conclude, because the reader cannot but like the person. Rather than a tautology, this points to the fact that, in essays, not only must the voice engage, but also *the essay's truth must come to reside in that character*, the person of the essayist. There is no room, no allowance, for a discrepancy between the voice we hear in the essay and the sense we have of the essayist. Here, inside and outside coincide: truth embodied.

One final point, and that emerges in the very last paragraph of Montaigne's great essay.

> Because Socrates alone had seriously digested the precept of his god—to
> know himself—and because by that study he had come to despise himself,
> he alone was deemed worthy of the name *wise*. Whoever knows himself
> thus, let him boldly make himself known by his own mouth. (275)

With these concluding words, Montaigne does not appear so different from T. S. Eliot, after all. This sounds, in fact, like Dr. Johnson in *Rasselas* and the *Rambler* essays, as well as Eliot in his great essay-poem *Four Quartets*. It is, in any case, the necessary first step in the long and arduous journey toward self-correction.

In balanced, carefully crafted verses, the young poet Alexander Pope describes the *ideal critic*:

> But where's the Man, who Counsel *can* bestow,
> Still *pleas'd* to *teach*, and yet not *proud* to *know*?
> Unbiass'd, or by *Favour* or by *Spite*;
> Not *dully prepossest*, nor *blindly right*;
> Tho' Learn'd, well-bred; and tho' well-bred, sincere;
> Modestly bold, and Humanly severe?
> Who to a *Friend* his Faults can freely show,
> And gladly praise the Merit of a *Foe*?
> Blest with a *Taste* exact, yet unconfin'd;
> A *Knowledge* both of *Books* and *Humankind*;
> *Gen'rous Converse*; a *Soul* exempt from *Pride*;
> And *Love to Praise*, with *Reason* on his Side? (*An Essay on Criticism* 31–42)

Just about a century before, the studious and worldly wise Francis Bacon offered in prose a similarly balanced and carefully crafted essay on the value of "Studies." The contrasts between the authors are as striking as the thoughts are similar.

Pope was just beginning his great career. A Roman Catholic in an Anglican land, he was denied a University education; an Augustan humanist, he was mightily suspicious of the "new science" and expressed his severe reservations, verging on horror, in his last, great poem, *The Dunciad*. Although he wrote in verse, mainly, Pope also favored the essay form, penning not just *An Essay on Criticism* but also *An Essay on Man* and the four *Moral Essays.* Bacon, on the other hand, enjoyed advantages unavailable to Pope: a member of Parliament in his twenties, he was always active in service and famously successful: Solicitor-General, Lord Keeper, Lord Chancellor, successively Baron Verulam and Viscount St Alban. In his "spare time," Bacon studied natural philosophy and developed a framework for nothing less than reform of the whole of human learning.

His essays are notoriously brief, and while labeled as Montaigne did his writings, they are anything but rambling, personal, reflective. They were first published in 1597: ten pithy writings expanded, and often lengthened considerably, to fifty-eight by the time of the third edition in 1625, titled *The Essayes or Counsels, Civill and Morall,* these words pointing to the crucial differences from Montaigne's *essais.* Bacon's are not trials or attempts, nor are they assays or efforts to mine experience for meaning; instead they are, frankly, counsels, written with the authority of one who has the breadth and the depth of experience *to know.* To Montaigne's defining *Que sais-je?* Bacon answers, "I at least know a lot." If Montaigne, in founding the essay, claimed he was writing for himself, his study long become himself, Bacon, very differently, writes to share the fruits of his impressive experience, his acquired knowledge, his earned wisdom. If for Montaigne, to cite Walter Pater, "not the fruit of experience, but experience itself, is the end," for Bacon, contrariwise, as Graham Good has noted, the essays represent the "fruits" rather than the "experiences," "the results of inquiry, not the process of inquiry" (45). As a result, Bacon may not exactly invite you in, as Montaigne does, but you cannot fail to feel that Bacon has your best interests in mind, so far as he understands them.

"Of Studies" is number fifty of the *Essayes or Counsels.* Little more than a single page, it is sometimes divided into three paragraphs. Frequently anthologized, it is one of Bacon's most famous—though one might be hard put to say "popular." Today it might be grouped with the essayistic equivalent of "flash fiction" or the "short short story," perhaps having a place in such a collection as *In Short.*

"Of Studies" is straightforward; its language, moreover, does not appear charged with meaning, for all its polish and craft. I shall begin by simply quoting, the opening paragraph first:

> Studies serve for delight, for ornament, and for ability. Their chief use for
> delight, is in privateness and retiring; for ornament, is in discourse; and

for ability, is in the judgment and disposition of business. For expert men can execute, and perhaps judge of particulars, one by one; but the general counsels, and the plots and marshalling of affairs, come best from those that are learned. To spend too much time in studies is sloth; to use them too much for ornament, is affectation; to make judgment wholly by their rules, is the humour of a scholar. They perfect nature, and are perfected by experience: for natural abilities are like natural plants, that need proyning by study; and studies themselves do give forth directions too much at large, except they be bounded in by experience. Crafty men contemn studies, simple men admire them, and wise men use them; for they teach not their own use; but that is a wisdom without them, and above them, won by observation. (439)

Several observations attend upon reading, to say nothing of the rhetorical devices, characteristic of Renaissance prose, on vivid and excellent display here. First, then, might be the fact, and the way, that the number *three* dominates, controlling structure and thinking alike—so much so that I am reminded of Swift's *Tale of a Tub*, whose Hack persona lists among his works published and unpublished "*A panegyrical Essay upon the Number Three*" (he also lists, his other mention of an essay, "*A critical Essay upon the Art of Canting, philosophically, physically, and musically considered*"!).

Second is the fundamental difference in play between studies and experience, with observation allied with the latter. The latter difference Bacon exploits in order ultimately to advance their necessary union. The former point marks the crucial role of the *sentence* in Bacon's essay—a legacy that the *familiar* essay still honors. In the essay, in fact, more than any other literary kind, the sentence matters: it is more than the "pack mule" of writing, it is the basis, the very fundament, of the essay, the writer always in quest of beautiful, witty, striking expression. For Bacon, it is apparent, studies provide the writer with the *form* of the sentence, while experience "fills" that form with matter.

"Of Studies," not unusually for Bacon, is tight, severely ordered. The prose is plain—although modern-day readers may at first think it artificial. It may appear studied, but it is always clear, accessible, only infrequently metaphorical or allusive. Sentences here consist of three points, rationally coordinated. So arranged, sentences mirror the *kind* of order Bacon finds operating in the world: if it is not rigid, it is at the very least palpable. It also differs from the kind of order apparent in, say, Lancelot Andrewes, a friend writing at exactly the same time. For Andrewes, order is supple; it turns on strict observation, too, but is directed toward the literary rather than either the ethical or the scientific. Andrewes's procedure is bookish, his mind textured. In Eliot's fine phrasing, Andrewes is "contemplative," his emotion "wholly evoked by the object of contemplation, to which it is adequate" (*Selected Essays* 351). Bacon, on the other hand, more resembles John Donne, as Eliot presents him in comparison with Bishop Andrewes. Bacon, too, "is much less the mystic; he is primarily interested in man," thus Modern in the way that Andrewes is Medieval (352). Where Bacon differs from, say, Donne (and joins with Andrewes) is precisely in avoiding the indulgence in *personality*. In short, Bacon takes the *essay* (as Montaigne had inaugurated it, with its focus on personality) and makes it *familiar*.

For all their differences, "Bacon and Montaigne are working in what is recognizably the same genre," claims Graham Good (43). Bacon even advances the "strategy of avoiding extremes" (47) characteristic of the *English* essay, as of Anglican thinking in general. There is, at the same time, a forward-looking quality unmistakable in Bacon's closely *reasoned* prose, especially when compared with Andrewes's prose, which, as Eliot acknowledged, "may seem pedantic and verbal." He "takes a word and derives the world from it"—for example, "turn" in a sermon on Lent—"squeezing and squeezing the word until it yields a full juice of meaning which we should never have supposed any word to possess" (*Selected Essays* 347–48). Much more interested in *res* rather than *verba*, the first English essayist, for all his learning, never shows any hint of pedantry, his writing directed toward humanity's improvement—thus toward the *common* reader, whom it readily accommodates, not least in either length or purely rational order. So repeating an essential structure, as in "Of Studies," thus serves, much as the recurrence of certain linguistic and descriptive "tags" did in oral epic, to make for ready consumption—Bacon, then, functions as teacher, lecturer. He can be said to forward the cause of reformation.

"Of Studies" changes direction slightly after the last sentence quoted above, the focus shifting to specifics of reading. The mood is now imperative, rather than declarative, Bacon having moved from description to counsel—excellent counsel at that. I cannot resist the temptation to reckon that when he urges us to read in order "to weigh and consider," he is advising us to *essay*. Again, I quote the paragraph whole.

> Read not to contradict and confute; nor to believe and take for granted;
> nor to find talk and discourse; but to weigh and consider. Some books
> are to be tasted, others to be swallowed, and some few to be chewed and
> digested; that is, some books are to be read only in parts; others to be read,
> but not curiously; and some few to be read wholly, and with diligence
> and attention. Some books also may be read by deputy, and extracts
> made of them by others; but that would be only in the less important
> arguments, and the meaner sort of books; else distilled books are like
> common distilled waters, flashy things. (439)

Certainly by this point, the reader understands the importance here of distinction, difference, and analysis. The distinction among kinds of books,
for example, derives from (prior) comparison.

From reading as procedure or process, Bacon turns now, in the third and
final paragraph of the essay, to the "fruits" of reading. I end, having thus
provided the whole of the essay.

> Reading maketh a full man; conference a ready man; and writing an
> exact man. And therefore, if a man write little, he had need have a great
> memory; if he confer little, he had need have a present wit; and if he
> read little, he had need have much cunning, to seem to know that he
> doth not. Histories make men wise; poets witty; the mathematics subtile;
> natural philosophy deep; moral grave; logic and rhetoric able to contend.
> "Abeunt studia in mores." Nay there is no stond or impediment in the
> wit, but may be wrought out by fit studies: like as diseases of the body
> may have appropriate exercises. Bowling is good for the stone and reins;
> shooting for the lungs and breast; gentle walking for the stomach; riding
> for the head; and the like. So if a man's wit be wandering, let him study
> the mathematics; for in demonstrations, if his wit be called away never
> so little, he must begin again. If his wit be not apt to distinguish or find
> differences, let him study the schoolmen, for they are *cymini sectores*. If
> he be not apt to beat over matters, and to call up one thing to prove and
> illustrate another, let him study the lawyers' cases. So every defect of the
> mind may have a special receipt. (439–40)

What could be more optimistic, hopeful, and progressive than the prospect
opened by the last line here: a treatment for "every defect of the mind."
Swift's Modern, aforementioned, promises to have written—in Bacon's

wake?—"*A Panegyric upon the World.*" There may be room as well as opportunity for *personal* improvement, but as the Modern writes, "I am so
entirely satisfied with the whole present procedure of human things, that
I have been preparing materials towards" not only that essay but also "a
second part entitled *A modest Defence of the Proceedings of the Rabble in all
Ages*" (270).

The essayist is an amateur, a Virginia Woolf who has merely done a little reading up. . . . Meditation is the essence of it; it measures meanings; makes maps; exfoliates.
—William H. Gass, "Emerson and the Essay,"
   in *Habitations of the Word*

"The Passionate Discourse of an Amateur"

John Dryden's Prose and Poetic Essays

TEACHING OFTEN BRINGS such heightened awareness and perhaps such intensity of consciousness as Zen labels mindfulness. At least I find it so. Most recently, as I struggled to show how Eliot both posits an "Impersonal theory of poetry" and commits himself to the usually reflective form known as the essay, all the while condemning Romantic poetry for precisely its reflectiveness, I read aloud the following passage in "Tradition and the Individual Talent": the poet, wrote Eliot, "will be aware . . . that he must inevitably be judged by the standards of the past. I say judged, not amputated, by them; not judged to be as good as, or worse or better than, the dead; and certainly not judged by the canons of dead critics. It is a judgment, a comparison, in which two things are measured by each other" (*Selected Essays* 15).

The point on which I was launched had to do with the *relation* of tradition and the individual, and I was intent on the sub-point of Eliot's sense of conformity, eager to show his complexifying and refusal to reduce. That point appears clearest in the very next sentences in Eliot's essay, of course: "To conform merely would be for the new work not really to conform at all; it would not be new, and would therefore not be a work of art. And we do not quite say that the new is more valuable because it fits in; but its fitting in is a test of its value . . ." (*Selected Essays* 15). With these words, Eliot emerges as a complicated Modern—or is it a complicated Ancient?—both one and the other, as *The Waste Land* dramatizes.

What struck me, upon reading all these sentences together in class that morning, was the tossed-off definition of comparison and judgment as two things "measured by each other." In one sense, I reckon, I had not *read* these fecund words before, certainly not with full consciousness or with attention to what they actually say. Reading them aloud, however, in the conditions of intensity that is the university classroom, and with confidence born of experience, I had something of an epiphany. I had, in other words, the experience and glimpsed the meaning of that experience. That entailed grasping how Eliot characteristically works with differences, relations, and even oppositions in such a way as to measure one by the other.

Hardly anything is more important to Eliot than the assertion of comparative judgment as "two things measured by each other." If it smacks ever so lightly of skepticism, it does not disguise its antidogmatism. Here lies, in any case, I believe, Eliot's greatest debt to John Dryden, whom he so admired and on whom he wrote so frequently and well. It may be that in the earlier poet-critic Eliot found needed clarification of a deep instinct, perhaps the articulation of what had lain inchoate in his own critical thinking. I return here to Dryden, both to his early and grand work *An Essay of Dramatick Poesie* (1668) and his equally grand essay-poem *Religio Laici or A Laymans Faith* (1682).

An Essay of Dramatick Poesie stands as a tour de force, a remarkable essay that combines creation and commentary (or criticism). Pope's *An Essay on Criticism* is frequently celebrated for bringing together, and being, both poetry and criticism, or in its own terms, wit and judgment: it *is* criticism in poetic form, poetry that is critical commentary. It deserves all the praise imaginable. Dryden's *Essay* deserves no less; even if it is less pyrotechnical, it is the work of a writer at the top of his powers.

And so does *Religio Laici*, to which I turn first, because it is not considered an essay, because it is a neglected masterpiece badly misread in the past, and because it shows the full development of something Dryden perhaps discovered fifteen or so years earlier in the *Essay of Dramatick Poesy*. I refer to that sense of *immanent form* and *purposive movement* that Dryden rather brilliantly represents in his poem and that I discussed in *Tracing the Essay: Through Experience to Truth* and that Walter A. Davis elaborated in 1978 in *The Act of Interpretation: A Critique of Literary Reason*. First, *Religio Laici or A Laymans Faith*.

Begin at the beginning, with the justly praised exordium, in which Dryden establishes its basic movement as well as its fundamental message:

> Dim, as the borrow'd beams of Moon and Stars
> To *lonely, weary, wandring* Travellers,
> Is *Reason* to the *Soul*: and as on high,
> Those rowling Fires *discover* but the Sky
> Not light us *here*; so *Reason*'s glimmering Ray
> Was lent, not to *assure* our *doubtfull* way,
> But *guide* us upward to a *better Day*. (1–7)

The triplet here, which Dryden infrequently used and then often for emphasis, alerts us to the poem's major thematic point as well as its basic direction: the poem *guides us upward*. Indeed the various sub-arguments that follow, with the Deist, the Roman Catholic, and the sectarian, end the same: "More Safe, and much more modest 'tis, to say / *God wou'd not leave Mankind without a way*" (295–96). And, more elaborately,

> Thus Man by his own strength to Heaven wou'd soar:
> And wou'd not be Oblig'd to God for more.
> Vain, wretched Creature, how art thou misled
> To think thy Wit these God-like Notions bred!
> These Truths are not the product of thy Mind,
> But dropt from Heaven, and of a Nobler kind.
> *Reveal'd Religion* first inform'd thy Sight,
> And *Reason* saw not, till *Faith* sprung the Light.
> Hence all thy *Natural Worship* takes the *Source*:
> 'Tis *Revelation* what thou thinkst *Discourse*. (62–71)

One after another, challenges and opposition fall away, *as the argument takes us—upward—to God as answer to our various questions, quests, and plight*. And so, from natural theology to revelation, from priestly power to

Scriptura sola, it is God and He alone whom we should seek, worship, and depend upon.

> The *welcome News* is in the *Letter* found;
> The *Carrier*'s not Commission'd to *expound*.
> It *speaks* it *Self*, and what it does contain,
> In all things *needful* to be *known*, is *plain*. (366–69)

Notable is not only the emergence of Dryden's lifelong and frequently bitter anticlericalism but also his perfervid literalism and insistence on the "letter." Through the "letter" you proceed to God, mediation being necessary—including that of this very essay-poem.

The terms for Dryden's strategy in *Religio Laici*, itself derived and developed from *An Essay of Dramatick Poesie*, I take from Walter A. Davis's previously mentioned and unduly neglected book. He writes: "Put in the simplest and most exacting terms, the task of interpretation is to apprehend the purposive principle immanent in the structure of a literary work which determines the mutual interfunctioning of its component parts" (2). Such a position effectively challenges our usual ways of proceeding as well as elucidates Dryden's literary practice, in prose and verse alike. Let us stay with Davis a moment, for his elaboration also helps us see what is at stake with this notion of immanence:

> the critic of forms tries to apprehend structure as the continuous mani-
> festation and development of an organizing purpose. . . . Purpose is often
> the last thing critics consider. Its status is generally no more than that
> of an abstract category under which to group the discussion of general
> artistic ends . . . which bear little or no relationship to a work's concrete
> movement and phenomenal integrity. Its connection with the rest of the
> text is of the loosest sort. Purpose floats above and beyond the work or
> is only present in it from time to time. The critic of forms, in contrast,
> conceives purpose as *an immanent or indwelling rather than transcendent
> cause*. He holds the connection between purpose and structure to be direct
> and continuous: rather than locating purpose in a *disembodied* realm of
> general artistic ends or abstract intentions, he strives to find it at work in
> the dynamic progression of the text. (2; italics added)

Nothing Gnostic or Manichean here, in other words. In any case, Davis concludes: "Purpose coincides with structure because it gives birth to it. It is the most concrete category in criticism because its embodiment is constant and comprehensive: the purpose that shapes a work of art is realized by no more and no less than that entire work of art" (ibid.). As well as any poem or prose work I know, *Religio Laici* dramatizes these notions, its "dynamic progression" revealing the essential argument.

The argument of *An Essay of Dramatick Poesie*, it is worth noting, implies a similar immanence. Consider: critical positions are *embodied,* thanks to Dryden's fiction, literature always being different from philosophy's penchant for *ideas,* disembodied. Moreover the setting for the *Essay* bears a great deal of thematic weight. It not only suggests the importance of the critical "warfare" (by juxtaposition with the literal battle then being fought as the English meet the Dutch sailing up the Thames, not far, in fact, from where the little boat moors), but that concrete and particular situation *roots* the critical discussion; that is to say, criticism is not an isolated matter, separate from "the real world" and questions of culture, politics, and history. The *Essay,* thus, in more than one fashion, works against "mere" transcendence.

Worthy of note, too, is Dryden's mature comparative method, subtler, in fact, than in the earlier *Essay.* There, Ancients and Moderns, English and French, are directly compared and contrasted: "two things measured by each other." Here, in the essay-poem, "dynamic progression" is less directly comparative: the faults in the Deist, the Roman Catholic, and the sectarian receive the attention, an alternative being implied. The *via media* emerges during the process of consideration and contestation. The positive, in other words, lies implicit, at least until the climactic penultimate verse paragraph, and even there it is offered as difference, as a middle ground between the various extremes the poem has revealed.

Eliot's edition of Dryden's *Essay,* published in 1928, is "preceded" by his "Dialogue on Poetic Drama." In the preface to that essay, he defends his decision not to attempt "a learned introduction," for the latter, he writes, would be "a presumption and a superfluity," given the commentary of W. P. Ker and David Nichol Smith. Instead he has opted to follow Dryden (in Pope's words, proceeding in "the same Spirit that its Author *writ*") by attempting a dialogue. "If I cannot add to the knowledge and understanding of Dryden, I can perhaps add to his glory *by the contrast.* But my purpose is, if possible, to throw the dialogue of Dryden into a rather new light, by the great *contrast* between the topics, and between the attitudes towards them" (ix; italics added). Eliot thus engages, characteristically, in "analysis and comparison," his aim as always "elucidation." Eliot goes on to embrace the lack of dogmatism the dialogue form ensures, denying that he himself has "clear opinions on this subject." He denies as well that the characters in his dialogue can be identified "with myself or anyone else," and even that they are "fictions." They are, instead, he claims, "merely voices; a half-dozen men who may be imagined as sitting in a tavern after lunch, lingering over port and conversation at an hour when they should all be doing something else" (x).

These last words mark the contrast with Dryden's *Essay*, where the four men *are* characters, can be identified with historical persons, and clearly include Dryden himself (as Neander, who gets the last word). Moreover in the *Essay* a certain leisureliness consorts with urgency: the importance of the literary-critical discussion is both suggested and magnified by Dryden's own comparative method. He, that is, measures the importance of the discussion by the speakers' particular historical and geographical location, which he describes as follows, writing in "To the Reader": "It was that memorable day, in the first Summer of the late War, when our Navy ingag'd the Dutch: a day wherein the two most mighty and best appointed Fleets which any age had ever seen, disputed the command of the greater half of the Globe, the commerce of Nations, and the riches of the Universe" (9). The effect is to heighten and elevate the critical "warfare" that follows, implying *its* significance, too. The *Essay* thus functions in a manner opposite that of the mock-heroic, for here the manner aggrandizes, rather than reduces, the matter.

Indeed the *Essay* serves as a panegyric on the present age, its promise, its early achievement, and, above all, its difference from the "previous age." Early on, in fact, Crites, defender of the Ancients and based on Dryden's father-in-law, Sir Robert Howard, slams one poet of the Cromwell era as "a very Leveller in poetry" and proceeds to this fulsome praise of scientific advances, which Swift and Pope would soon lampoon, but which the *Essay* sets up as a prelude to literary advances: is it not evident now, he asks, "when the Study of Philosophy has been the business of all the *Virtuosi* in *Christendome*" that

> almost a new Nature has been reveal'd to us? that more errours of the
> School have been detected, more useful Experiments in Philosophy

have been made, more Noble Secrets in Opticks, Medicine, Anatomy, Astronomy, discover'd, than in all those credulous and doting Ages from *Aristotle* to us? so true it is that nothing spreads more fast than Science, when rightly and generally cultivated. (16–17)

As was not the case, so goes the implication, when the Puritans ruled. As to the arts, particularly poetry, says Eugenius a bit later, "the Muses, who ever follow Peace, went to plant in another Countrey; it was then that the great Cardinal of *Richelieu* began to take them into his protection" (34). But the French, the *Essay* insists, are a "servile" lot, and we should not mirror their servility, following them uncritically.

Nor, Dryden insists, should we forget the great disaster from which we have only recently emerged. The Fire was more recent, the Plague even more so, but Dryden recalls in no uncertain terms the war that "turned the world upside down":

And though the fury of a Civil War, and Power, for twenty years together, abandon'd to a barbarous race of men, Enemies of all good Learning, had buried the Muses under the ruines of Monarchy; yet with the restoration of our happiness, we see reviv'd Poesie lifting up its head, & already shaking off the rubbish which lay so heavy on it. (62–63)

Dryden's terms say it all: from fury and barbarism to "the restoration of our happiness."

The Civil War was extremism in desperate action, the Puritan Commonwealth another extremism, thoroughgoing in its mission and purifying in intent—consider, merely, the closing of the theaters. The essayist resists such immoderation, such violence. Even the famous definition of a play—rendered up by Lisideius, not Neander-Dryden—reflects the tension violated and vitiated in the Puritan regime: "*A just and lively Image of Humane Nature, representing its Passions and Humours, and the Changes of Fortune to which it is subject; for the Delight and Instruction of Mankind*" (16). "Delight and instruction" derive, of course, from Horace, but "just and lively" is Dryden's yoking of difference that, in the event, serves as the thematic link for the *Essay*'s central argument.

Neander makes the crucial point, contra Lisideius, regarding the English and the French. I grant, he says, that "the French contrive their plots more regularly, and observe the laws of comedy, and decorum of the stage (to speak generally), with more exactness than the English." But that is only part of the story, only one half of the accepted definition of "what a play ought to be." The other half, the more important actually, has to do with liveliness:

> For the lively imitation of Nature being in the definition of a Play, those which best fulfil that law ought to be esteemed superiour to the others. 'Tis true, those beauties of the French poesie are such as will raise perfection higher where it is, but are not sufficient to give it where it is not: they are indeed the Beauties of a Statue, but not of a Man, because not animated with the Soul of Poesie, which is imitation of humour and passions. (44)

Regularity or exactness thus serves as *outer* to the *inner* that is liveliness or soul, the animating, active force.

These terms control the ensuing, and climactic, "examen" of Ben Jonson's *The Silent Woman* as well as the comparison of Jonson and Shakespeare, itself a model of the kind of analysis and comparative judgment that Eliot came to revere. The subject throughout is, as Neander tells us, "relations." In a major passage, he makes explicit what the definition of a play and the preceding analyses at least imply, measuring the French by the English, whom he has shown to be superior:

> To conclude on this subject of Relations, if we are to be blam'd for showing too much of the action, the French are as faulty for discovering too little of it: a mean betwixt both should be observed by every judicious Writer, so as the audience may neither be left unsatisfied by not seeing what is beautiful, or shock'd by beholding what is either incredible or undecent. (50–51)

Of course, *Religio Laici* later argues likewise for the established church as precisely fulfilling the need for a position "betwixt" the two extremes of Roman Catholicism and Protestant sectarianism.

The same structure applies in the consideration fundamental to the *Essay of Dramatick Poesie*, the battle between the Ancients and the Moderns. In an eloquent and moving passage, near the end, Neander enunciates a middle-ground position not unlike Eliot's own in "Tradition and the Individual Talent." The point at issue is rhyme in plays. Neander reflects:

> But it is to raise envy to the living, to compare them with the dead. They are honour'd, and almost ador'd by us, as they deserve; neither do I know

any so presumptuous of themselves to contend with them. Yet give me leave to say thus much, without injury to their Ashes; that not onely we shall never equal them, but they could never equal themselves, were they to rise and write again. We acknowledge them our Fathers in wit; but they have ruin'd their Estates themselves before they came to their childrens hands. There is scarce an Humour, a Character, or any kind of Plot, which they have not blown upon: all comes sullied or wasted to us: and were they to entertain this Age, they could not make so plenteous treatments out of such decay'd Fortunes. This therefore will be a good Argument to us either not to write at all, or to attempt some other way. There is no bayes to be expected in their Walks; *Tentanda via est, qua me quoque possum tollere humo.* (71–72)

No mindless, or servile, imitation of the Ancients, then; no "thoroughgoing" conformity to the past or tradition. Dryden, like Eliot later, chose "to attempt some other way," to *essay*, in fact.

In the *Essay of Dramatick Poesie*, Dryden clearly embraces modernity, optimistic, even sanguine, with "the restoration of our happiness." The "new age" has left the fury and the barbarism of the preceding age behind, although it is far from forgotten—and never will be. On the other hand, this Modern pointedly does not transcend the Ancients. They remain alive, figured in Crites. All begins with them, of course, and the *Essay* returns to Crites for further argument on the (new) subject of rhyme. And although Crites is (twice) bested, and Neander obviously wins out, the "losing" side in these staged debates does not feel reduced; it is rendered with both seriousness and respect. If no "betwixt" emerges here, and could not given the issues, the manner and method of Dryden's writing nevertheless suggests no (thoroughgoing) separation or division. These "combatants" are, after all, friends, and remain so. The "new man" Neander, who comes off best in the drama, is represented at the end in terms not altogether flattering ("*Neander* was pursuing this discourse so eagerly, that *Eugenius* [advocate of regularity] had called to him twice or thrice ere he took notice that the Barge stood still, and that they were at the foot of *Somerset* Stairs, where they had appointed it to land") (79). Still the four part amicably, "*Eugenius* and *Lisideius* to some pleasant appointment they had made, and *Crites* and *Neander* to their several Lodgings" (80). If anticipations of "enthusiasm" perhaps appear in Neander, no signs of individualism appear anywhere in the *Essay.*

In *Religio Laici,* of course, separation, division, enthusiasm, the "private spirit," and individualism abound, objects of Dryden's often-scathing satire. Here Dryden struggles with the fact of the Reformation and the changes it wrought. He writes, directly, that "this good had full as bad a Consequence" (299): freeing his fellow laity from the shackles of a self-interested and corrupt priesthood, but in creating a priesthood of all readers of Holy Scripture, ushering in opportunities for new and greater abuses—

> So all we make of Heavens discover'd Will
> Is, not to have it, or to use it ill.
> The Danger's much the same; on several Shelves
> If *others* wreck *us,* or *we* wreck our *selves.* (423–26)

There is no going back—a lesson Eliot learned well—to the way it was before. And indeed Dryden does not want that. Instead, he accepts, however critically and cautiously, the present as inescapable and unavoidable. The past is both past *and* present, not *merely* past *nor* merely present. What to do with this present is the question—neither to be "amputated" by the past nor drown in the present.

R. P. Blackmur once described criticism as "the passionate discourse of an amateur." Embracing the notion, Allen Tate, no mean critic in his own right, reckoned that Blackmur meant "the man *devoted* to the object of his attention—literature, in this case—the man whose developing awareness and possession of the imaginative object becomes in the end self-knowledge" [Foreword xiv]. Tate's italics point to the religious character of the critic's commitment, and the whole smacks of the essay as we have been tracing it here. In working out a position for the layman that both accepts his freedom and entails his responsibilities, Dryden wrote in *Religio Laici* as an amateur, one whom he pointedly distinguished from the professional and self-seeking (who would, of course, avoid self-knowledge). Focusing on Scripture, moreover, he wrote as well as a "common reader," his poem effectively linking layman, amateur, common reader, and essayist, four aspects of one basic idea.

I know of no work that more fully and effectively embodies Blackmur's description of criticism than *An Essay of Dramatick Poesie.* This is no mere professional document, the dialogue instead that of "men of letters." These are amateurs and, in Virginia Woolf's understanding, "common readers." Anything else, anything more narrow, would violate Dryden's entire effort to show precisely the social and cultural importance of dramatic poetry.

There is something else in Blackmur's description that is relevant to Dryden's *Essay*: his term "passionate." Everywhere the *Essay* reveals, as it argues for, passion and liveliness, both inseparable, of course, from the central notion of importance. Crites, Eugenius, Lisideius, and Neander all speak passionately because they *love* literature and recognize its significance—they are "devoted" to it.

In the essay from which I have drawn, itself devoted to the criticism of the sadly neglected Andrew Lytle, his friend Allen Tate proceeds to fine remarks on reading, apposite to our discussion. After describing Lytle's essays as "creative," he writes of them as "close translations of works which Lytle has read, reread, read once again, so that his last reading assumes so complete a mastery of the text that he no longer needs to refer to it" (Foreword xv). Mastery here means, I take it, not control over the text-become-slave to the reader's will but, instead, surrender and submission, so that, in the terms of *Religio Laici*, you can hear the text "*speak . . . it Self.*" It is an "inside" position. So much so, in fact, that Tate even says, "For reading is translation" (ibid.).

Writing then follows; it is, Geoffrey Hartman once declared, the difference that reading makes. Of Lytle, Tate says this: "This sentence is his modest declaration of purpose for his critical writing: 'It is part of the author's discipline to read well, and to read well you must write it down'" (xv). Lytle thus, and Tate too, reveals the inseparable link between reading and writing. If writing "completes" the act of reading, it does not transcend it in the sense of moving on and leaving it behind, in part because the act of writing finely involves reading (what one writes). Writing, then, is dependent upon reading, through and by means of which writing must proceed.

Eliot knew as much, as did Dryden. The earlier poet, the earlier essayist, did not need to teach the later the significance of poesy. But he did show him, differently from the way Georg Lukács described, *how* to reveal the importance of critical reflection. Determined, at least from the time of "Tradition and the Individual Talent" in 1920, that "two things are measured by each other," Eliot obviously knew the *relation* between reading and writing: each needs the other and should be considered in relation to one another. According to Dryden, his reading of Henry Dickinson's translation of Father Richard Simon's *Critical History of the Old Testament* "bred" his layman's faith: "which better thou hast read, / Thy Matchless Author's work: which thou, my Friend, / By well translating better dost commend" (227–29). Reading, translating, writing—they are entangled. As are Dryden, the essay, and Eliot.

We emerge from consideration of Dryden's most famous essay and his great essay-poem with new appreciation of Eliot's statement in "Tradition and the Individual Talent" regarding the relation of "two things." As can be seen, he sometimes draws out the inseparability of such apparent opposites as faith and doubt, as well as thought and feeling. At other times, the emphasis falls on the most striking aspect of the pattern, Incarnation: the way is in, through, and by means of Christ, man, the literal, the body. The *via media* then arises as a necessary "third," an in-between all important. Now we understand there also functions a relation that stems from comparison whereby "two things are measured by each other," the result being such elucidation of each as separate consideration probably could not produce.

A byproduct, as it were, of our effort here, this essay: comparing *An Essay of Dramatick Poesie* and *Religio Laici*, a prose essay and a poem, shows us that a poem and an essay are not absolutely different; on the contrary, they share a great deal, and most important is their common essayistic basis, their foundation in the matter of the form we call the essay. Comparing these two particular works produces further insight: although they share the embodiment of ideas and positions, they diverge, as we have seen, in both treatment of ineffective ideas and positions—the antitheses—and the texture of the thesis. Dryden certainly does not extend to the sectarians in *Religio Laici* the respect shown to, and due, the Ancients and the French, although neither the Deist nor the Papist is exactly savaged. And indeed, in the *Essay*, Dryden, as Neander, does directly argue the position of the English, although *he* is not the defender of the Moderns, that being left to Eugenius. In *Religio Laici*, differently, neither Dryden nor anyone else *asserts* or even describes in particular the preferred, Anglican position. Instead the thesis *emerges*. The method of argument is, in fact, negative, with the antitheses revealed or, better, exposed, and that procedure, I reckon, embodies the Anglican way: it is the *via media*. That way simply arises *as alternative*, which points to the glory of the "middle way," the Church of England, and the essay; it represents the quiet that the poem praises, as well as the sensibleness that avoids extremes. It is, in short, a way of being— and so must be represented in persons—rather than a disembodied idea, a manner of proceeding, a matter of character, just as Dryden began to see in *An Essay of Dramatick Poesie* and developed in *Religio Laici or A Laymans Faith*.

These ideas are endemic to the essay, and Eliot's reading in the seventeenth century would have exposed him to them, particularly when he measured them against Montaigne, whom he so much admired and feared. I rather suspect, however, that Eliot took more from John Dryden than we have thought, more than he ever directly acknowledged. The need persists for extended measurement of Eliot by Dryden and of Dryden by Eliot. What we observe, as students of the essay, is that that form mirrored the very problems Dryden saw around him in politics, religion, and culture; in addressing one situation, he therefore addressed another.

Particularly important is the sense that Dryden conveys of *pattern*, or structure, the underlying figure in such tapestries as he weaves in both *An Essay of Dramatick Poesie* and *Religio Laici or A Laymans Faith*. From the latter, more so than the former, Eliot pretty clearly drew a sense of the essay's potential virtually obliterated in the later eighteenth and the entire nineteenth century. Dryden, in fact, faced squarely the challenges the "new" form imposed, especially its strident individualism, and tried to turn the essay in another direction. Pope followed suit, in his various versified and *familiar*—rather than personal—essays. For Dryden, the essay, too, like the Reformation, was an undeniable good with as bad a consequence. He made it the vehicle for traditional values and surrender of the assertive and aggressive self to a power outside. He did more, building on the sense of the *via media* already there, at least in Bacon, and realizing the essay's potential as incarnational structure. Two centuries later, Eliot returned to the challenge, renewing Dryden's effort, his essay, sometimes in prose, sometimes in verse, like his mentor, the capacious poet-essayist.

Very few people, I suspect, know how to read—in the sense
of being able to read for a variety of motives and to read a
variety of books each in the appropriate way. . . . Philosophy
is difficult, unless we discipline our minds for it; the full
appreciation of poetry is difficult for those who have not trained
their sensibility by years of attentive reading.
—T. S. Eliot, preface, *Thoughts for Meditation*, selected and
arranged by N. Gangulee

With Wit Enough to Manage Judgment

Alexander Pope's An Essay on Criticism

YOU CAN REST CONFIDENT in very few positive statements regarding the essay. One of the safest, it has long seemed, is that, no matter
what else the essay is or is not, it is written in prose. This assumption baffles
me—even more than the truism that the essay is a piece of writing that you
can manage to read in one sitting. Virginia Woolf called *A Room of One's
Own* an essay, and although it is certainly powerful, gripping reading, I
for one cannot read—or re-read—it in one sitting; not only is it around
150 pages, but it is also "language charged with meaning," thus requiring
"attentive reading" and thoughtfulness. John Locke's *An Essay on Human
Understanding* is even longer, of course, its difficulty stemming from its being philosophy, for which I for one lack the necessary discipline. As to the
essay's being a prose creature, there are the well-known and illustrious instances of Alexander Pope's poetic essays *An Essay on Criticism, An Essay on
Man,* and the so-called Ethic Epistles or *Moral Essays,* to say nothing of less
obvious although still important predecessors in the seventeenth century.
Truth is, neither length nor mode—that is, verse or prose—determines

whether a piece of writing deserves the label "essay." I would hesitate to question such a fastidious and exacting writer as Pope.

Thus I include—without apology and without a felt need to justify its title—Pope's verse masterpiece *An Essay on Criticism*, one of at least six essays he penned as poetry. I choose this verse-essay for several reasons, including the likelihood that it would appeal least to today's student or general reader! It also treats topics central to our concerns throughout the present book. Moreover the fact that I have written about it elsewhere, more than once in fact, and extensively, will allow me to forgo some reflections and analyses that, were I to attempt to do full justice to the work here, would greatly exceed my stringent limitations of space. I can do no more here than to initiate a reading, in hopes that the inspired reader will, as appropriate, turn to other commentary and, better, continue the work of reading that I have only just begun.

I focus, then, on Pope's advice, as relevant today as when he wrote three centuries ago. What strikes immediately is his judiciousness, as well as his wisdom, his amazing capacity to bring together what so often is separated and, worse, made into oppositions. *An Essay on Criticism* is both a magnificent work of criticism and a great poem (regarding the latter, see, for instance, my article on the poem's usually slighted second section). In the terms of the poem, *An Essay on Criticism* is a work of both wit and judgment, and one as the other: poetry made of criticism. The achievement is remarkable—especially so for one who could have been no older than twenty-three, and maybe, as he was not above suggesting, years younger!

The issues, along with Pope's strategies and his values, are marked early on. Thus he writes, regarding the central concern:

> Some, to whom Heav'n in Wit has been profuse,
> Want as much more, to turn it to its use;
> For *Wit* and *Judgment* often are at strife,
> Tho' meant each other's Aid, like *Man* and *Wife*. (80–83)

Between 1711, when the poem first appeared, and 1743, its last appearance in Pope's lifetime, the first couplet was perhaps even clearer in significant intent: "There are whom Heav'n has blest with store of Wit, / Yet want as much again to manage it." In his magisterial introduction to *An Essay on Criticism* in the Twickenham Edition, Aubrey Williams superbly points to the issues at stake. Whereas Pope thus refuses to separate wit and judgment, many of his near-contemporaries were doing just that, including Thomas Hobbes and the aforementioned John Locke, following the lead of Peter Ramus, who notoriously rearranged the five parts of the art of rhetoric, removing invention, arrangement, and memory from rhetoric, giving them to dialectic, and leaving rhetoric with only expression (or style) and delivery. This position would prevail, with disastrous consequences for poetry. Williams spells them out:

> The ultimate effect of such a line of thought as this would be the trivialization of poetry itself: the faculty of Wit and the figurative language it inspires are seen as unrelated to truth and real knowledge, to "things as they are." Since figurative language is of the essence of poetry, the denial of its ability to express truth is the denial of the value and dignity of poetry. At best, the main role of Wit or of poetry becomes (as in Ramistic theory) the mere ornamentation of those truths provided for it by the judgment, and it is scarcely conceivable that Pope, for whom Wit in the *Essay* is synonymous on occasion with Genius and Art itself, would or could share in assumptions so prejudicial to his art. (217)

From here, Williams proceeds, with equal authority and definition, to a reading of lines 80–83 of the poem, quoted above. Unmistakable, indeed, is Pope's

> insisting that Wit, rather than Judgment or Sense, can manage Wit. Wit thus becomes not only a faculty which provides quickness of insight and liveliness of expression, but also a controlling and ordering faculty. Wit and Judgment seem to be . . . differing aspects of the same faculty. (218)

If judgment already exists within wit, then criticism lies within literature, which offers access to it as part of itself. The implications are momentous. Judgment is no exterior force, power, or capacity; indeed it is secondary to wit or literature. My own experience as a writer supports this, for, I find, judgment is not a second phase of a process. Instead judgment occurs alongside "creation" or imaginative conception. *Within the imaginative, synthetic, and creative moment itself,* I know whether there is adequacy and accuracy. How this happens, I am no more prepared to say than I am to posit when one develops the capacity.

Although writing is Pope's main concern in *An Essay on Criticism*, both the primary sort that is poetry and the secondary that is commentary and evaluation, he also discusses reading, albeit not nearly so extensively. What he says about criticism must, of course, have to do with reading. On reading specifically, his most direct and valuable advice is that with which such later—and different—critics as Virginia Woolf and C. S. Lewis concur: "A perfect Judge will *read* each Work of Wit / With the same Spirit that its Author *writ*" (233–34)—this is, note, different from E. D. Hirsch's admonition to quest for the writer's "intention." That "perfect Judge" Pope describes later on in detail, absence of pride being very nearly the fundamental requirement:

> But where's the Man, who Counsel *can* bestow,
> Still *pleas'd* to *teach*, and yet not *proud* to *know*?
> Unbiass'd, or by *Favour* or by *Spite*;
> Not *dully prepossest*, nor *blindly right*;
> Tho' Learn'd, well-bred; and tho' well-bred, sincere;
> Modestly bold, and Humanly severe?
> Who to a *Friend* his Faults can freely show,
> And gladly praise the Merit of a *Foe*?
> Blest with a *Taste* exact, yet unconfin'd;
> A *Knowledge* both of *Books* and *Humankind*;
> *Gen'rous Converse;* a *Soul* exempt from *Pride*;
> And *Love to Praise*, with *Reason* on his Side? (631–42)

Much here applies more or less directly to any reader.

In a very real sense, of course, Pope's entire poem concerns reading and how fairly and judiciously to manage it. Behind him stands John Dryden, who made reading the focus of his essay-poem *Religio Laici or A Laymans Faith*, which makes reading a key to one's position relative to God. Pope is a moral critic, through and through. "LEARN then what MORALS Criticks ought to show," he writes, beginning the third and final section of *An Essay on Criticism*, "For 'tis but *half* a *Judge's Task*, to *Know*" (560–61). As in the depiction of the ideal critic, so here Pope insists on the whole, not merely a part, of truth. Lines 631–42 *express*, not merely state, the point that the ideal critic combines disparate and seemingly opposite qualities, abilities, and values. Similarly, knowing is but half of a critic's task. Manner counts too, fully as much, in fact, as matter; and you must know how to write as well as how to read if you are to be a critic—"*Nature's chief Master-piece is writing well,*" Pope quotes the Duke of Buckingham as saying in his *Essay on Poetry* (724). Pope sums up the requirement in writing: "Nor in the *Critick* let the *Man* be lost! / *Good-Nature* and *Good-Sense* must ever join; / To Err is *Humane*; to Forgive, *Divine*" (523–25).

In face of the expressed need to attend to wholes, our all-too-familiar pattern in reading consists of privileging a part. It may be one aspect of poetry, imagery, say, or meter; or it may be that we attend carefully and afford a fair hearing only to those of our own party or sect. It may be, too, that we are biased in favor of the Ancients or the Moderns. The "perfect Judge" will, however, "Survey the *Whole*" (235) rather than make the whole depend upon a favored or privileged part:

> Most Criticks, fond of some subservient Art,
> Still make the *Whole* depend upon a *Part*,
> They talk of *Principles*, but Notions prize,
> And All to one lov'd Folly Sacrifice. (263–66)

How right Pope remains.

As criticism consists of both wit and judgment, matter and manner, so does reading in general. Sympathy and judgment must come together in the *whole* act that we call reading, although the temptation remains strong to make that whole depend upon a part: we either give ourselves to our author, as Woolf urges, or we judge immediately, even before finding out what he or she is saying (as do many of my students nowadays). But if wit manages judgment, and literature has within itself judgment, then surely judgment already exists within that sympathetic engagement essential to reading, by any and all of us, critics or "common readers."

A fundamental point for Pope is one none of us wishes to hear. Not only is "A *little Learning* . . . a dang'rous Thing" (215), but "Pride, where Wit fails, steps in to our Defence, / And fills up all the *mighty Void* of *Sense*" (209–10). Therefore the most important criticism is self-criticism: "Trust not your self; but your Defects to know, / Make use of ev'ry *Friend* —and ev'ry *Foe*" (213–14). In any case, again, "*Good-Nature* and *Good-Sense* must ever join; / To Err is *Humane*; to Forgive, *Divine*."

Character thus matters—it may be the most important thing for a critic. He or she must forgo or avoid the great temptation toward part-iality of one sort or another and combine frequently separated qualities: knowing "*Humankind*" as well as "*Books*" and having "a Taste exact, yet unconfin'd."

The demand is considerable: nothing less than "a *Soul* exempt from *Pride.*" Then, and only then, may appear the ideal of "*Gen'rous Converse.*"

Criticism should be just that, a noble idea: conversational rather than pedantic or dogmatic, and generous. This essay-poem ends exactly so, the poet-critic "Not *free* from Faults, nor yet too vain to *mend.*"

Together with the injunction to read with the same spirit as that with which the poet wrote, this representation entails knowing the work in and of and for itself. Sympathy is thus crucial, and I infer that Pope would have us figure judgment as residing inside sympathy, just as criticism does literature. If judgment does not exist outside, distant and separate, it will not be harsh, at least not unfairly so. What a difference that would make in our reading and, more, in our commentary.

Let us now draw out Pope's thinking, extending it if need be. In order to do so, I turn to T. S. Eliot's hugely influential early essay "Tradition and the Individual Talent," a part of *The Sacred Wood.* In a sense, *An Essay on Criticism* is about the same or similar concerns. Certainly Pope prizes tradition as Eliot does, and they both wish to subordinate the individual to tradition and engage him or her fully in it. Moreover Pope and Eliot share a kind of thinking that I would describe, borrowing from Montaigne (on Seneca), as "*ondoyant et divers.*" It accepts and embraces tension, keeping difference in play while resisting freezing it into absoluteness or opposition. Take Eliot, again, in this important paragraph:

> In a peculiar sense [the poet] will be aware also that he must inevitably
> be judged by the standards of the past. I say judged, not amputated by
> them; not judged to be as good as, or worse or better than, the dead;
> and certainly not judged by the canons of dead critics. *It is a judgment,*
> *a comparison, in which two things are measured by each other.* To conform
> merely would be for the new work not really to conform at all; it would
> not be new, and would therefore not be a work of art. And we do not
> quite say that the new is more valuable because it fits in; but its fitting
> in is a test of its value—a test, it is true, which can only be slowly and
> cautiously applied, for we are none of us infallible judges of conformity.
> We say: it appears to conform, and is perhaps individual, or it appears
> individual, and may conform; but we are hardly likely to find that it is one
> and not the other. (15–16; italics added)

Eliot's commentary is typically comparative, comparison being, he says, along with "analysis" "the tools of criticism" ("Imperfect Critics," in *The Sacred Wood* 33).

Comparison is one of the two essential and *defining* tools of criticism, says Eliot, and when he, who wields this tool more surely and productively than anyone else I know, compares John Donne and Lancelot Andrewes, say, or Bishop King or Lord Herbert of Cherbury and Tennyson, he draws out differences *and* reveals both better and worse writing. The issues emerge crisply as well as succinctly, and I feel both enlightened and confident in the revelations. Comparison, at least as Eliot manages it, is never one-sided or extreme; it allows for, and produces, balance and fairness. No either/or but both/and — reminiscent of Pope's handling of diverse qualities in, for example, his representation in *An Essay on Criticism* of the ideal critic.

In Eliot's comparing, the result is not, then, triumph of one over the other; although neither wins, neither loses. Comparing thus prevents too positive a conclusion. The game concerns elucidation and clarification, certainly precision of perception, instead of winning. You know each text "not positively, but negatively, in its differences from" another, "not in its own properties" (J. H. Newman, qtd. in Dawson 106). Or, rather, the text's "own" properties emerge in, through, and by means of the revealed differences from another. In any case, comparison is a *via media* instrument; in mitigating the positive, it works against the building of an argument. It produces something else of vital importance. It steadfastly works against, and in Eliot certainly deters, individualistic interpretation, the personal, or the part-ial, mitigated if not obviated, for comparing virtually removes the focus from the reader and puts it on the object(s), where it belongs. I do not think that this has been sufficiently noted.

Question yourself, your opinions, your judgment, Pope urges; "trust not yourself," but instead turn to others, friend and foe alike, to reveal your errors, missteps, imprecision. More than one is essential. "Avoid *Extremes*" (384), counsels Pope, and like Eliot, he urges, immerse yourself in the whole tradition:

Be *Homer's* Works your *Study*, and *Delight*,
Read them by Day, and meditate by Night,
Thence form your Judgment, thence your Maxims bring,

And trace the Muses *upward* to their *Spring*;
Still with *It self compar'd,* his *Text* peruse;
And let your *Comment* be the *Mantuan Muse.* (124–29)

Judgment *is* thus inseparable from the literature from which it springs and that effectively manages it. The individual cannot know by himself or herself, nor can he know a work by itself, in and of itself.

Wit and *Judgment* often are at strife,
Tho' meant each other's Aid, like *Man* and *Wife.*
'Tis more to *guide* than *spur* the Muse's Steed;
Restrain his Fury, than Provoke his Speed;
The winged Courser, like a gen'rous Horse,
Shows most true Mettle when you *check* his Course. (82–87)

Pope's essay-poem thus teaches *and* delights, teaching not least in, through, and by means of delighting. That delight stems, in part, from the sheer mastery of both language and poetic form. *An Essay on Criticism* appears all the richer, affording you more pleasure and instruction, when you read it in relation—comparing it—with other essays.

"A Modest Proposal," perhaps the most enigmatic and widely read essay in English.
—Lydia Fakundiny, *The Art of the Essay*

It's Not an Essay

Jonathan Swift's "A Modest Proposal" and the Immodesty of Satire

SATIRE IS A PARTICULAR LITERARY FORM. So is the essay. Unfortunately sometimes these forms are confused, even fused, their essential differences elided. Some irony attends here, for in fact satire consists of the elimination of precisely such differences as play between itself and the essay.

The inclusion of Jonathan Swift's great satire "A Modest Proposal" among essays betrays the need for distinction. It reveals the poverty of inclusive accounts of the essay. Despite the undeniable impossibility of defining this protean form, to house almost anything in prose under the rubric—while, incidentally, denying the title, or honorific, to even those works in verse that call themselves essays—is folly. It is sloppy criticism, absent the precision of scholarship and devoid of literary commentary's most striking and necessary components: comparison and analysis.

The plot of "A Modest Proposal" is entirely familiar. The speaking voice advocates cannibalism of young Irish children as a reasonable and indeed responsible way of dealing with pressing Irish problems. Clearly we cannot take this at face value for one reason: the *author* is himself a churchman (although contemporary readers might well not have known that Jonathan Swift is the author). Just as clearly, the diverse and monstrous problems besetting the Irish emerge in all their horror, along with English perfidy and Irish culpability. Moreover, not long into the piece, whatever this bizarre writing is, we realize that the speaker is not to be trusted. Before we have been with him for a page, we hear him refer to (human) babies being "dropped" from their "dam," and a clear picture of his nature, if not exactly his character, begins to emerge. In modern-day terms, he would be a human engineer, a social scientist of the worst cloth, who proceeds only according to the dictates of disengaged reason, thus subject to the drive and will of logic alone, distanced, supposedly objective, and absent any feelings common to the animal we call man. These very qualities of sound reasoning and dispassion, this voice parades, proclaims, and attempts to verify. He denies any self-interest, representing himself as motivated solely by concern for the public good, preeminently in the last paragraph, which by itself makes clear the character of the speaker:

> I profess in the sincerity of my heart that I have not the least personal interest in endeavouring to promote this necessary work, having no other motive than the *public good of my country, by advancing our trade, providing for infants, relieving the poor, and giving some pleasure to the rich.* I have no children by which I can propose to get a single penny; the youngest being nine years old, and my wife past child-bearing. (446)

To my mind, the voice in "A Modest Proposal" thus prefigures the bourgeoisie of *Madame Bovary*, if he does not anticipate "the State" as Orwell presents its hegemony in *Animal Farm* and *Nineteen Eighty-Four*. In any case, we can be sure that this speaker—to be ruthlessly distinguished from his author—plays a major, and determinative, role in this satire, as is typical of Swift (see, for example, *A Tale of a Tub* and *Gulliver's Travels*).

As we continue to read, we dismiss the proposals being advanced and distance ourselves from him who makes them, both equally and at the same time: the voice is hardly less horrid than his proposal; only this kind of person must offer this kind of solution. Swift often literalizes metaphors, here the English eating the Irish alive, and his speaker becomes the epitome of all things inhuman, not merely *inhumane*, as he reminds us, although he is worse, of those "rational creatures" the Houyhnhnms in *Gulliver's Travels*. As we know from a letter to his good friend Alexander Pope, written as he was composing that great satire, Swift believed man only "*rationis capax*." But the speaker of "A Modest Proposal" and the horses of the fourth and final book of *Gulliver's Travels* know next to nothing of either body or soul. In other words, Swift's speaker is "thoroughgoing."

As satire typically works, there is both a thesis and an antithesis: both what the author opposes and what he advocates. The satirist, for all his wit and complexity, indeed ingenuity, must be clear—otherwise he will offend the wrong people just as he appears to embrace the wrong people, Daniel Defoe being a case in point with his *Shortest Way with Dissenters*, which enraged both sides. Sides are the issue, in fact the problem, for the satirist takes sides, represents problems in terms of the wrong side being taken, the right being opposed to it. It is not, then, that taking sides is necessarily a problem, certainly not *the* problem, for the satirist tacitly assumes that a right side exists and that his or her readers can perhaps be "cured" of wrong tendencies and brought onboard. Either/or prevails, not neither/nor, even less both/and. In other words, "A Modest Proposal" works by being *pointed*, its satire sharp rather than blunt.

And Swift manages to make his side clear, the antithesis to the thesis that is the inhumanity that leads to cannibalism. Were it not for one thing, that antithesis—the alternative to the horrid, the monstrous—would be what we ordinarily *think of* as the opposite. It would simply be implicit, unstated, and merely emerging. But "A Modest Proposal" becomes a satire, in part, because Swift leaves nothing to chance. He makes explicit, as well as pointed, overtly declaring what he himself espouses behind his speaker's back. What that speaker denounces and dismisses is, given the satiric structure, what is actually being promoted. It is quite reasonable, but not extreme; here, common sense prevails, compassion alongside reason, humanity thus present. This we find, in italics, the speaker having made his particular and pointedly disinterested case:

> Therefore let no man talk to me of other expedients: *Of taxing our ab-*
> *sentees at five shillings a pound: Of using neither clothes, nor household*
> *furniture, except what is of our own growth and manufacture: Of utterly*
> *rejecting the materials and instruments that promote foreign luxury: Of curing*

the expensiveness of pride, vanity, idleness, and gaming in our women: Of
introducing a vein of parsimony, prudence, and temperance: Of learning to
love our country, wherein we differ even from Laplanders, *and the inhabitants*
of Topinamboo: *Of quitting our animosities and factions, nor act any longer*
like the Jews, *who were murdering one another at the very moment their city*
was taken: Of being a little cautious not to sell our country and consciences
for nothing: Of teaching landlords to have at least one degree of mercy towards
their tenants. Lastly, *of putting a spirit of honesty, industry, and skill into our*
shopkeepers, who, if a resolution could now be taken to buy only our native
goods, would immediately unite to cheat and exact upon us in the price, the
measure and the goodness, nor could ever yet be brought to make one fair
proposal of just dealing, though often and earnestly invited to it. (445)

Any lingering complexity stems from Swift's inclusive, sweeping satire: everyone is indicted. Only he without blemish might cast the first stone; the speaker casts stones aplenty, but he is hardly without fault. His solution is, of course, a large part of the problem, more so for us who have survived the twentieth century and the poverty of scientism and so-called objectivity. Despite its ridiculousness—or, maybe because of it—we cannot fail to appreciate the relevance and timelessness of Swift's dramatic representation, especially of his insouciant speaker.

Nothing reveals the difference between "A Modest Proposal" and the essay better than this speaker. He alone should prevent us from thinking of this satire as an essay. To be sure, this "objective" speaker is personal in the sense that he refers more than once to his own situation, adducing his family situation, for instance, as evidence of that disinterestedness. And yet we cannot confidently say that he is personal in any real sense, for he is not a person—rather, a monster. Monsters do not write essays, nor do essayists adopt monstrous personas.

Swift's speaker is, of course, grossly unaware of his own monstrousness. He lacks, indeed, any self-consciousness. In this regard, he resembles Gulliver, who, we know, is not a little too confident in his opinions, although Gulliver is at least right about the Yahoos he despises, even as he fails to recognize that he himself is one of them:

But the Houyhnhnms, who live under the government of reason, are
no more proud of the good qualities they possess, than I should be for

not wanting a leg or an arm, which no man in his wits would boast of, although he must be miserable without them. I dwell the longer upon this subject from the desire I have to make the society of an English yahoo by any means not insupportable, and therefore I here entreat those who have any tincture of this absurd vice, that they will not presume to appear in my sight. (239)

After this: "Finis."

The point, though, concerns more, much more, than the "character" of the speaker. Of course the essay as form is highly dependent on the voice we hear: if we do not like that, avers Annie Dillard, we most likely will toss the essay aside. Somewhat differently, E. B. White declared that candor is the one essential quality in the essayist. As a result, essays incarnate familiar and agreeable voices, even if that voice be critical. In my judgment, Thoreau fails as an essayist in large part because of his unrelenting, sanctimonious, and quite unsympathetic voice.

More than character, however, is involved. In "A Modest Proposal," Swift's voice is created and fictional. It is not his. There is room for disagreement here, some readers regarding that voice as Swift's persona (the late, great biographer—and my teacher—Irvin Ehrenpreis, for one) while others judge the voice we hear in "A Modest Proposal" to be that of a fictional character, someone totally divorced from Swift. I subscribe to this latter notion, considering the speaker as like in kind, if not in degree, the much more developed Lemuel Gulliver. For our purposes here, it may not much matter which way we tend, for in either case, the voice of "A Modest Proposal" is *thoroughgoing* in his difference from the biographical Swift.

Essays, on the other hand, require that the voice be that of the author. To be sure, that voice may be shaved and shaped to fit the artistic integrity of the work: essayists as alike and different as Edward Hoagland and Sam Pickering have long maintained that creativity enters the form, which is, after all, a kind of *creative* nonfiction. Simply put, a tension obtains in the essay between fact and fiction, the imagined and the truthfully represented (White's candor, I reckon). In "A Modest Proposal," there is no such tension, as I have been suggesting.

The satirist, quite unlike the essayist, is out to persuade: as James Sutherland once wrote in his Clark Lectures published as *English Satire*: "he must compel his readers to agree with him; he must persuade them to accept his judgment of good and bad, right and wrong" (5). Furthermore, "If the satirist habitually simplifies and exaggerates, if he deals with only one side of a question or one aspect of a man's character—above all, if he is interested only in what he finds and never asks himself how or why it came to be there—" (17–18), well, then, you have a crucial difference from the essayist, who is never so sure or so simplistic. According to Sutherland, "The satirist, like the magistrate on the bench, is there to administer the law, to uphold the order of a civilized community; he brings men and women to the test of certain ethical, intellectual, social, and other standards" (19). The essayist, differently, is not given to judgment so much as to sympathy, finding himself unable to judge because she recognizes both her own complicity and his kinship with those who falter. There is not, then, the detachment required of satire. The essayist is, moreover, there not to administer laws or to uphold civilized order—in other words, functionary—but, rather, to open even that order to scrutiny and criticism and, more important perhaps, to remind us of ways and values in danger of being forgotten or lost, to preserve not so much by supporting as by keeping alive the memory of those alternative ways and procedures. There is, for the essay, always an intriguing other-ness, which, it happens, the satirist tends to distrust and reject.

Let us not forget, either, the thesis/antithesis structure that characterizes satire, with its fear and denunciation of otherness. As I have remarked, satire is pointed, as well as sure of itself and its position. It divides, positing, and thereby furthering, opposition, not just difference. There is right and wrong, and if you do not agree with the satirist, you are wrong. Delicacy has no place in satire, but in essays it peers around every corner, blunting sharpness and defusing confrontation.

Satire is as positive as the essay is exploratory, inquisitive, and tentative. Indeed satire is positive even in its negativity, its opposition. There *is* a position, a proper one, taken, defended, and represented as right. Matters are clear-cut, but not normally with the essay. I think no one has written better of the essay's particular nature—its *via media* nature—than John Henry Newman, describing quite another institution: "it is not known positively, but negatively, in its differences from the rival [forms], not in its own properties, and can only be described as a third system, neither the one nor the other, partly both, cutting between them, and, as if with a critical fastidiousness, trifling with them both" (qtd. in Dawson 106).

Nothing precludes the essayist from having a position or taking a stand, but those do not mark the essayist nor determine her or his work. On the other hand, the essayist is neither (necessarily) pacifistic nor weak. Certainly he is not indifferent or chary or cowardly. Nor does he pick his battles based on shrewdness. He tends to come with a definite moral and cultural stance, but he is, as Montaigne said of Seneca, "*ondoyant et divers*," neither doctrinaire nor sectarian. As a consequence, you respect him as a man, not for his opinions. There is a wholeness, then, about the essay that satire cannot approach.

The essay is skeptical, rather than affirmative of a definite and single position. It may be affirmative of "life's newness and joy," but the essay *does not know enough* — "que sais-je?" Montaigne is known to have asked — to be particularly positive, or to defend a position in any thoroughgoing way. In fact the essay shies away from making positive statements. Some do occur, naturally, but for the most part they derive from concrete and particular experience represented, from which meaning has been extracted and then offered up. Of course Emerson and Thoreau spring immediately to mind as exceptions. The former certainly engages in philosophical-moral analysis and exhortation, the latter in moral and political harangue. But that means, in my judgment, that Emerson and Thoreau are actually writing something different from and other than essays, a point to which I return in treating them in this book. Richard Selzer has said it well, in "A Worm from My Notebook": "There are no 'great' subjects for the creative writer; there are only the singular details of a single human life. . . . Always, it is the affliction of one human being that captures the imagination." Always, too, Selzer continues, essayist and surgeon, the writer—I would say especially the writer, she or he, of essays— "ceases to think of his character as an instrument to be manipulated and think[s] of him as someone with whom he has fallen in love. For it is always, must always be, a matter of love" (434–35). How different is "A Modest Proposal."

Lacking positive force and flourishing in its differences from various rivals rather than "in its own properties," the essay can be no other than modest and humble. It directly advocates little while reminding us of what we need, because people always have needed *that*, to carry on, to make the most of our little time. I would not, then, call the essay a "second-class citizen," unless with the irony of a satirist.

Dr. Samuel Johnson . . . didn't persuade you; he just told you. There was no arguing with him. But he did it in such a bluff way, appealing to you as the sensible fellow that you really are, that nobody could take offence. He is never the "superior person" that Addison was: he never talks down to you. [H]e is not preaching tolerance and understanding, he is exhibiting them, not without humour.

—Bonamy Dobrée, *English Essayists*

Turning Inside Out

Samuel Johnson's "The Solitude of the Country"

DR. JOHNSON'S ESSAYS are much closer to Bacon's than to Montaigne's. They show next to none of the latter's self-expressiveness while based in and deriving from the latter's English, and Anglican, proclivity for balance. You can find no more originality of thought or feeling than you can "enthusiasm." They are public rather than private, their truth general and common instead of individual and particular. They make not for fun reading, but they do—still—"furnish . . . mankind with the two noblest of things, which are sweetness and light" (Swift, *The Battle of the Books* 368).

Their author was a sort of Renaissance man of letters: poet, critic, dictionary maker, maker of the fictional tale we know as *Rasselas*, itself composed of narrative essays. Samuel Johnson wrote journalistic essays for *The Rambler*, penned *The Idler* papers for *The Universal Chronicle or Weekly Gazette*, and wrote for Hawkesworth's *Adventure* and *The Gentleman's Magazine*. As a contributor of essays to (emerging) periodicals, Johnson deserves mention alongside Addison and Steele, who certainly paved the way for his more profound and capacious writing. I cannot but think Bonamy Dobrée's assessment accurate: "While Addison's standard was the social one, Johnson's was the ethical one, with the result that he seems less out of date, since manners change more than ethics do. Like Bacon, he challenges us to thought, and to read him is to be stimulated" (24).

In Dr. Johnson, common sense reigns, along with universal opinion and judgment, but they exist as part of a larger whole of sensibility, rich with compassion. He can be satirical, as in the poems "London" and "The Vanity of Human Wishes," but he never belittles or reduces, and while—in *Rasselas*, for instance—he decries humanity's inveterate wishfulness, he never lacks for sympathy for our plight, from which it never seems he feels himself exempt or above. Essentially made up of dramatized essays, *Rasselas*, in fact, emphasizes "the dangerous prevalence of imagination," the title of chapter XLIV. There, Johnson has his favorite Imlac, who, nevertheless, has been said in XI to have "felt the enthusiastic fit" (528), confide to the Prince, regarding "choices of life": "'This, Sir, is one of the dangers of solitude, which the hermit has confessed not always to promote goodness, and the astronomer's misery has proved to be not always propitious to wisdom,'" for, isolated and alone, bereft of necessary human contact and of that otherness we require as a species, his reason has taken leave, leaving him subject to flights of fancy and fits of enthusiasm (596–97).

With this introduction, with this bit of knowledge concerning Johnson, we turn to "The Solitude of the Country," with, as Phillip Lopate has recently put it, his refusal "to sugar-coat things" (136). Historically this essay is important, because it comes on the cusp of Romanticism with its idealization of country life, solitude, and the joys—and centrality—of the inner life. The value is not, however, limited to the historical. Take this short paragraph, for instance, which effectively responds to, and in my judgment refutes, Montaigne in his *apologia* for personal essaying:

> But though learning may be conferred by solitude, its application must
> be attained by general converse. He has learned to no purpose, that is
> not able to teach; and he will always teach unsuccessfully, who cannot
> recommend his sentiments by his diction or address. (142–43)

The points here are perhaps even more valuable today.

At any rate, the opening of "The Solitude of the Country" recalls *Rasse-*

las and at the same time harks back to another Augustan humanist—and Anglican—and his similar asseverations against what he called in the thematically central chapter of *A Tale of a Tub* "A Digression Concerning the Original, the Use, and Improvement of Madness in a Commonwealth." I refer, of course, to Jonathan Swift, whose *Tale* has, to my knowledge, never been considered in the context of the essay and that form's rise to prominence. First, note the opening paragraphs of Johnson's essay:

> There has always prevailed among that part of mankind that addict
> their minds to speculation, a propensity to talk much of the delights of
> retirement; and some of the most pleasing compositions produced in
> every age, contain descriptions of the peace and happiness of a country
> life. I know not whether those who thus ambitiously repeat the praises
> of solitude, have always considered, how much they depreciate mankind
> by declaring, that whatever is excellent or desirable is to be obtained by
> departing from them; that the assistance which we may derive from one
> another, is not equivalent to the evils which we have to fear; that the
> kindness of a few is overbalanced by the malice of many; and that the
> protection of society is too dearly purchased, by encountering its dangers
> and enduring its oppressions. (141)

Now, Montaigne had, of course, famously retired, young (at least, by our standards), from public life and in that relative leisure began to make his *essais*. Abraham Cowley followed suit, devoting himself upon retirement to botany and essay writing: to "learn the art and get the habit of thinking," he wrote in the essay "Of Solitude" (49). Introducing her anthology *The Art of the Essay*, Lydia Fakundiny expresses both sympathy and agreement: "You want a place for looking at it all, taking it all in somehow: the shifting human scene and yourself perilously in it" (12). Henry David Thoreau famously retired from Concord, Massachusetts, in the mid-nineteenth century in order to spend a couple of years, alone for the most part, at Walden Pond; there he hoped to get to the core of life, its wild heart. Alice Meynell is but one other essayist drawn to discuss solitude, this in the essay that I read elsewhere in this volume. Johnson appears to take a rather unessayistic stance, no friend of solitude and suspicious of anything that smacks of the deprivations and depletions of the private.

In this regard, he reminds us of Swift in his enormously complex satire *A Tale of a Tub*, decades earlier. Made of two interlocking components, the religious allegory of the Three Brothers and their father's Will and a series of "digressions," linked thematically by issues of reading and misreading, the satire has not, I think, been appreciated as an expose of essaying. By the time one has reached the conclusion, which, like Johnson's *Rasselas*, is merely an end "in which nothing is concluded," one cannot but think of the essay. For here is what the satirized persona, a Hack writer, says:

> I am now trying an experiment very frequent among modern authors; which is to write upon *Nothing*; when the subject is utterly exhausted, to let the pen still move on; by some called the ghost of wit, delighting to walk after the death of its body. And to say the truth, there seems to be no part of knowledge in fewer hands, than that of discerning when to have done. (352)

Especially is such a passage resonant to the reader who recalls that Hilaire Belloc penned volumes of essays with the unassuming titles *On Everything*, *On Something*, simply *On*, and *On Nothing and Kindred Subjects*. This last consists of thirty-one familiar essays, each of them bearing the tiny preposition "on" as first word in the title. There is, in addition, an opening "letter," which might be called an essay "On Nothing."

Here Belloc explains how, in Normandy, in summer, "it was determined among us (the jolly company!) that I should write upon Nothing, and upon all that is cognate to Nothing, a task not yet attempted since the Beginning of the World." Such writing, he soon realized, "might be very grave," and indeed, he writes, he has proceeded "in spite of my doubts and terrors" (*On Nothing* ix). What Belloc offers recalls the Hack's account of the Tale proper, itself an instance of reading, of course:

> [A]t a Grand Committee some days ago, this important discovery was made by a certain refined and curious observer — that seamen have a custom when they meet a whale, to fling him out an empty tub by way of amusement, to divert him from laying violent hands upon the ship. This parable was immediately mythologized; the whale was interpreted to be Hobbes's *Leviathan*, which tosses and plays with all other schemes of Religion and Government, whereof a great many are hollow, and dry, and empty, and noisy, and wooden, and given to rotation. This is the *Leviathan* from whence the terrible wits of our age are said to borrow their weapons. The ship in danger is easily understood to be its

old anti-type, the Commonwealth. But how to analyze the tub, was
a matter of difficulty; when after long enquiry and debate, the literal
meaning was preserved; and it was decreed, that in order to prevent these
Leviathans from tossing and sporting with the Commonwealth (which of
itself is too apt to fluctuate) they should be diverted from that game by a
Tale of a Tub. (263)

An admission of sorts, then, that the Hack has already written on nothing.

Belloc's satire too bites and stings. But he himself, unlike Swift who
is buffered by his persona, waxes enthusiastic, and ends up, his subject exhausted, letting his pen simply move on (not unlike the Hack, incidentally,
who, in trying to say what wisdom is, a passage that moves via metaphor to
one rapid description after another, remains convinced that it is an interior
matter, later contradicted, of course):

> Many things have I discovered about Nothing, which have proved it—to
> me at least—to be the warp or ground of all that is holiest. It is of such
> fine gossamer that loveliness was spun, the mists under the hills on an
> autumn morning are but gross reflections of it; moonshine on lovers is
> earthly compared with it; song sung most charmingly and stirring the
> dearest recollections is but a failure in the human attempt to reach its
> embrace and be dissolved in it. It is out of Nothing that are woven those
> fine poems of which we carry but vague rhythms in the head: —and that
> Woman who is a shade, the Insaisissable, whom several have enshrined in
> melody—well, her Christian name, her maiden name, and as I personally
> believe, her married name as well, is Nothing. (xiv–xv)

At this point, Nothing takes a perhaps surprising—and un-Swiftian—turn,
morphing into something, or rather, into space, opening, gap, thus acquir-
ing philosophical substance that Swift reaches via the satire itself:

> I never see a gallery of pictures now but I know how the use of empty
> spaces makes a scheme, nor do I ever go to a play but I see how silence is
> half the merit of acting and hope some day for absence and darkness as
> well upon the stage. . . . Nothing is the reward of good men who alone
> can pretend to taste it in long easy sleep, it is the meditation of the wise
> and the charm of happy dreamers. So excellent and final is it that I would
> here and now declare to you that Nothing was the gate of eternity, that by
> passing through Nothing we reached our every object as passionate and

happy beings—were it not for the Council of Toledo that restrains my
pen. (xv)

Now Belloc is nigh on to his friend G. K. Chesterton's acute observation
that you know nothing until you know nothing. We cannot but recall
Odysseus's necessary encounter with the Nothingness that is death, preparation sufficient for his heart to come to heel (because healed).

We return to *A Tale of a Tub*, now contextualized, which is the aim as well
of our ultimate return to Johnson's essay "The Solitude of the Country."
In the *Tale*, the narrator admits his penchant for solitude and his deprived
situation—"the shrewdest pieces of this treatise were conceived in bed in
a garret; at other times . . . I thought fit to sharpen my invention with
hunger; and in general, the whole work was begun, continued, and ended,
under a long course of physic, and a great want of money"—and, further,
he suggests a direct, positive connection between such a (retired) situation
and writing (265). The Hack's Modern pride and arrogance are nowhere
more evident or greater.

> [E]ven I myself, the author of these momentous truths, am a person,
> whose imaginations are hard-mouthed, and exceedingly disposed to run
> away with his reason, which I have observed from long experience to be a
> very light rider, and easily shook off; upon which account, my friends will
> never trust me alone, without a solemn promise to vent my speculations
> in this, or the like manner, for the universal benefit of human kind; which
> perhaps the gentle, courteous, and candid reader, brimful of that modern
> charity and tenderness usually annexed to his office, will be very hardly
> persuaded to believe. (336)

The controlling metaphor here is the same as that in the aforementioned
section IX where "enthusiasm" is dissected: "But when a man's fancy gets
astride on his reason, when imagination is at cuffs with the senses, and
common understanding, as well as common sense, is kicked out of doors,
the first proselyte he makes is himself" (331).

In the case of the Hack, there is no doubt about the source of his inspiration, or even his knowledge:

> because, memory being an employment of the mind upon things past,
> is a faculty for which the learned in our illustrious age have no manner

of occasion, who deal entirely with invention, and strike all things out of themselves, or at least by collision with each other. (312)

The difference adumbrated here is that between the Ancient and the Modern, which *The Battle of the Books*, the *Tale*'s companion satire, represents as that between the bee and the spider. In the bee's stinging words, the issue is whether product or achievement results from what is within the isolated, private individual or from without the self.

> You boast, indeed, of being obliged to no other creature, but of drawing and spinning out all from yourself; . . . So that in short, the question comes all to this—which is the nobler being of the two, that which by a lazy contemplation of four inches round, by an overweening pride, feeding and engendering on itself, turns all into excrement and venom, produces nothing at last, but fly-bane and a cobweb; or that which, by an universal range, with long search, much study, true judgment, and distinction of things, brings home honey and wax. (367)

What is most apparent about the speaking voice of *A Tale of a Tub*, the solitary Hack writer, is his self-dramatization. As T. S. Eliot observed, perhaps most notably in the essay "Shakespeare and the Stoicism of Seneca," such attention began in the Renaissance—at the time, indeed, of the "invention" of the essay, although he does not say so. The cult of personality then arises, one figure after another—Hamlet, to take a notable instance— "dramatizing himself against his environment" (*Selected Essays* 131). I strongly suspect that Swift had the essay in mind as he wrote, recognizing its basis, its implicit values, and—from his perspective as an Ancient—its considerable dangers. Belloc may later have determined to save the essay by making writing about nothing something, but the Hack whose voice we hear in the *Tale* merely strikes all out from his demented and corrupting self, taking the essay form to its exaggerated conclusion, the true conclusion of one of the greatest satires ever penned, in any language.

We ordinarily do not associate Dr. Johnson with *im*-personality. On the contrary, his unique, garrulous personality appears, as they say, larger than life. That is due, however, primarily to the engaging, magisterial biography done by his Scottish friend James Boswell. The essays, poems, and critical lives do not reveal Johnson's personality, although they seem somewhat different from Eliot's essays. As I said, Johnson is much closer to Bacon than to Montaigne.

Still Johnson joins with Eliot in offering his *observations*, rather than reflections, and certainly not "speculations" such as Swift's Hack indulges. Johnson specifically, in fact, denounces the very products of the imagination that the Hack praises. Where the Hack engages in panegyric, Johnson practices clear-sightedness, and for him, that means spilling the beans on the emptiness, the nothing-ness, of wishful thinking. Thus the

> specious representations of solitary happiness, however opprobrious to
> human nature, have so far spread their influence over the world, that
> almost every man delights his imagination with the hopes of obtaining
> some time an opportunity of retreat. Many indeed, who enjoy retreat only
> in imagination, content themselves with believing, that another year will
> transport them to rural tranquillity, and die while they talk of doing what
> if they had lived longer they would never have done. (141)

So scrupulous is Johnson, so nuanced in his thinking, that he immediately allows that there are some who earnestly essay the state of solitude. Throughout, Johnson is guided by that traditional Western, and biblical, understanding of the necessity of demythologizing incumbent upon "sacred discontent."

"The greater part of the admirers of solitude," Johnson insists, are interested only in the immediate "gratification of their passions." Others, differently, seek to escape from, or at least to avoid, "grossness, falsehood and brutality" and so turn, hopefully, "to find in private habitations at least a negative felicity, and exemption from the shocks and perturbations with which public scenes are continually distressing them." Johnson pulls no punches:

> To neither of these votaries will solitude afford that content, which she
> has been taught so lavishly to promise. The man of arrogance will quickly
> discover, that by escaping from his opponents he has lost his flatterers,
> that greatness is nothing where it is not seen, and power nothing where
> it cannot be felt: and he, whose faculties are employed in too close an
> observation of failings and defects, will find his condition very little

mended by transferring his attention from others to himself; he will probably soon come back in quest of new objects, and be glad to keep his captiousness employed on any character rather than his own.

Others, continues Johnson, are "seduced into solitude" by the supposed experience and testimony of "great names," while others still "consider solitude as the parent of philosophy, and retire in expectation of greater intimacies with science" (142). Some, he grants, have found what they seek, and solitude can, indeed, provide solace from fatigue as well as stimulate study and discovery.

And yet Johnson remains wary, suspicious of motive as well as result, reasonable in the sense of knowing full well the seductions of *partial* truth. Just here, in fact, in the sentences on learning, solitude, and teaching that I quoted earlier, his eloquence rises, his structure mirroring that balance:

> But though learning may be conferred by solitude, its application must be attained by general converse. He has learned to no purpose, that is not able to teach; and he will always teach unsuccessfully, who cannot recommend his sentiments by his diction or address. (142–43)

The lines are successfully expressive, the message *embodied* in the speaker.

Johnson is not done yet, for he proceeds with a longer paragraph, an elaboration on these points, in the manner of his various revelations, including that of the deluded Astronomer in *Rasselas*—and pointedly unlike Swift's Hack Modern, a specialist in the very enthusiasm against which Johnson animadverts here:

> Even the acquisition of knowledge is often much facilitated by the advantages of society: he that never compares his notions with those of others, readily acquiesces in his first thoughts, and very seldom discovers the objections which may be raised against his opinions; he, therefore, often thinks himself in possession of truth, when he is only fondling an error long since exploded. He that has neither companions nor rivals in his studies, will always applaud his own progress, and think highly of his performances, because he knows not that others have equalled or excelled him. And I am afraid it may be added, that the student who withdraws himself from the world, will soon feel that ardour extinguished which praise or emulation had enkindled, and take the advantage of secrecy to sleep rather than to labour. (143)

Missing, in other words, says Johnson, is *comparison*, which age teaches as being an instrument not only of criticism but also of truth. Lack of comparison bedeviled Swift's Brobdingnagians and spelled literal disaster for the Phaiacians in *The Odyssey*.

The final element to discuss in "The Solitude of the Country" is the religious "recluses," toward whom Johnson says both respect and reticence are due. He grants, first of all, without—notice—denying, that they "retire from the world, not merely to bask in ease or gratify curiosity, but that being disengaged from common cares, they may employ more time in the duties of religion, that they may regulate their actions with stricter vigilance, and purify their thoughts by more frequent meditation" (143). Still and all, these are very special persons, few in number, and Johnson sets them aside, his interest and concern in us ordinary mortals, "common readers" or not.

> To men thus elevated above the mists of mortality, I am far from presuming myself qualified to give directions. On him that appears "to pass through things temporary," with no other care than "not to lose finally the things eternal," I look with such veneration as inclines me to approve his conduct in the whole, without a minute examination of its parts; yet I could never forbear to wish, that while vice is every day multiplying seducements, and stalking forth with more hardened effrontry, virtue, would not withdraw the influence of her presence, or forbear to assert her natural dignity by open and undaunted perseverance in the right.

An essayist at the core, Johnson concludes these sentiments, these observations, rather pointedly, hardly advocating the monastic life:

> Piety practised in solitude, like the flower that blooms in the desert, may give its fragrance to the winds of heaven, and delight those unbodied spirits that survey the works of God and the actions of men; but it bestows no assistance upon earthly beings, and however free from taints of impurity, yet wants the sacred splendor of beneficence. (143)

Little could be more telling than Johnson's reference here to "unbodied spirits," for as a devout Anglican, as well as an astute essayist, he well knows that for men and women embodiment—Incarnation—is truth, "the hint *half* guessed, the gift *half* understood."

Johnson's conclusion follows directly therefrom; it is eloquent and moving, beneficent and judicious, both drawn from and directed toward "general converse" and no less aware than Swift of the connection between the private and the "tender," and the public and the clear-sighted:

> Our Maker, who, though he gave us such varieties of temper and such difference of powers yet designed us all for happiness, undoubtedly intended that we should obtain that happiness by different means. Some are unable to resist the temptations of importunity, or the impetuosity of their own passions incited by the force of present temptations: of these it is undoubtedly the duty, to fly from enemies which they cannot conquer, and to cultivate, in the calm of solitude, that virtue which is too tender to endure the tempests of public life. But there are others, whose passions grow more strong and irregular in privacy; and who cannot maintain an uniform tenor of virtue, but by exposing their manners to the public eye, and assisting the admonitions of conscience with the fear of infamy: for such it is dangerous to exclude all witnesses of their conduct, till they have formed strong habits of virtue, and weakened their passions by frequent victories. But there is a higher order of men so inspirited with ardour, and so fortified with resolution, that the world passes before them without influence or regard: these ought to consider themselves as appointed the guardians of mankind; they are placed in an evil world, to exhibit public examples of good life; and may be said, when they withdraw to solitude, to desert the station which Providence assigned them. (143–44)

In short, for the Augustan, for the Anglican, the individual needs the public life and its response to contain, to restrain the flights of fancy and the lure of enthusiasm to which we, fallen creatures, are all subject. The public thus plays the same role in Johnson's essay as tradition does in Dryden's essay-poem *Religio Laici*.

Johnson appears as leery of thoroughgoing commitment to the country as he is of enthusiastic engagement with solitude. In criticizing both solitude and country life, with which he offers public life and the city as alternatives (theses to those antitheses), he is pointedly anti-Romantic. The essay and Romanticism are, of course, bosom friends, sharing so many values that Wordsworth even called his (and Coleridge's) revolutionary *Lyrical Ballads* "short essays."

    "The Solitary of the Country" thus stands, I submit, not just as an anti-Romantic work but, as such, in clear opposition to the essay in its personal, individualist, Montaignian manner. It may be a brief for the "familiar" form of that form. It is, in any case, in a line from Bacon that leads on to T. S. Eliot, his similar anti-Romanticism, his paean to tradition rather than the individual, and his attempts to turn the essay (back) toward observation and away from (Romantic) reflection. "The Solitude of the Country" makes no small contribution to this ongoing effort, part of the age-old and perennial "battle of the books."

Walking, rambling, sauntering, strolling, wandering are more than
recurrent topics of essay writing; they're images by which essayists like
to figure their particular mode of discoursing, tropes of essaying itself.
—Lydia Fakundiny, *The Art of the Essay*

An Allegory of Essaying?

Process and Product in William Hazlitt's
"On Going a Journey"

"THE SOUL OF A JOURNEY," writes William Hazlitt, friend of
Wordsworth, Coleridge, and Charles Lamb and one of the premier
nineteenth-century essayists, "is liberty, perfect liberty, to think, feel, do
just as one pleases" (93). For such perspectives, Tom Paulin has recently
written of, and embraced, his "radical style." As an essayist, Hazlitt anticipates Thoreau, in "Walking," who likewise "saunters" (a *sans terre*, opines
the latter, in one of his more egregious puns), but the differences tell more
than the similarities. Hazlitt is more companionable, despite his well-
known anger and despite his preference for solitary walking, less a "hair-
shirt of a man" (E. B. White). Unlike Thoreau, who, although he hoped to
walk "at least" four hours a day, Hazlitt allows that "We *go a journey* chiefly
to be free of all impediments and of all inconveniences" (ibid.; italics mine).
For him, journeying, which carries an altogether richer connotation than
mere walking, provides a needed respite and particular, distinct opportu-

nities. It is not a way of life; and if he would, for the nonce, rid himself of inconveniences, Thoreau, more radically, would reduce the exigencies of living to a few bare necessities. Thoreau, in fact, welcomes the very inconveniences that Hazlitt would avoid. The latter "goes a journey," as he puts it, because he is not merely walking or strolling or sauntering but "because I want a little breathing-space to muse on indifferent matters," where Contemplation is his boon companion. Rather than a paean to walking, "On Going a Journey" is a plea for and a demonstration of mental journeying.

The essay as form has itself been received as expressive; it is often said to mimic the peregrinations discussed. Whether or not an allegory of essaying, "On Going a Journey" raises questions about process and product—and appears to make its position clear. Process seems to triumph, in both the telling and the interpretation of journeying.

Consider the opening paragraph, which extends to more than three full pages (in Lydia Fakundiny's *The Art of the Essay*), constituting in the process more than a third of the essay. No self-respecting college or university teacher of composition would allow—or give a decent grade to—such apparently hapless self-indulgence and inattention to—nay, flouting of—form. To make matters worse, there is the final paragraph, of only four, made of stops, starts, swerves, and frequent dashes, indicating change of focus, return, and then further change—all this introduced with the sophomoric admission anathema to "the well-written" paper: "—To return to the question I have quitted above" (99).

Worse still may be the fact of the very different third paragraph, devoted to philosophical reflection of a rather high order. Indeed this excursus is about as philosophical as the personal or familiar essay ever gets, this on the succession of ideas and the mind's inherent limitations. The turn is abrupt and, I think, unexpected, despite the supplied link to journeying:

There is hardly anything that shows the short-sightedness or capriciousness of the imagination more than travelling does. With change of place we change our ideas; nay, our opinions and feelings. We can by an effort indeed transport ourselves to old and long-forgotten scenes, and then the picture of the mind revives again; but we forget those that we have just left. It seems that we can think of but one place at a time. The canvas of the fancy has only a certain extent, and if we paint one set of objects upon it, they immediately efface every other. We cannot enlarge our conceptions; we only shift our point of view. The landscape bares its bosom to the enraptured eye; we take our fill of it; and seem as if we could form no other image of beauty or grandeur. We pass on, and think no more of it: the horizon that shuts it from our sight also blots it from our memory like a dream. In travelling through a wild barren country, I can form no idea of a woody and cultivated one. It appears to me that all the world must be barren, like what I see of it. In the country we forget the town, and in town we despise the country. (98–99)

I for one find some of this untrue, for example the last sentence—indeed, in town, I think of and long for the country. But evaluation and critique are not yet our concern, which is to read the essay and find how it works. What follows there smacks of the peregrinations of the form we call the essay as it displays its characteristic humility.

All that part of the map that we do not see before us is a blank. The world in our conceit of it is not much bigger than a nutshell. It is not one prospect expanded into another, county joined to county, kingdom to kingdom, lands to seas, making an image voluminous and vast;— the mind can form no larger idea of space than the eye can take in at a single glance. The rest is a name written on a map, a calculation of arithmetic. . . . Things near us are seen of the size of life: things at a distance are diminished to the size of the understanding. We measure the universe by ourselves, and even comprehend the texture of our own being only piece-meal. In this way, however, we remember an infinity of things and places. The mind is like a mechanical instrument that plays a great variety of tunes, but it must play them in succession. (99)

"One idea recalls another," Hazlitt proceeds to write, but he also says that one idea "excludes all others" (ibid.). I cannot help but then apply what he says to my reading of "On Going a Journey." Are we similarly limited, unable to hold in mind more than what lies immediately before us? Does succession rule? To return to Hazlitt:

In trying to renew old recollections, we cannot as it were unfold the whole web of our existence; we must pick out the single threads. So in coming to a place where we have formerly lived and with which we have intimate associations, everyone must have found that the feeling grows more vivid the nearer we approach the spot, from the mere anticipation of the actual impression: we remember circumstances, feelings, persons, faces, names, that we had not thought of for years; but for the time all the rest of the world is forgotten! (ibid.)

The paragraph ends, as I have noted, with the unimpressive admission of having strayed from the matter at hand: "—To return now to the question I have quitted above." Does this mean that the third paragraph, with its philosophical musings, could be extracted without damage to the essay? Hazlitt suggests as much. I, however, think otherwise. It may not be logically necessary, but at the very least it adds texture, richness, dimension, and layering—as well as, one might say, gravitas.

In fact, it does more. To appreciate that, we must now return to the essay's very first words. Unlike Hilaire Belloc's "The Mowing of a Field," with its extended opening physical and natural descriptions, and Zora Neale Hurston's "How It Feels to Be Colored Me," which takes its time as a point of being "civilized," "On Going a Journey" gets right down to business. The opening sentence repeats the title ("One of the pleasantest things in the world is going a journey; but I like to go by myself"), and although the ensuing paragraph does divagate, Hazlitt is in no evident hurry; the opening declaration remains in control of the essay's progression. The reader may wander with Hazlitt's details, but I do not think that he ever loses focus. What he gives us, I think it will be clear from our reading, matches the essayist Edward Hoagland's description of the personal essay. It is, he writes in "What I Think, What I Am," "like the human voice talking, its order the mind's natural flow, instead of a systematized outline of ideas" (691). More than most, Hazlitt happens to be interested in ideas. They are, in fact, the reason for his "going a journey."

Before we proceed with our reading, we must stop and consider. Hazlitt writes: "I would attempt to wake the thoughts that lie slumbering on golden ridges in the evening clouds: but at the sight of nature my fancy, poor as it is, droops and closes up its leaves, like flowers at sunset. I can make nothing out on the spot:—I must have time to collect myself" (95–96). These words help to establish Hazlitt's procedure. "On Going a Journey" is not at all a record of a particular travel; journeying matters for the ideas its experience inspires and generates—it *enables*. And what Hazlitt gives us in the essay when it rambles—in its rambles—does not mimic walking but mental traveling. Time has intervened, and Hazlitt has "collected" himself. "On Going a Journey" thus differs from Wordsworth's revolutionary definition of poetry as "emotion recollected in tranquillity," for Hazlitt deals with ideas, in the first place—of course, he *is* writing an essay, not poetry. Moreover Hazlitt *collects* what memory working on experience provides to him; it is a present activity, rather than a "re-collection." Hence, I think, the sense we inevitably have that Hazlitt gives a picture of himself *in the process of writing*. The writing itself, in other words, is responsible for (the fact and the nature of) the third paragraph, as well as for the length of the first and the fitfulness of the last.

In the preceding paragraph, that is, the second, Hazlitt has made clear, amid its fleshed-out musings and laconic descriptions of time spent at inns, that "I have certainly spent some enviable hours" there—"sometimes when I have been left entirely to myself, and have tried to solve some metaphysical problem, as once at Witham-common, where I found out the proof that likeness is not a case of the association of ideas" (97). His later lucubrations may be seen as another example of such philosophical problem solving—although Hazlitt does not represent it as inspired or generated by any particular journey. Already, though, in the first paragraph, this time about one-third through, he clearly anticipates that later excursus, noting Mr. Cobbett's observation that " 'an Englishman ought to do only one thing at a time,' " to which he adds, "So I cannot talk and think, or indulge in melancholy musing and lively conversation by fits and starts" (94). Similarly he praises his friend Coleridge for his ability to "do both," that is, unite understanding and speaking.

His subject, Hazlitt repeatedly makes clear, is "the involuntary impression of things upon the mind" (94), recognizing, as his friend Wordsworth put it at the end of his great autobiographical poem *The Prelude*, that "the mind of Man becomes / A thousand times more beautiful than the earth" (14.450–51). Still it is to nature that Hazlitt would precisely *repair*. And there he would journey alone. Walking with a companion or as a party is fraught with unsurpassable dangers to the needed respite, inspiration, and generation of ideas (later: "These eventful moments in our lives are in fact too precious, too full of solid, heartfelt happiness to be frittered and dribbled way in imperfect sympathy. I would have them all to myself, and drain them to the last drop: they will do to talk of or to write about afterwards" [96]). He wishes to store up.

You cannot read the book of nature, without being perpetually put to the trouble of translating it for the benefit of others. I am for the synthetical method on a journey, in preference to the analytical. I am content to lay in a stock of ideas then, and to examine and anatomise them afterwards. I want to see my vague notions float like the down of the thistle before the breeze, and not to have them entangled in the briars and thorns of controversy. For once, I like to have it all my own way; and this is impossible unless you are alone, or in such company as I do not covet. (94)

Although of a different texture and intellectual intensity, the third paragraph is not only related to such musing, but it also follows, more or less naturally, from this kind of reflection.

Thus, on the first page of the essay, Hazlitt grants that "no one likes puns, alliterations, antitheses, argument, and analysis better than I do; but," he adds, "I sometimes had rather be without them" (93). Going a journey, he prefers synthesis to analysis. Nowhere is the focus of the essay clearer than early in that paragraph when Hazlitt writes, accentuating the thinking that journeying in nature both allows and prompts:

Give me the clear blue sky over my head, and the green turf beneath my feet, a winding road before me, and a three hours' march to dinner — *and then to thinking!* It is hard if I cannot start some game on these lone heaths. I laugh, I run, I leap, I sing for joy. From the point of yonder rolling cloud, I plunge into my past being, and revel there. . . . Then long-forgotten things . . . burst upon my eager sight, and I begin to feel, think, and be myself again. Instead of an awkward silence, broken by attempts at wit or dull common-places, mine is that undisturbed silence of the heart which alone is perfect eloquence. (ibid.; italics added)

Still, within paragraphs, while the focus is maintained, it is not sharp. Hazlitt takes a line out for a walk, and the walk takes him along a path hardly narrow or direct. The nearly three-page second paragraph provides striking instances. The subject is inns, and Hazlitt is simply expansive, giving rein not to the imagination or fancy but to memory, which he indulges: journeying has indeed given him something to think about and to write about, and here he cashes in. Thus he tells us of "luxuriating in books," for example at an inn at Bridgewater, after being "drenched" in an all-day rain, sitting up half the night to read *Paul and Virginia*, which he picked up there; then at an inn at Llangollen, where, on April 10, 1798, which he notes as his birthday, he "sat down to a volume of the *New Eloise* . . . over a bottle of sherry and a cold chicken"—if these are not enough details, Hazlitt goes on to explain, "The letter I chose was that in which St. Preux describes his feelings as he first caught a glimpse from the heights of the Jura of the Pays de Vaud, which I had brought with me as a *bonne bouche* to crown the evening with" (97).

And then there is the last paragraph. To be sure, Hazlitt has not forgotten his focus: "In setting out on a party of pleasure, the first consideration always is where we shall go: in taking a solitary ramble," as is his preference, "the question is what we shall meet with by the way." He writes, of course, in like manner: the question being what memories and what thoughts and ideas will rise on his journey down the page. Here he continues: "The mind then is 'its own place'; nor are we anxious to arrive at the end of our journey" (99). The journey itself does matter to Hazlitt, and he never seems in a hurry to arrive at the end of the writing, prolonging it, in fact (see just below). The end, we might say, occurs in the journeying, the purpose realized and fulfilled in the act—product *in* the process.

Here Hazlitt has not only remembered his focus, but he also recalls what he "quitted above": "I have no objection to go to see ruins, aqueducts, pictures, in company with a friend or a party, but rather the contrary, for the former reason reversed" (99). After some reflection comes a dash, and Hazlitt now writes: "As another exception to the above reasoning, I should not feel confident in venturing on a journey in a foreign country without a companion." Then soon, another dash and this: "Yet I did not feel this want or craving very pressing once, when I first set my foot on the laughing shores of France" (100). Finally yet another dash, and Hazlitt is off on his final point, which he would have be concluding. The essay's last sentence is as follows: "I should . . . like well enough to spend the whole of my life in traveling abroad, if I could anywhere borrow another life to spend afterwards at home!" (101).

The whole last paragraph feels to me tacked on, rather than strictly necessary. It neither adds much nor leads to a satisfying conclusion. In my judgment, "On Going a Journey" could have ended after the third paragraph without great loss. I suspect that Hazlitt, for whatever reason or reasons, felt after that thoroughgoing philosophizing a need to return to the focus on journeying. He then walks around the subject a bit longer, thinking of first this point, then another, another still, and so on. The dashes, indicative of starts and stops, may not represent a certain discomfort or unease as they both interrupt and initiate a different "take," but, instead, register a certain "informally dialectical manner of thinking": "the thinking/writing process not as linear and consistent but as discontinuous and drawn to contraries" (Lydia Fakundiny, letter to author). Truth to tell, any apparent dis-ease will be greater than need be, for the sections of this last paragraph are not as disparate or disconnected as Hazlitt's punctuation, and his rhetorical strategy, lead us to believe. Still, at this point although not before, process triumphs over product.

Then I dare; I will also essay to be.
—Ralph Waldo Emerson, journal

Emerson's ambitions were enormous, and endangered his desires.
"He burst into conclusions at a spark of evidence," Henry Seidel
Canby said, accurate about Emerson's urgency, Emerson's need to be
immense. He was the Horatio Alger of our youthful hopes. He would
Do & Dare. He would Strive & Succeed, and drag us, as unwilling as
we often were, into virtuous accomplishment. . . . He sometimes
seemed a grimacing spout to a drenched roof. He did fancy the idea,
though: that passing through him (as if he were the categories of our
consciousness) flesh would become symbol; matter would be refined
like ethyl and emerge as volatile, ignitable mind.
—William H. Gass, "Emerson and the Essay,"
  in *Habitations of the Word*

The Risk of Not Being

Ralph Waldo Emerson's "Illusions"

I WOULD AVOID EMERSON IF I COULD. He is difficult, and I
never feel that I (can) understand him. Harold Bloom thinks him essential, the very fount of the literature that we call American. I find him a
thoroughgoing Transcendentalist, and I do not much care for either Transcendentalists or the "thoroughgoing." He is, I reckon, much that Eliot
rejected when he chose England and left the Unitarianism of his youth for
Anglo-Catholicism, itself the incarnation of the pattern (of Incarnation)
that Emerson could never quite see, his eyeball transparent.

I cannot avoid Emerson, however, but not because of Harold Bloom,
but rather William H. Gass and his magnificent essay on Emerson titled
"Emerson and the Essay," included in his *Habitations of the Word*, published twenty or so years ago. That essay, tendentious, extreme, rollicking,
and percipient—brilliantly original—remains among the most insightful
introductions to the essay that I know. I admire it more than I respect
Emerson.

"Emerson and the Essay" is scintillating. It is also richly imaginative, rather than darkly theoretical, an instance of "creative criticism." As such, it is exactly what T. S. Eliot excoriates: a mixture of the creative and the critical. It is, then, what Geoffrey Hartman endorses and promotes: criticism as literature.

On Emerson in general, Gass is terrific, although not original, the work of Joel Porte and David Porter, in particular, standing behind and supporting him. With the help of the latter, Gass shows that "if Emerson was to be, he *would* have to 'essay it'" (31). Porte has said that "essaying to be"

> is the fundamental conceit of this greatest of American essayists. He too dares, endeavors, tries, attempts, essays . . . to create himself in the very process, in the very act, of setting words on paper or uttering them aloud. In order to exist, he must speak, for the speech validates itself—brings into being that which is envisioned or hoped for and gives Emerson a solid platform on which to stand. (qtd. in Gass 16–17)

No one has written better, more definitively, and I doubt ever will, than Gass on the thinking that Emerson pursues in, through, and by means of his essaying. Process and product unite, Gass finds:

> Emerson made the essay into the narrative disclosure of a thought. It became an act of thinking, but not of such thinking as had actually occurred. Real thought is gawky and ungracious; it goes in scraps, gaps, and patches, in sidles and byways, hems and haws; it is both brutal and careless, unpredictable and messy. Instead, Emerson's essays present us with an ideal process, an *ought*; yet it is, again, not one of rational confirmation; it is not the logician's order we encounter; it is the orator's: an order of revelation and response, the intertwined exfoliation of fact, feeling, and idea. In this sense, exposition becomes the narrative, and the form that of a fiction. (34–35)

Achieved, Gass goes on to claim, for audience and essayist alike, is nothing else than "a kind of reassociation of . . . sensibility" (35).

Just here, with this somewhat ironic echo of T. S. Eliot, we smack against Emerson's difference from the essayist of "The Metaphysical Poets," for, as David Porter has written, Emerson "'reattached language to process rather than to conclusion, to the action of the mind wonderfully finding the words adequate to its experience'" (qtd. in Gass 34). Is this not a reinvention of Emerson's fellow-Romantic Wordsworth's famed notion of poetry as emotion "recollected" in tranquillity? It is certainly an embrace of Montaigne.

The Emersonian idea also recalls its opposite as Eliot has described it in his brilliant essay on the seventeenth-century Anglican Divine Lancelot Andrewes:

> Andrewes's emotion is purely contemplative; it is not personal, it is wholly evoked by the object of contemplation, to which it is adequate; his emotions wholly contained in and explained by its object. But with Donne [in contrast] there is always the something else. . . . Donne is a "personality" in a sense in which Andrewes is not: his sermons, one feels, are a "means of self-expression." He is constantly finding an object which shall be adequate to his feelings; Andrewes is wholly absorbed in the object and therefore responds with the adequate emotion. (*Selected Essays* 351)

With Emerson, one feels, the situation is more complicated and complex than with Donne, with whom he yet shares a certain penchant for self-dramatization. Andrewes submits himself to, and essentially becomes one with, an object outside the self; Emerson, quite differently, and, as a Romantic, an avatar of process, has no object with which to struggle other than his own mind, his experience; any sense of adequacy can only attach to that experience.

Their worlds are different: Emerson's from Andrewes's, and from Eliot's too. Gass offers this description of Emerson, withholding most criticism:

> "Life is a series of surprises," he says, but we can no longer be surprised by the absence of any disciplined philosophy. He dislikes distinctions. Clarity dismays him, makes him suspicious. He dotes on degrees but damns kinds. He is dangerously devoted to the continuum. He does not want to finely, plainly *think*; scrub things clean, draw cutting lines, laboriously link. He wants to writhe. (36)

Indeed, Gass immediately adds: "The power of the process fills him with light. It is like that. Montaigne attests to it." As to his orating, his famous lectures that Gass represents as themselves essay*ings*,

> Emerson's verbal maneuvers concluded, his listeners are sent away with their hearts a little higher in their chests, in a Dionysian mood, intoxicated

by their own powers and possibilities, not by bottled artificialities, drugs, the falsehoods of gambling and war, or still further fraudulent rites. (37)

Emerson—with Gass more or less happily beside him and in tow—emerges for the Ancient mind as a thoroughgoing Modern, on whose reason fancy has gotten astride and ridden with gusto to the enthusiasm that Swift, for one, links with madness.

On the essay as form, Gass offers so many crucial insights that I shall not attempt to rehearse them here, but merely highlight a few of them. He distinguishes the essay, to begin with, from its "opposite," "that awful object, 'the article'" (25), which he—in thoroughgoing fashion—represents in unsparing prose calculated to elicit the reader's contempt. Philosophy, writes Gass, himself a philosopher by trade, "turns into literature by being tied to a temperament, a tone, a style, a time of life, a rhetoric, a scaffold of categories, a schedule of rhymes" (19). In fact, "the hero of the essay is its author in the act of thinking things out. Feeling and finding a way" (19–20). In other words:

> The essay induces skepticism. It is not altogether the fault of Montaigne. The essay is simply a watchful form. . . . Halfway between sermon and story, the essay interests itself in the narration of ideas—in their *un-folding*—and the conflict between philosophy or other points of view becomes a drama in its hands; systems are seen as plots and concepts as characters. (23)

It is, the essay, "a sort of secular sermon, inducing skepticism, and written by the snake" (27). "The words of others . . . most often bring the essay into being" (26), and that being exists as "a converse between friends [that] can be made into an actual invitation," for the essay works against "*absence of community*" (24).

I have chosen to read "Illusions," anthologized by Lydia Fakundiny in *The Art of the Essay* and included by Joel Porte in the Norton Critical Edition of *Emerson's Prose and Poetry*. "Illusions" is a medium-length essay, rather short, actually, by Emerson's standards. It is like the essay generally in being impure: it begins with an autobiographical narrative, moves to reflections on that recounted experience, engages in deep philosophical speculation, and even brings philosophy down to everyday life with the following application, emphasis being ethical, the mood imperative—it instances the kind of "oppositional or contrary thinking" that we observed in Hazlitt (Lydia Fakundiny, letter to author):

> In this kingdom of illusions we grope eagerly for stays and foundations. There is none but a strict and faithful dealing at home, and a severe barring out of all duplicity or illusion there. Whatever games are played with us, we must play no games with ourselves, but deal in our privacy with the last honesty and truth. I look upon the simple and childish virtues of veracity and honesty as the root of all that is sublime in character. Speak as you think, be what you are, pay your debts of all kinds. I prefer to be owned as sound and solvent, and my word as good as my bond, and to be what cannot be skipped, or dissipated, or undermined, to all the *éclat* in the universe. This reality is the foundation of friendship, religion, poetry, and art. At the top or at the bottom of all illusions, I set the cheat which still leads us to work and live for appearances, in spite of our conviction, in all sane hours, that it is what we really are that avails with friends, with strangers, and with fate or fortune. (*Essays and Lectures* 1122)

This brief on behalf of honesty and candor represents no mean apology for the essay as a form, perhaps the principal form, of nonfiction. Emerson would dispel illusions as Swift would the deceptions prompted by enthusiasm or the unreined fancy or imagination; the latter's interest is psychological, moral, and ultimately theological, however, whereas Emerson's concern lies with the ontological and the moral.

"Illusions" begins with Emerson's brief narrative of a visit to the famous Monmouth Cave in Kentucky where he was treated to the illusion, deep below the earth among the stalactites and stalagmites, that he was able to witness the stars and even a comet. The truth was, of course, otherwise: "Some crystal specks in the black ceiling high overhead, reflecting the light of a half-hid lamp, yielded this magnificent effect" (1115–16). Emerson was displeased: "I own, I did not like the cave so well for eking out its sublimities with this theatrical trick." In fact, of course, as he readily acknowledges, illusion is quite familiar to human experience: "The senses interfere everywhere, and mix their own structure with all they report of. . . . In admiring the sunset, we do not yet deduct the rounding, coordinating, pictorial powers of the eye" (1116). Attention, and focus, thus shift to the observer, the subject.

Here, says the Transcendentalist, lies our first illusion. "Our first mistake," Emerson continues, "is the belief that the circumstance gives the joy which we give to the circumstance." The point is thoroughgoing Romanticism, prominent in Wordsworth and Coleridge. In short, writes Emerson, triumphantly, "We live by our imaginations, by our admirations, by our sentiments" (1116).

"Illusions" is not about the imagination's "creative" powers, however, at least not primarily. Rather it concerns deception, and "we rightly accuse the critic who destroys too many illusions. Society does not love its unmaskers." Among them is Emerson, of course, who, here, unmasks this large truth: "We are coming on the secret of a magic which sweeps out of men's minds all vestige of theism and beliefs which they and their fathers held and were framed upon" (1120). The great illusion, then, is that creative power resides outside the self. "What if you shall come to discern that the play and playground of all this pompous history are radiations from yourself, and that the sun borrows his beams?" (ibid.).

Careful to acknowledge that he himself is by no means exempt from illusions, Emerson goes on to explain, and to distinguish, that there "are deceptions of the senses, deceptions of the passions, and the structural, beneficent illusions of sentiment and of the intellect" (1120). Illusions abound, different in kind, including those of love and of time. Though, he says, "the world exists from thought" (1120),

> what avails it that science has come to treat space and time as simply
> forms of thought, and the material world as hypothetical, and withal
> our pretension of *property* and even of self-hood are fading with the rest,
> if, at last, even our thoughts are not finalities; but the incessant flowing
> and ascension reach these also, and each thought which yesterday was a
> finality, to-day is yielding to a larger generalization? (1121)

The prospects are gloomy, Emerson as dour as Dr. Johnson, but without the consolations of the latter's abiding faith: "Well 'tis all phantasm; and if we weave a yard of tape in all humility, and as well as we can, long hereafter we shall see it was no cotton tape at all, but some galaxy which we braided, and that the threads were Time and Nature" (1121).

The following reflections feel genuine, certainly they are powerful, and they lead directly to Emerson's homely advice that I quoted above. His plaintive questions echo Montaigne.

We cannot write the order of the variable winds. How can we penetrate the law of our shifting moods and susceptibility? Yet they differ as all and nothing. Instead of the firmament of yesterday, which our eyes require, it is to-day an eggshell which coops us in; we cannot even see what or where our stars of destiny are. From day to day, the capital facts of human life are hidden from our eyes. Suddenly the mist rolls up, and reveals them, and we think how much good time is gone, that might have been saved, had any hint of these things been shown. A sudden rise in the road shows us the system of mountains, and all the summits, which have been just as near us all the year, but quite out of mind. But these alternations are not without their order, and we are parties to our various fortune. If life seem a succession of dreams, yet poetic justice is done in dreams also. The visions of good men are good; it is the undisciplined will that is whipped with bad thoughts and bad fortunes. When we break the laws, we lose our hold on the central reality. Like sick men in hospitals, we change only from bed to bed, from one folly to another; and it cannot signify much what becomes of such castaways, — wailing, stupid, comatose creatures, — lifted from bed to bed, from the nothing of life to the nothing of death. (1121–22)

Emerson does not shy from truth, and honesty, as he sees them; the language is sometimes harsh. It is also often lyrical and poetic.

William H. Gass thinks Emerson an essayist who dabbled in poetry, most often unsuccessfully. I do not agree. I think Emerson a poet — perhaps, to borrow a term, an "intellectual poet" — whose poetry transcends verse and can exist in prose, not least in the ideas that matter maybe above all else.

It matters that a poem serves as epigraph to "Illusions," although Lydia Fakundiny does not include it. In their Norton Critical Edition of *Emerson's Prose and Poetry*, Joel Porte and Saundra Morris introduce it with this observation: "This epigraph is one of Emerson's best when considered as an independent poem" (290n1). Here it is:

Flow, flow the waves hated,
Accursed, adored,
The waves of mutation:
No anchorage is.
Sleep is not, death is not;

Who seem to die live.
House you were born in,
Friends of your spring-time,
Old man and young maid,
Day's toil and its guerdon,
They are all vanishing,
Fleeing to fables,
Cannot be moored.
See the stars through them,
Through treacherous marbles.
Know, the stars yonder,
The stars everlasting,
Are fugitive also,
And emulate, vaulted,
The lambent heat-lightning,
And fire-fly's flight.

When thou dost return
On the wave's circulation,
Beholding the shimmer,
The wild dissipation,
And, out of endeavor
To change and to flow,
The gas become solid,
And phantoms and nothings
Return to be things,
And endless imbroglio
Is law and the world,—
Then first shalt thou know,
That in the wild turmoil,
Horsed on the Proteus,
Thou ridest to power,
And to endurance.

Emerson justifies both his inclusion of the poem and my claim regarding his central interest in poetry when he writes, in "Illusions," "The intellect is stimulated by the statement of truth in a trope" (1123). At any rate, the consolation offered in the poem is not religious. In its implied panegyric to the god of flux, here Proteus, it is in fact anti-Christian.

Transcendence supposedly aims at—and achieves—escape from just this changeableness, and even here, in this essay, Emerson makes clear that commitment. The last paragraphs of "Illusions" treat this issue, its difficulty manifest. The diagnosis remains accurate.

> One would think from the talk of men, that riches and poverty were a great matter; and our civilization mainly respects it. But the Indians say, that they do not think the white man with his brow of care, always toiling, afraid of heat and cold, and keeping within doors, has any advantage of them. The permanent interest of every man is, never to be in a false position, but to have the weight of Nature to back him in all that he does. Riches and poverty are a thick or thin costume; and our life—the life of all of us—identical. For we transcend the circumstance continually, and taste the real quality of existence; as in our employments, which only differ in the manipulations, but express the same laws; or in our thoughts, which wear no silks, and taste no ice-creams. We see God face to face every hour, and know the savor of Nature. (1122–23)

The issue is thus joined, Emerson deeper and deeper into the essential problem, which he proceeds to state precisely:

> The early Greek philosophers Heraclitus and Xenophanes measured their force on this problem of identity. Diogenes of Apollonia said, that unless the atoms were made of one stuff, they could never blend and act with one another. But the Hindoos, in their sacred writings, express the liveliest feeling, both of the essential identity, and of that illusion which they conceive variety to be. "The notions, '*I am*,' and '*This is mine*,' which influence mankind, are but delusions of the mother of the world. Dispel, O Lord of all creatures! the conceit of knowledge which proceeds from ignorance." And the beatitude of man they hold to lie in being freed from fascination. (1123)

Emerson writes, as we have seen, that "the intellect is stimulated by the statement of truth in a trope," but what he adds in that sentence is just as important: "and the will by clothing the laws of life in illusions." Thus we seem to be in a position of both/and, accepting both truth and illusions, another instance of Emerson's dialectical way of thinking/writing.

At this point, circling about the issue now fully joined, Emerson offers clarification with distinction.

But the unities of Truth and of Right are not broken by the disguise. There need never be any confusion in these. In a crowded life of many parts and performers, on a stage of nations, or in the obscurest hamlet in Maine or California, the same elements offer the same choices to each new comer, and, according to his election, he fixes his fortune in absolute Nature. It would be hard to put more mental and moral philosophy than the Persians have thrown into a sentence: —

"Fooled thou must be, though wisest of the wise:
Then be the fool of virtue, not of vice." (1123)

Significantly the truth that Emerson prizes and endorses appears "in a trope," *as poetry*, thus attesting to the "clothing [of] the laws of life in illusions." Every person, I reckon Emerson is saying, will buy into and suffer from, indulging, illusions. That will be; so the issue comes down to which illusions he will embrace, all the while aiming at the process of disillusionment. Truth exists—even if we cannot (always) attain to it or grasp it.

This, I think, constitutes the point of Emerson's last, great paragraph in "Illusions," which is worth quoting in full. It takes on directly, by assuming something close to Alexander Pope's sense of the Great Chain of Being, the notion already stated and accepted that change and flux *appear* everywhere.

There is no chance, and no anarchy, in the universe. All is system and gradation. Every god is there sitting in his sphere. The young mortal enters the hall of the firmament: there is he alone with them alone, they pouring on him benedictions and gifts, and beckoning him up to their thrones. On the instant, and incessantly, fall snow-storms of illusions. He fancies himself in a vast crowd which sways this way and that, and whose movement and doings he must obey: he fancies himself poor, orphaned, insignificant. The mad crowd drives hither and thither, now furiously commanding this thing to be done, now that. What is he that he should resist their will, and think or act for himself? Every moment, new changes, and new showers of deceptions, to baffle and distract him. And when, by and by, for an instant, the air clears, and the cloud lifts a little, there are the gods still sitting around him on their thrones, — they alone with him alone. (1123–24)

Emerson's response, thus, to Plato's Allegory of the Cave.

His is a trope, a fiction, clothing the truth that comes on to "the secret of a magic which sweeps out of men's minds all vestige of theism and beliefs which they and their fathers held and were framed upon" (1120). Self-reliance cohabits with self-assertion.

"Illusions" is mixed and impure writing, even as it reeks of the old Puritan impossibilities. Emerson's sense of both/and, owing perhaps to a sound and insightful intuition that his conclusion vitiates, appears to be a poetic and imagined notion of harmony. I shall leave unresolved just how that butts up against the very different essayistic understanding of critical and perhaps salvific tension.

If you have built castles in the air, your work need not be lost; that is where they should be. Now put the foundations under them.
— Henry David Thoreau, *Walden*

Welcome, O life! I go to encounter for the millionth time the reality of experience and to forge in the smithy of my soul the uncreated conscience of my race.
— Stephen Dedalus, in *A Portrait of the Artist as a Young Man* by James Joyce

Forging in the Smithy of the Mind

Henry David Thoreau's "Walking" and the Problematic of Transcendence

LYDIA FAKUNDINY IS RIGHT, AS USUAL: "Walking, rambling, sauntering, strolling, wandering are more than recurrent topics of essay writing; they're images by which essayists like to figure their particular mode of discoursing, tropes of essaying itself" (15). The titles of early "essay periodicals" (as Fakundiny calls them) affirms the point: if not already Addison and Steele's *Spectator* very early in the eighteenth century, certainly by the time Dr. Johnson called his *The Rambler*, then *The Adventurer*, and finally *The Idler*. Understandably essayists are fond of walking and of walking as subject; see, to name only those who spring immediately to mind, Hazlitt, Chesterton, Max Beerbohm, Edward Hoagland, Alfred Kazin. Surely the most famous of these sojourners, these "Sainte-Terrers" as he himself labels his ilk, these saunterers, is Henry David Thoreau, the so-called hermit of Walden Pond, who left town—and the mass of men who lead lives of quiet desperation—and headed out, alone, to forge a new life, a new way of living, one built on ultimate simplicity.

In the excellent introduction to her equally excellent anthology *The Art of the Essay*, Fakundiny writes, shedding light at once on the essay and on the author of such essays as "Civil Disobedience," "Life Without Principle," those that constitute *Walden*, and the inimitable "Walking":

> In the essay's long preoccupation with these figures, rambling, sauntering, and the rest stake out the broader idea of walking as if to preserve its sense of leisure, of not keeping to a straight path in a predetermined amount of time. Although the walker necessarily strikes out in some one direction rather than another—you must go east or west, as Thoreau says in "Walking"—the route is not planned beforehand, or if planned, then only in a general way. There is room for being dilatory, time for digression. There is the prospect, too, of an occasional sally: a spirited little foray to some appealing spot ahead or sideways, some object or sight that calls for a closer look. The route is mapped in the going. And except for a general familiarity with the terrain to be walked, there's no anticipating what will come your way; you set out to see what is out there to be seen. (16)

So described, walking is the heart of liberty, bound to appeal to the arch-individualist who generally accepted his Concord friend Ralph Waldo Emerson's paean to "self-reliance." A surveyor by trade, moreover, Thoreau was well aware that the essayist engages in "home-cosmography" (in the last essay in *Walden* he in fact quotes Sir William Habington's seventeenth-century poem from which this apt term comes): the mapping of both the close region that one physically inhabits and that "home" that is the self. Thoreau thus announces on the very first page of *Walden* that

> [i]n most books, the *I*, or first person, is omitted; in this it will be retained; that, in respect to egotism, is the main difference. We commonly do not remember that it is, after all, always the first person that is speaking. I should not talk so much about myself if there were anybody else whom I knew as well. Unfortunately, I am confined to this theme by the narrowness of my experience. (259)

This last sentence marks a significant confession.

"Walking" opens boldly, assertively, even defiantly, Thoreau never one to accommodate, welcome, or invite us into his world, nor one to mince words, or admit of a complexity when simplification looms possible. The set-off first paragraph establishes the theme and the tone for the entire essay, nearly forty pages of strident prose whose wildness mirrors the topic:

> I wish to speak a word for Nature, for absolute freedom and wildness, as contrasted with a freedom and culture merely civil—to regard man as an inhabitant, or a part and parcel of Nature, rather than a member of society. I wish to make an extreme statement, if so I may make an emphatic one, for there are enough champions of civilization: the minister and the school committee and every one of you will take care of that. (592)

Difference prevails, difference rendered "extreme," frozen into opposition, without compromise, moderation, or any apparent hope of a *via media*. Thoreau extends no invitation to his audience to go along with him.

When he turns to the topic of walking, it is clear that Thoreau believes that he will—to borrow from Joyce in the epigraph above—create the uncreated conscience of walking: "I have met with but one or two persons in the course of my life who understood the art of Walking, that is, of taking walks—who had a genius, so to speak, for *sauntering*." Thoreau then indulges his penchant for etymological speculation, linking "saunterer" to "a *Sainte-Terrer*," or "Holy-Lander" (592). Some, he allows, "would derive the word from *sans terre*, without land or a home, which, therefore, in the good sense, will mean, having no particular home, but equally at home everywhere." If the relevance of all this seems doubtful, it will soon become clear that Thoreau—wild as he may occasionally be—is actually advancing a position. Indeed, he avers, "every walk is a sort of crusade, preached by some Peter the Hermit in us, to go forth and reconquer this Holy Land from the hands of the Infidels" (593). The religious terms are thus apt, Thoreau a peripatetic fundamentalist, an extremist, who "cannot preserve my health and spirits, unless I spend four hours a day at least—and it is commonly more than that—sauntering through the woods and over the hills and fields, absolutely free from all worldly engagements" (594). That spirit of unbridled and uncompromising freedom and independence, without ties to any "nets" flung out to bind the soul, permeates Thoreau's essay. And for his reader? Thoreau is no more accommodating than compromising: "If you are ready to leave father and mother, and brother and sister, and wife and child and friends, and never see them again— if you have paid your debts, and made your will, and settled all your affairs, and are a free man—then you are ready for a walk" (593). This "crusader," this "Walker,

Errant," is "a sort of fourth estate, outside of Church and State and People" (594). "Errant" also rather well describes the sauntering movement of this essay.

What Thoreau is about, this errant Transcendentalist, differs, obviously, from what William Hazlitt is about, interested not so much in walking as in "going a journey." Thoreau, it is immediately clear, cares less about the physical act of walking, and the adventures that it may provide, than something spiritual. There is no point, he affirms, in "direct[ing] our steps to the woods, if they do not carry us thither"; there is no point if "I have walked a mile into the woods bodily, without getting there in spirit." Still, he writes, finely, that, out walking, too often "the thought of some work will run in my head and I am not where my body is—I am out of my senses. In my walks I would fain return to my senses" (597–98).

In his senses or not, Thoreau resists the narrow. Even the very notion of "way" gives him pause, opposed as he is to that of "village," on which word he expatiates wildly:

> The word is from the Latin *villa*, which together with *via*, a way, or more anciently *ved* and *vella*, Varro derives from veho, to carry, because the villa is the place to and from which things are carried. They who got their living by teaming were said *vellaturum facere*. Hence, too, the Latin word *vilis* and our vile, also *villain*. This suggests what kind of degeneracy villagers are liable to. They are wayworn by the travel that goes by and over them, without traveling themselves. (599–600)

Thoreau is, in any case, decidedly "latitudinarian," as the following striking passage makes clear. It is Thoreau's philosophy in a nutshell, delivered as prophecy—fences do not make for good walking, the broad way often not the most traveled:

> At present, in this vicinity, the best part of the lane is not private property; the landscape is not owned, and the walker enjoys comparative freedom. But possibly the day will come when it will be partitioned off into so-called pleasure-grounds, in which a few will take a narrow and exclusive pleasure only—when fences shall be multiplied, and man-traps and other engines invented to confine men to the *public* road, and walking over the surface of God's earth shall be construed to mean trespassing on some gentleman's grounds. To enjoy a thing exclusively is commonly to exclude

yourself from the true enjoyment of it. Let us improve our opportunities, then, before the evil days come. (602)

When he goes out walking, Thoreau finds that he "finally and inevitably" heads southwest, as if drawn to that symbolic representation of the future, the "more unexhausted and richer": "Eastward I go only by force; but westward I go free. Thither no business leads me" (603). Consequently "I must walk toward Oregon, and not toward Europe." *In the essay*, Thoreau is clearly laying the groundwork for his developing focus on his stated mission in "Walking," which is to speak for "absolute freedom and wildness," as opposed to "civilization." Thus he now writes:

> We go eastward to realize history and study the works of art and literature, retracing the steps of the race; we go westward as into the future, with a spirit of enterprise and adventure. The Atlantic is a Lethean stream, in our passage over which we have had an opportunity to forget the Old World and its institutions. (604)

Then another prophecy: "If we do not succeed this time, there is perhaps one more chance for the race left before it arrives on the banks of the Styx; and that is in the Lethe of the Pacific, which is three times as wide" (604).

Thoreau believes America to be variously blessed—naturally, that is. Because there is an evident correspondence between landscape and climate, on the one hand, and intellect, spirit, and the heart, on the other—so grand and fortuitous is everything here and now—he, this Modern, this "enthusiast," expects great things to be achievable:

> we shall be more imaginative, . . . our thoughts will be clearer, fresher, and more ethereal, as our sky—our understanding more comprehensive and broader, like our plains—our intellect generally on a grander scale, like our thunder and lightning, our rivers and mountains and forests— and our hearts shall even correspond in breadth and depth and grandeur to our inland seas. . . . As a true patriot, I should be ashamed to think that Adam in paradise was more favorably situated on the whole than the backwoodsman in this country. (608)

Not just space but also time applies: having seen "a panorama" of the Mississippi, and juxtaposed its glories with the supposedly lesser glories in the

Old Countries, Thoreau concludes that "*this was the heroic age itself*," for after all, "the hero is commonly the simplest and obscurest of men" (609). As a result of such optimism, Thoreau writes, for example: "It is too late to be studying Hebrew; it is more important to understand even the slang of today" (608).

At this point, "Walking" makes explicit the connection between "the West" and "the Wild." In "Wildness," he asserts, ever wilder in his interpretations, "is the preservation of the World" (609). Nothing less than "life consists with wildness. The most alive is the wildest" (611). Rather than in "lawns and cultivated fields," certainly "not in towns and cities," "hope and the future" lie "in the impervious and quaking swamps" (611), for "a swamp [is] a sacred place, a *sanctum sanctorum*." Indeed "in such a soil," claims Thoreau, with brazenness enough for Legion, "grew Homer and Confucius and the rest, and out of such a wilderness comes the Reformer eating locusts and wild honey" (613) — thus does Thoreau connect with the opening of the essay. From here, he proceeds to claim — "argue" is much too strong a word — that "in literature it is only the wild that attracts us," that English literature is "essentially tame and civilized, . . . reflecting Greece and Rome," and that the prized wildness that he glorifies is such as "no *culture*, in short, can give" (615–16).

These are, Thoreau readily admits, "wild fancies," and he embraces them because they "transcend the order of time and development" (618). He would have wild men, rather than tame ones. "Who but the Evil One," he asks, "has cried 'Whoa' to mankind?" The following nicely sums up Thoreau's position here, this wild man, who stands tall, above ordinary men, themselves no better, he considers, than beasts of burden:

> I rejoice that horses and steers have to be broken before they can be made
> the slaves of men, and that men themselves have some wild oats still left to
> sow before they become submissive members of society. Undoubtedly, all
> men are not equally fit subjects for civilization; and because the majority,
> like dogs and sheep, are tame by inherited disposition, this is no reason
> why the others should have their natures broken that they may be reduced
> to the same level. Men are in the main alike, but they were made several in
> order that they might be various. If a low use is to be served, one man will
> do nearly or quite as well as another; if a high one, individual excellence
> is to be regarded. . . . Confucius says, "The skins of the tiger and the

leopard, when they are tanned, are as the skins of the dog and the sheep tanned." But it is not the part of a true culture to tame tigers, any more than it is to make sheep ferocious; and tanning their skins for shoes is not the best use to which they can be put. (619)

Suddenly "Walking" veers. The final ten pages, about one-fourth of the whole, are strikingly different: evocative more than polemical and horta-tory, nearly poetic in texture and structure. First Thoreau treats names, surprising me with the focus ("there is nothing in a name," we are given to believe, this followed by the assertion that now "our only true names are nicknames" [620]). Then comes an excursus on culture, Thoreau repeat-ing his earlier denunciations but proceeding to an all-too-brief account of a "wild and dusky knowledge," "a kind of mother-wit" (619). In fact Thoreau promotes "a Society for the Diffusion of Useful Ignorance," ulti-mately claiming that "the highest we can attain to is not Knowledge, but Sympathy with Intelligence"—this could all be fruitfully pursued (622–23). But Thoreau immediately connects this point with the following:

> There is something servile in the habit of seeking after a law which we
> may obey. We may study the laws of matter at and for our convenience,
> but a successful life knows no law. It is an unfortunate discovery certainly,
> that of a law which binds us where we did not know before that we were
> bound. Live free, child of the mist—and with respect to knowledge we are
> all children of the mist. The man who takes the liberty to live is superior
> to all the laws. (623–24)

A clue to what Thoreau is doing in these last pages is provided by a short section, of only one paragraph, which follows a brilliantly imagined and richly textured account of a Wordsworthian experience regarding Spauld-ing's Farm. Here is that clue, which, in beginning with the natural from which it soars higher and higher, reflects the principle being discussed:

> We are accustomed to say in New England that few and fewer pigeons
> visit us every year. Our forests furnish no mast for them. So, it would
> seem, few and fewer thoughts visit each growing man from year to year,
> for the grove in our minds is laid waste—sold to feed unnecessary fires
> of ambition, or sent to mill—and there is scarcely a twig left for them to
> perch on. They no longer build or breed with us. In some more genial

season, perchance, a faint shadow flits across the landscape of the mind, cast by the *wings* of some thought in its vernal or autumnal migration, but, looking up, we are unable to detect the substance of the thought itself. Our winged thoughts are turned to poultry. They no longer soar, and they attain only to a Shanghai and Cochin-China grandeur. Those *gra-a-ate thoughts*, those *gra-a-ate men* you hear of! (627)

Thoreau would soar like Stephen Dedalus, that Icarian and Luciferian figure, who proclaims more than once, "I will not serve." For Thoreau, here, there is this recapitulation: "We hug the earth — how rarely we mount! Methinks we might elevate ourselves a little more" (ibid.).

In the last pages of "Walking" Thoreau shows just how this might be, writing, to my mind, more effectively than earlier in the essay. Thoreau is very good indeed when he "hugs the earth"; but when he waxes ethereal, he becomes very nearly embarrassing — for instance: "If you have built castles in the air, your work need not be lost; that is where they should be. Now put the foundations under them" (443). Note first, as to instances of his strength, the remainder of the paragraph that opens with the last sentence I quoted just above, where observation leads to concrete and particular writing:

We might climb a tree, at least. I found my account in climbing a tree once. It was a tall white pine, on the top of a hill; and though I got well pitched, I was well paid for it, for I discovered new mountains in the horizon which I had never seen before — so much more of the earth and the heavens. I might have walked about the foot of the tree for threescore years and ten, and yet I certainly should never have seen them. But, above all, I discovered around me — it was near the end of June — on the ends of the topmost branches only, a few minute and delicate red conelike blossoms, the fertile flower of the white pine looking heavenward. I carried straightway to the village the topmost spire, and showed it to stranger jurymen who walked the streets — for it was court week — and to farmers and lumber-dealers and woodchoppers and hunters, and not one had ever seen the like before, but they wondered as at a star dropped down. Tell of ancient architects finishing their works on the tops of columns as perfectly as on the lower and more visible parts! Nature has from the first expanded the minute blossoms of the forest only toward the heavens, above men's heads and unobserved by them. We see only the flowers that are under our feet in the meadows. The pines have developed their delicate blossoms on the highest twigs of the wood every summer for ages, as well over the heads of Nature's red children as of her white ones; yet scarcely a farmer or hunter in the land has ever seen them. (627–28)

The effectiveness here—and it is considerable—derives from the minuteness of the detail and the scrupulousness of Thoreau's observation and subsequent representation.

Immediately afterward, he switches modes, becoming hortatory again—and in the event, losing me. "Above all," he writes, possibly with a pun, "we cannot afford not to live in the present." So far, so good, but then Thoreau becomes characteristically extreme—and wild: "He is blessed over all mortals who loses no moment of the passing life in remembering the past" (628). His "gospel according to this moment" represents one of the most extreme paeans.

The very next section returns to the mode and prevailing tone of the penultimate one. It is even more poetic, directly recalling Wordsworth's famous realization upon Mount Snowdon in the concluding, fourteenth book of *The Prelude*. I shall quote entire the two paragraphs, for they deserve it—the long, beautifully pointed second sentence reflects, I reckon, the accumulating details that go into this remarkable observation. As in Wordsworth, light figures, and prefigures, the paradisiacal, what M. H. Abrams once finely termed "natural supernaturalism":

> We had a remarkable sunset one day last November. I was walking in a
> meadow, the source of a small brook, when the sun at last, just before
> setting, after a cold, gray day, reached a clear stratum in the horizon, and
> the softest, brightest morning sunlight fell on the dry grass and on the
> stems of the trees in the opposite horizon and on the leaves of the shrub
> oaks on the hillside, while our shadows stretched long over the meadow
> eastward, as if we were the only motes in its beams. It was such a light
> as we could not have imagined a moment before, and the air also was so
> warm and serene that nothing was wanting to make a paradise of that
> meadow. When we reflected that this was not a solitary phenomenon,
> never to happen again, but that it would happen forever and ever, an
> infinite number of evenings, and cheer and reassure the latest child that
> walked there, it was more glorious still.
>
> The sun sets on some retired meadow, where no house is visible, with

all the glory and splendor that it lavishes on cities, and perchance as it has never set before—where there is but a solitary marsh hawk to have his wings gilded by it, or only a musquash looks out from his cabin, and there is some little black-veined brook in the midst of the marsh, just beginning to meander, winding slowly round a decaying stump. We walked in so pure and bright a light, gilding the withered grass and leaves, so softly and serenely bright, I thought I had never bathed in such a golden flood, without a ripple or a murmur to it. The west side of every wood and rising ground gleamed like the boundary of Elysium, and the sun on our backs seemed like a gentle herdsman driving us home at evening. (629–30)

All this is well said, but Thoreau leaves off reporting, when—to invoke Swift's denunciation of enthusiasm in *A Tale of a Tub*—fancy gets astride upon the reason, and there quickly follows the attempt to convert others; Thoreau all too rarely forgoes preaching.

In fact, immediately after these brilliant paragraphs of observation, he ends, preaching. He evidently did not know when to stop; he could not control himself. Here, in trying to link up with the beginning of the essay, Thoreau pushes hard:

So we saunter toward the Holy Land, till one day the sun shall shine more brightly than ever he has done, shall perchance shine into our minds and hearts, and light up our whole lives with a great awakening light, as warm and serene and golden as on a bankside in autumn. (630)

What Thoreau lacks, I am tempted to say, is that "dull equanimity" against which he himself rails. He senses, to be sure, a way—a *via media*—that he will not allow himself to explore, correctly acknowledging—without stopping to reflect—that "for my part, I feel with regard to Nature I live a sort of *border life*, on the confines of a world into which I make occasional and transient forays only, and my patriotism and allegiance to the state into whose territories I seem to retreat are those of a moss-trooper" (625; italics added).

I now needed to live, with the top layer of my person known to the
outside world and displayed for social purposes. But, close to the bone,
there had to be an inner stratum, formed and cultivated in solitude
where the essence of what I was, am now, and will be, perhaps, to the
end of my days, hides itself and waits to be found by the lasting silence.
— Doris Grumbach, *Fifty Days of Solitude*

Estranging the Familiar

Alice Meynell's "Solitudes"

THIS BEAUTIFUL LITTLE ESSAY—less than three pages in Lydia
Fakundiny's anthology *The Art of the Essay*—is to be read in solitude, sa-
vored, perused, meditated upon. Published in 1928 in the collection *The
Spirit of Place* and reprinted thirty years later in *Wayfaring*, it needs be set
against William Hazlitt's "On Going a Journey" and Thoreau's "Walking,"
as well as Samuel Johnson's "The Solitude of the Country," which has little
good to say about any solitude but says what it says in a manner controlled
and erudite. In "Solitudes," with its proclamation of different kinds of
aloneness, the matter is fully as much manner and style as either subject or
"perspective." Meynell's sensibility is less Romantic than classical, although,
unlike Johnson, she embraces such solitude as the Romantics sought and
found bracing, if not essential. But she is less a friend of reflection than an
embodiment of meditation. Language matters greatly to this unfairly neglected essayist, poet, and editor. Virginia Woolf understood her, not least
because Meynell too worked in "language charged with meaning"—and
of course Woolf and Meynell shared many views regarding women, their

history, and their capacity to contribute, especially to the world of letters. Alice Meynell is no more a woman's writer, however, than Jane Austen or Woolf herself.

Introducing *Alice Meynell: Prose and Poetry*, the Centenary Edition, published in 1947, the inimitable Vita Sackville-West described her work as having the "elaborate finish" of objects made "with an etching pen." She elaborates as follows, a bit preciously and condescendingly in my judgment: "Reading her essays, one is reminded of old jewellers sometimes perceived seated at a cluttered table in the back room of a little shop, a cylindrical magnifying-glass fixed in one eye, bent over a skeleton framework, and with infinite delicacy dripping rather than dropping the tiny glittering stones into the setting from the tip of a pair of pincers." Yet Sackville-West is surely right in adding that "such precision was Alice Meynell's in her choice of words" (17). Introducing "Solitudes," Lydia Fakundiny observed, further, that "the occasionally dense sentence, the elliptical summation, the startlingly chosen word, force a more careful pace, a dislocation from the preconceived and the obvious" (177). Precision marks Meynell's work, but then so do framework and design—intelligent design. She is less like Emerson, didactic and hortatory, and, I think, more like T. S. Eliot, although she appears less literary and more concerned with the familiar. That *familiar* she thinks about closely, more closely than Emerson, much more so than Thoreau, who mixes observation and reflection. Meynell is thoroughly within her subject, no observer distanced spatially or temporally. This is not experience reflected in tranquility or otherwise.

If Meynell recalls Dr. Johnson's supreme, balanced, and oh-so-ordered conclusions, she stands in Bacon's shadow. But she is less pontifical than either—and more human because more humble, certainly compassionate and capacious. Her "civilization" is never paraded, but incarnated in the sensibility that cannot be separated from manner, behavior, and style. Here she is opening "Solitudes":

> The wild man is alone when he wills, and so is the man for whom civilization has been kind. But there are the multitudes to whom civilization has given little but its reaction, its rebound, its chips, its refuse, its shavings, sawdust, and waste, its failures; to them solitude is a right forgone or a luxury unattained; a right forgone, we may name it, in the case of the nearly savage, and a luxury unattained in the case of the nearly refined.

We realize soon enough that Meynell's subject *is* civilization, nothing more or less.

Her very next sentence wrenches us to attention: "Thus has the movement of the world thronged together into some blind by-way." Of these persons, about whom Meynell declines to wax sentimental even as her sentiment is made manifest, she then writes, taking words with the seriousness that we observe in such "squeezers" of words as Lancelot Andrewes:

> Their share in the enormous solitude which is the common, unbounded, and virtually illimitable possession of all mankind has lapsed, unclaimed. They do not know it is theirs. Of many of their kingdoms they are ignorant, but of this most ignorant. They have not guessed that they own for every man a space inviolate, a place of unhidden liberty and of no obscure enfranchisement. They do not claim even the solitude of closed corners, the narrow privacy of lock and key. Nor could they command so much.
> (272–73)

Completely within her subject, Meynell we now enjoy as we observe her *thinking through writing*. She genuinely "essays," first maintaining that solitude "lies in a perpetual distance," England offering it in abundance and making it available in countless places and countless ways. "Or rather," Meynell then writes, "solitudes are not to be measured by miles" but instead "numbered by days," her verbs as precise as her distinction between space and time. Soon, she qualifies: "Nay, solitudes are not to be numbered by days, but by men themselves. Every man of the living and every man of the dead might have had his 'privacy of light'" (273). Light, by the way, as Vita Sackville-West acknowledges, is very important to Meynell; Sackville-West links it, on the one hand, with the clarity of her expression and, on the other, with "the quality of light, perhaps the light of Rome, which she loved so much, but in any case a Latin light never veiled by northern mists of vagueness or vacillation" (17). No Romanticism or enthusiasm, either, if not exactly a *via media*.

For "the mass of men [and women] who lead lives of quiet desperation" (Thoreau), Meynell has said: "For the solitude that has a sky and a horizon they do not know how to wish." Solitude, she is convinced, "needs no park. It is to be found in the merest working country; and a thicket may be as secret as a forest." Size counts no more than location. It does not hide, the "best solitude": "This the people who have drifted together into the streets live whole lives and never know" (273). Solitude thus appears a matter of choice, available to any and all who will but accept it.

Meynell is most sensitive and sympathetic, it seems, to those, "the men, and the many women, who have sacrificed all their solitude to the perpetual society of the school, the cloister, or the hospital-ward." These, she writes, "walk without secrecy, candid, simple, visible, without moods, unchangeable, in a constant communication and practice of action and speech." Their loss is neither "barren [n]or futile," and they appear to Meynell to have "the conviction," which they "bestow": the conviction "of solitude deferred" (274). The observation is at once subtle and astute, keen and sympathetic.

Even the rich, who can afford solitude, know little of it; of them, to be sure, it is "a prepared, secured, defended, elaborate possession," and yet they know nothing of that most delicious, delicate, and significant solitude, which Meynell, the mother of seven, offers as "the natural solitude of a woman with a child." What follows, coming after a short paragraph on Millet's painting of the solitary as "alone and inaccessible," could, but does not, smack of the sentimental. The scene Meynell paints is far more effective, I find, than Wordsworth's account of "the blessed babe." According to the essayist, "All is commonplace until the doors are closed" upon mother and child. Then, writes Meynell in prose stunningly beautiful, as only a mother, surely, could do. Although the writing is poetic, the passage is not prose poetry; it lacks artifice, or the pretense toward poetry, secure in its precision of thinking:

> This unique intimacy is a profound retreat, an absolute seclusion. It is
> more than single solitude, it is a multiplied isolation more remote than
> mountains, safer than valleys, deeper than forests, and further than mid-
> sea. That solitude partaken—the only partaken solitude in the world—is
> the Point of Honour of ethics. Treachery to that obligation and a betrayal
> of that confidence might well be held to be the least pardonable of all
> crimes. There is no innocent sleep so innocent as sleep shared between a
> woman and a child, the little breath hurrying beside the longer, as a child's
> foot runs.

Meynell ends with sentences that offer stinging social critique, made all the more effective by the play on language at the end that is, like all child's play, more than childish: "But a favourite crime of the modern sentimentalist is that of a woman against her child. Her power, her intimacy, her opportunity, that should be her accusers, excuse her" (274).

Next Meynell shocks the reader attentive to her style and manner, for abruptly she returns to the notion of the park, which she had quitted three paragraphs earlier. There, you will recall, she led off by writing, "It [solitude] needs no park." Here she writes, "A conventional park is by no means necessary for the preparation of a country solitude" (274). Her interest lying in both similarity and difference, in difference and identity, Meynell moves from that earlier meditation that reflected no necessity of seclusion to a consideration of the country. That earlier paragraph began with "the merest working country" and moved swiftly to the city, where there is no "hiding-place" and where people, with never an hour alone, "live in reluctant or indifferent companionship, as people do in a boarding-house, by paradoxical choice, familiar with one another and not intimate" (273). Here, in the essay's penultimate paragraph, Meynell actually develops the point about parks, inching toward a conclusion regarding solitude as uncontrived. Solitude, as she prefers it, is less a positive quality than something known in its difference.

> Indeed, to make those far and wide and long approaches and avenues to peace seems to be a denial of the accessibility of what should be so simple. A step, a pace or so aside, is enough to lead thither. Solitude is not for a lifetime, but for intervals. A park insists too much, and, besides, does not insist very sincerely. In order to fulfil the apparent professions and to keep the published promise of a park, the owner thereof should be a lover of long seclusion or of a very life of loneliness. He should have gained the state of solitariness which is a condition of life quite unlike any other. (274–75)

A remarkable thought! As this essay, as well as others, shows, Meynell highly values secrecy.

At this point in the paragraph, Meynell veers, swerves, moving abruptly—again thinking through the writing—to a meditation on difference from what she has just described (note, for example, the way the simple word "wild" resonates and reverberates, as well as the rapid and unforced shifts of perspective):

The traveller who may have gone astray in countries where there is an almost life-long solitude possible is aware how invincibly apart are the lonely figures he has seen in desert places there. Their loneliness is broken by his passage, it is true, but hardly so to them. They look at him, but they are not aware that he looks at them. Nay, they look at him as though they were invisible. Their un-selfconsciousness is absolute; it is in the wild degree. They are solitaries, body and soul. Even when they are curious, and turn to watch the passer-by, they are essentially alone. (275)

Now Meynell shifts back, this move not jarring at all: she thus returns to "the country" and that notion of "park" from which she switched focus in order to make a difference. She even skillfully picks up the earlier, seemingly tossed-off allusion to the painter Millet, weaving as if magically her tapestry that *might* have appeared careless or haphazard, subject to far less rhetorical and artistic control than Meynell exhibits:

Now, no one ever found that attitude in a squire's figure, or that look in any country gentleman's eyes. The squire is not a life-long solitary. He never bore himself as though he were invisible. He never had the impersonal ways of a herdsman in the remoter Apennines, with a blind, blank hut in the rocks for his dwelling. Millet would not even have taken him as a model for the solitary in the briefer and milder sylvan solitudes of France. And yet nothing but a life-long, habitual, and wild solitariness would be quite proportionate to a park of any magnitude. (ibid.)

By the time we reach these words, and the explicit reference now to "park," we cannot but marvel at Meynell's *essaying*: the way she moves, meditating on solitudes (the plural is significant, as Lydia Fakundiny allows) from many angles, truly "*ondoyant et divers*."

Her skill is not exhausted, her essaying yet incomplete. Meynell brings her essay to a close—not so much a "conclusion"—in the final paragraph by returning to the difference between solitude and loneliness, and that between solitude and crowd. We are back, in other words, on the street, far from the "wild," in London, even Paris, and the loneliness of crowds, of being subject to crowds, Meynell focused intently and squarely on *the look* that reveals all, just what the painter Millet knew and represented:

If there is a look of human eyes that tells of perpetual loneliness, so there is also the familiar look that is the sign of perpetual crowds. It is the London expression, and, in its way, the Paris expression. It is the quickly caught, though not interested look, the dull but ready glance of those who do not know of their forfeited place apart; who have neither the open secret nor the close, neither liberty nor the right of lock and key; no reserve, no need of refuge, no flight nor impulse of flight; no moods but what they may brave out in the street, no hope of news from solitary counsels. Even in many men and women who have all their rights over all the solitudes—solitudes of closed doors and territorial solitudes of sward and forest—even in these who have enough solitudes to fulfil the wants of a city, even in these is found, not seldom, the look of the street. (275–76)

Meynell's sympathy is strongest not just for those who do not *see* but for those who do not *know* enough for hope.

Meynell's little essay thus deserves, and stands, comparison with Walter Benjamin's subtle and acute explorations of the Parisian flaneur. Meynell, in any case, is an artist rather than a philosopher. "Solitudes" stands somewhere, on a very sturdy pole, between philosophy and literature, closer to the latter, to be sure, but without sacrificing the meaning that emerges in meditation (rather than from reflection). Whatever she is, Alice Meynell is, as Vita Sackville-West has written, "never heavy-handed, never dull" (26). That commentator thought it possible, more than half a century ago, that Meynell's reputation might "grow increasingly as a critic, independent and fearless, incisive and acute, uninfluenced by fashion" (25). Of course fashion has brought theory to the fore and left Meynell even farther behind. As an essayist, however, familiar as well as critical, Meynell deserves reading, by women and men alike. For those to whom language matters, and design, and above all precision of thought, expression, and execution, Alice Meynell's essays offer countless pleasures—and a great deal of wisdom.

[Tradition] cannot be inherited, and if you want it you must obtain it
by great labour.
—T. S. Eliot, "Tradition and the Individual Talent"

So that in short the question comes all to this—whether is the nobler
being of the two, that which by a lazy contemplation of four inches
round, by an overweening pride, feeding and engendering on itself,
turns all into excrement and venom, producing nothing at last but
fly-bane and a cobweb; or that which by an universal range, with long
search, much study, true judgment, and distinction of things, brings
home honey and wax.
—Jonathan Swift, *The Battle of the Books*

"By Indirections Find Directions Out"

Hilaire Belloc's "The Mowing of a Field"

IN 1910 GEORG LUKÁCS PUBLISHED what turned out to be a
seminal discussion of the essay. The Hungarian theorist modestly represented "On the Nature and Form of the Essay" as "a letter to a friend"—the
kind of "arrogant courtesy" he himself ascribes to "the great Sieur de Montaigne," acknowledged father of the form Lukács is celebrating. Lukács's
great contribution lies in positing irony as fundamental to the essay, to
be found, he claims, "in the writings of every truly great essayist": "And
the irony I mean consists in the critic always speaking about the ultimate
problems of life, but in a tone which implies that he is only discussing
pictures and books, only the inessential and pretty ornaments of real life—
and even then not their innermost substance but only their beautiful and
useless surface." A smallness thus striates the essay, suggested by Abraham
Cowley in an essay published in 1668. For Lukács, the essayist "ironically
adapts himself to this smallness—the eternal smallness of the most profound work of the intellect in face of life—and even emphasizes it with
ironic modesty" (9–10). Nearly seventy years later, E. B. White echoed the
substance (if not the form) of Lukács's reflections, referring to himself and

others who don the mantle of Montaigne as "second-class citizens" who had better not set their sights on literary prizes (vii).

Irony may be too strong a term for the way the essay proceeds, too high-falutin a concept for this surely modest form; it seems not quite to reflect its quiet texture. Better fitting, I have suggested in *Tracing the Essay*, is "sneaki-ness," the kind of stealth you find, say, in Hilaire Belloc's modest little essay "The Mowing of a Field," written a few years before Lukács offered his commentary and published in a volume of familiar essays titled *Hills and the Sea*. Modesty, as well as courtesy, marks every essay and collection Belloc ever penned, as represented by the titles of such volumes as *On Something*, *On Everything*, *On Nothing*, and simply *On*. In an essay on his favorite fountain pen—the 1905 Waterman Ideal—Belloc even denied he "created" anything at all, preferring the term "maker" for his little efforts. And yet "The Mowing of a Field" sneaks up from its modest title and humble be-ginnings and subject matter onto major moral and cultural critique. In its engagingly and seductively indirect manner, it may be seen as a "common reader" or layperson's essay on "tradition and the individual talent."

Although few if any of my students—despite being in Kansas—have ever mowed a field, they are smitten with Belloc's essay. From the start, he draws you in, making you feel there with him, in the south of England, in springtime, returning after too long an absence. It isn't Wordsworth re-turning to Tintern Abbey and discovering difference; what Belloc uncovers is sameness, continuation, living tradition. By the time they have finished the essay, my students understand how the essay works as form: we begin with the small, or in this case the quite mundane, but by the end we have moved outward, *through* that necessary detour-that-is-not-really-detour, to large and complex issues—and enjoyed every minute of the journey.

Belloc opens "The Mowing of a Field" with a detailed, bucolic descrip-tion, making his reader feel a part of the scene and welcome in this beau-tiful land isolated and separated—preserved, we shall come in time to appreciate—from the busy world (a point to which he will return toward the end). This is the opening paragraph, the first sentence suggestive of story and action to come; the whole of the paragraph we shall fully appre-ciate only in time, setting the stage, as it does, for a story that opts not for the easy or the latitudinarian:

> There is a valley in South England remote from ambition and from fear,
>   where the passage of strangers is rare and unperceived, and where the scent

of the grass in summer is breathed only by those who are native to that unvisited land. The roads to the Channel do not traverse it; they choose upon either side easier passes over the range. One track alone leads up through it to the hills, and this is changeable: now green where men have little occasion to go, now a good road where it nears the homesteads and the barns. The woods grow steep above the slopes; they reach sometimes the very summit of the heights, or, when they cannot attain them, fill in and clothe the combes. And, in between, along the floor of the valley, deep pastures and their silence are bordered by lawns of chalky grass and the small yew trees of the Downs. (143)

The following paragraphs establish time as one of the essay's prime concerns, as well as its difference from *pure* memoir or autobiography. Description here gives way to reflection, and as the contemporary poet Anne Carson avers, reflection marks the essay, distinguishing it from related forms. Though Belloc is no Wordsworth, he engages in similar reflection, his thoughts bred by both "this place [to which] very lately I returned" (144) and its difference from that which had for some time been his. He pointedly differs from the Romantic poet in denying that memory had glorified the surrounding and exalted it—a difference that the essay will, in fact, both elaborate and extend, even if implicitly. What matters to Belloc is not the past but the present—or perhaps the past in the present:

> The many things that I recovered as I came up the countryside were not less charming than when a distant memory had enshrined them, but much more. Whatever veil is thrown by a longing recollection had not intensified nor even made more mysterious the beauty of that happy ground; not in my very dreams of morning had I, in exile, seen it more beloved or more rare. (144)

I do not assume that Wordsworth lurked in the back of Belloc's mind as he wrote "The Mowing of a Field." The allusion—if allusion there is—is certainly indirect and may be a product of the reader's engagement. Memory, in any case, proves for Belloc less satisfying than the scene there before him: "And all these things fulfilled and amplified my delight, till even the good vision of the place, which I had kept so many years, left me and was replaced by its better reality" (144). This is, I might say, alluding to J. Hillis Miller's book on modern poetry, the art of reality, or, to invoke the essayist Wendell Berry, the art of the commonplace.

And art there is, in Belloc's mind and on his page. Art he approaches, in fact, through consideration of time. Looking about him, Belloc recognizes that the grass is just now ready for the scythe. Observation breeds reflection, the mind rooted in present reality and at the same time given to large exploration and probing. The reflections, whether particular or grandiose, derive from direct observation. Experience, not thought, is fundamental and primary.

> Death should be represented with a scythe and Time with a sickle; for
> Time can take only what is ripe, but Death comes always too soon. In a
> word, then, it is always much easier to cut grass too late than too early;
> and I, under that evening and come back to these pleasant fields, looked
> at the grass and knew that it was time. June was in full advance: it was the
> beginning of that season when the night has already lost her foothold of
> the earth and hovers over it, never quite descending, but mixing sunset
> with the dawn. (145)

It has been fourteen years since "I had last gone out with my scythe." That great span of time Belloc treats summarily, forgoing any temptation to expatiate (in Wordsworthian fashion perhaps) on the evils of the city. "In between that day and this," writes Belloc simply, "were many things, cities and armies, and a confusion of books, mountains and horrible great breadths of sea"—no laments or lamentations (145–46).

There was work to be done, and Belloc brings that same attitude to his account of it. The first order of business—although Belloc would find the term "business" abhorrent—is the preparation of the instrument for the mowing. The sharpening of the scythe involves art; it is the second of the arts Belloc mentions, the first being the apprehension of the right time to pursue the work of mowing. In detail he describes the proper sharpening, but as specific as he is, he never *indulges*, never loses sight of the reader, who wants just the right amount of detail. So he, the essayist, must know just how much to give, when, and where, and what kind, just as the mower must know just when to begin, and how to proceed. It is all a matter of art, and when you work well, the result may be art. Belloc does not exactly say this, and perhaps would not, but I think he himself achieves art in the following description:

> To tell when the scythe is sharp enough this is the rule. First the stone
> clangs and grinds against the iron harshly; then it rings musically to one

note; then, at last, it purrs as though the iron and stone were exactly suited. When you hear this, your scythe is sharp enough; and I, when I heard it that June dawn, with everything quite silent except the birds, let down the scythe and bent myself to mow. (146)

Preparation involved ritual, and mowing itself is nothing else, almost religious in texture. "Being suited" is what "The Mowing of a Field" is all about, and the foregoing paragraph rings and purrs as it moves against a later account of the unsuited mower, the mower disrespectful, individualistic—Promethean, says Belloc, with indignation.

Already the reader has felt *invited* into the world Belloc quietly and lovingly represents. The essayist engages in telling a story, and the reader is always there, listening attentively, patiently: "There is a valley in South England remote from ambition and from fear." Like all other essays, "The Mowing of a Field" implies this reader, you and I, and precisely imagines us *as another person of essentially the same nature and on the same level.* Thus I, the reader, cannot but think of the essay, and the experience represented there, with its meaning mined and assayed, as a "thou," not an "it," as with that "awful object, 'the article'" (Gass 25). The essay is a happy product of the sympathetic imagination.

That "The Mowing of a Field" is a familiar rather than personal essay is suggested by its very first sentence and supported by the opening two paragraphs. The speaker, who we may safely say *is* Hilaire Belloc, is the medium of the essay's message, not at all its focus. Indeed, at this point, the scythe having been readied, the essay becomes all the more pointed, eventually as honed and sharp as the scythe blade: description now serves the purpose of argument, and argument there is of a decidedly ethical and cultural nature. Belloc modulates into it just as he has been moving slowly but ever so surely outward, from the grass, to the scythe, to the mowing—and now the value of such work, its meaning and significance:

When one does anything anew, after so many years, one fears very much for one's trick or habit. But all things once learnt are easily recoverable, and I very soon recovered the swing and power of the mower. Mowing well and mowing badly—or rather not mowing at all—are separated by very little; as is also true of writing verse, of playing the fiddle, and of dozens of other things, but of nothing more than of believing. (146–47)

So, we say to ourselves, this essay is not just about mowing—the stakes are high. Now Belloc raises the level of discourse, more intense, more dramatic as he first describes the antithesis, the jerk, which is followed immediately by a description of the hero, the thesis of this satire (the passage is best read aloud, the pitch rising with the tumble of the syntax until Belloc whacks us with the last clause here):

> For the bad or young or untaught mower without tradition, the mower Promethean, the mower original and contemptuous of the past, does all these things: He leaves great crescents of grass uncut. He digs the point of the scythe hard into the ground with a jerk. He loosens the handles and even the fastening of the blade. He twists the blade with his blunders, he blunts the blade, he chips it, dulls it, or breaks it clean off at the tip. If anyone is standing by he cuts him in the ankle. He sweeps up into the air wildly, with nothing to resist his stroke. He digs up earth with the grass, which is like making the meadow bleed. (147)

The individual without tradition, ignorant of it, oblivious to it, the mower Promethean, encounters no resistance, will brook none, and so goes awry. The proper mower proceeds quietly, making no fuss, disturbing nothing, respectful of everything:

> the good mower who does things just as they should be done and have been for a hundred thousand years, falls into none of these fooleries. He goes forward very steadily, his scythe-blade just barely missing the ground, every grass falling; the swish and rhythm of his mowing are always the same. (147)

"Always the same"—the value of tradition, its basis in custom and ritual: Belloc will return to this issue toward the end of "The Mowing of a Field" when he dramatizes how to secure needed labor (or employment) and when he tells the story of the buying of a pig (or land).

Such thematically resonant and rhetorically magnificent passages sneak up on you in Belloc's essay; you expect neither such elegance nor such grandeur of thought—such gravitas. The importance lies on the surface, not below it but lateral to the mundane occasion and to accounts of the quite ordinary. That importance derives ultimately from the mind— Belloc's—that sees, understands, and grasps, probing and pursuing implications, all in a manner unassuming, restrained, and poised until it can no longer bear the moral offensiveness against which it then appropriately declaims. Nothing appears to be left unsaid or merely implied—it's all out in the open, not apparent only in spirit. The literal rules, manifest in a statement such as that concerning prayer: "mowing should be like one's prayers—all of a sort and always the same, and so made that you can establish a monotony and work them, as it were, with half your mind: that happier half, the half that does not bother" (148). Missing here, sadly for Romantics, is interiorization.

Of primary interest is not Belloc's mind but at once the quality of his response and "the world" he experiences. Natural description early on, which draws us in, soon gives way to accounts of the arts of sharpening the scythe, thence of mowing, interspersed with observations that move outward to greater and greater implications of the ways we do seemingly ordinary and even minor acts. "The world is too much with us," lamented Wordsworth, and Belloc too resides, as did Montaigne before either of them, apart from its "getting and spending." But Belloc more resembles Alice Meynell; he leaves the world only temporarily, for refreshment, and rather than forsake it, like Thoreau, he works out alternatives. Rather than escape, his strong cultural criticism is aimed at recognition, judgment, and change.

Time is a subject here, as it is in Scott Russell Sanders's "Under the Influence"—as it is, indeed, in perhaps all essays. In Sanders's fine essay, about which more directly, reflection on the past serves to enlighten and possibly to unburden the present; in "The Mowing of a Field," differently, the past lives on in the present, its virtues passed on and, one hopes, kept intact. Arguably time constitutes the essay's—the form's—true subject matter: not just what to do with it, as if in a retirement mode, but how to cope with and understand its ravages. Eliot's *Four Quartets*, an essay-poem, is perhaps the paradigmatic treatment of time; and in any case, E. B. White often treats time in his essays. Concerned with the present in whatever manner, essays reflect the present's supreme value, meaning and truth, here and now. For Belloc tradition connects present and past, endowing the present with meaning and acting as resistance. The past is a moral reminder—and remainder—a call to truth.

Belloc lacks the pretension and arrogance—no Promethean, he—to suggest that mowing is an allegory (although I suspect he was aware of the tradition in Renaissance literature of "mower" poems, themselves representations, willy-nilly, of Christ). And yet mowing shares with other activities certain unsurpassable values; it participates, no meaner or richer than any other, in the range of human endeavor, every act of which deserves respect and bears significance. Mowing is no more a metaphor for writing than writing is for mowing; they may or may not be equal in some scheme of importance that, in any case, man is incapable of ascertaining. Mowing and writing sit alongside one another, alike in the structure that Belloc invokes: they instance work, neither of them (as he suggests elsewhere regarding writing) "creative"; more modestly, both are developmental, a matter of cultivating a germ that owes its existence to a power other and greater than man.

In this essay, unlike White's "Death of a Pig," say, I never worry about a difference or discrepancy between speaker and author (the widest such difference being "A Modest Proposal," discussed earlier). The speaker in "The Mowing of a Field" is to be identified with Hilaire Belloc—it is he, in fact. And it is he who embodies the touted virtues of patience and respect. In embodying truth, the truth the essay is built upon and advocates, Belloc stands forth as our best access to it, a perhaps necessary mediation; at any rate, Belloc is the modal point—or site—at which, I am inclined to conclude, transcendence intersects with immanence. He makes concrete and human the values, the truth, represented in the various accounts narrated and described. In Belloc, *embodied truth* becomes "immanent form": form, which is the same thing as truth, is fleshed out and represented in a person.

But Belloc is not yet done with mowing. He has more to say yet about, first, what mowing allows you to see and understand, what you can see *in, through, and by means of it,* and, second, how the effective, good mower actually goes about his work. Belloc always makes comparisons, relating mowing to other activities, the religious again prominent among them:

> Mowing is a thing of ample gestures, like drawing a cartoon. Then, again, get yourself into a mechanical and repetitive mood: be thinking of anything at all but your mowing, and be anxious only when there seems some interruption to the monotony of the sound. In this mowing should be like one's prayers—all of a sort and always the same, and so made that you can establish a monotony and work them, as it were, with half your mind: that happier half, the half that does not bother. (148)

As with this last sentence, Belloc has a way, which some find annoying, of surprising by being blunt; what he says may stick in the craw of some Protestants.

But if so, not for long, for Belloc says so much that is good, that is refreshing, that is wise. The following precedes the above passage, focusing on respect:

> So great an art can only be learnt by continual practice; but this much is worth writing down, that, as in all good work, to know the thing with which you work is the core of the affair. Good verse is best written on good paper with an easy pen, not with a lump of coal on a white-washed wall. The pen thinks for you; and so does the scythe mow for you if you treat it honourably and in a manner that makes it recognize its service. (147)

In this regard, the pen resembles the scythe, which Belloc has treated honorably, both in practice and in representing it on the page. As to his pen, see the essay I alluded to earlier, "On the Pleasure of Taking Up One's Pen."

Thus prepared, Belloc set to work, mowing until the Angelus rang. Taking a short break, he observes "coming up to my field a man whom I had known in older times, before I had left the Valley." He describes him as a member of "that dark silent race," perhaps Iberian, or Celtic, that is, however, never named: "the permanent root of all England, [it] makes England wealthy and preserves it everywhere." The man clearly seeks employ, just as Belloc is interested in his labor. To accomplish their respective ends, the two men proceed indirectly, engaging in a ritual based in patience and respect: "For it is a good custom of ours always to treat bargaining as though it were a courteous pastime; and though what he was after was money, and what I wanted was his labour at the least pay, yet we both played the comedy that we were free men, the one granting a grace and the other accepting it" (149; who does which is not clear, which just may be Belloc's point). This is another world—different from what prevails beyond the Valley: "For the dry bones of commerce, avarice and method and need, are odious to the Valley; and we cover them up with a pretty body of fiction and observances" (149–50). No one is fooled; everyone knows what is going on, and yet they proceed to enact a comedy that self-consciously pretends otherwise. Although Belloc nowhere says so, that play is civilization itself, and his essay thus becomes cultural critique of a fundamental sort.

Once more, Belloc becomes indirect, interrupting his story of the day worker to elaborate on the custom embodied in the Valley: "Thus, when it comes to buying pigs, the buyer does not begin to decry the pig and the vendor to praise it, as is the custom with lesser men"; instead, "tradition makes them do business" in an indirect manner, patient, respectful: "There is no haste at all; great leisure marks the dignity of their exchange." Negotiation ensues until "all ritual is duly accomplished; and the solemn act is entered into with reverence and in a spirit of truth." In that way, Belloc says, completing his idealized account, "in the quiet soul of each runs the peace of something accomplished" (150).

Before he describes his own exchange with the familiar, dark man seeking employ, Belloc elaborates on the Valley's ways, offering a trenchant contrast with the ways of "commerce, avarice and method and need." What he is doing, it hardly needs to be stressed, is adding body to those "dry bones"—and through body spirit can emerge. In many ways, this account functions as the essay's climax, for in it themes come together, and the argument, if that is not too pointed a word for the thrust of the entire essay, is rounded off. Here "The Mowing of a Field" fulfills its promise as cultural criticism, its satire only once before sharper than in this description of the embodied speaking voice's—Belloc's—very antithesis:

> Thus do we buy a pig or land or labour or malt or lime, always with
> elaboration and set forms; and many a London man has paid double and
> more for his violence and his greedy haste and very unchivalrous higgling.
> As happened with the land at Underwaltham, which the mortgagees
> had begged and implored the estate to take at twelve hundred, and had
> privately offered to all the world at a thousand, but which a sharp *direct*
> man, of the kind that makes great fortunes, a man in a motor-car, a man
> in a fur coat, a man *of few words*, bought for two thousand three hundred
> before my very eyes, protesting that they might take his offer or leave it;
> *and all because he did not begin by praising the land.* (150–51; italics added)

What follows feels anticlimactic, thematic representation and reflection having given way to pure description of the mowing.

The final paragraph is, however, quietly beautiful, as well as poignant. Their efforts done for now, the day worker paid (and here called "my companion"), the two men rest a bit, appreciating the "beneficent and deliberate evening" and participating in "a complete silence"—the part of the worshipful service just preceding the going of one's own way. Of course, it is Belloc's boon "companion" who goes off, unobtrusively as he had appeared, a part too of this world, leaving Belloc where he was, reflecting, sympathetic, appreciative.

> He went off with a slow and steady progress, as all our peasants do, making their walking a part of the easy but continual labour of their lives. But I sat on, watching the light creep around towards the north and change, and the waning moon coming up as though by stealth behind the woods of No Man's Land. (152)

After coming together, in "business" made from need and carried on with mutual respect and according to tradition, peasant and landowner part company for the nonce, one walking, the other still sitting. Difference is thus maintained and reasserted, but quietly, and under the carapace of the night and with the blessing of such light as is available.

In Belloc *embodied truth* becomes *immanent form*: form, which is the same thing as truth, is fleshed out and represented in a person. Belloc's good friend Chesterton may have been unable, or so he claims in "A Piece of Chalk," to see through creatures to the form they embody, but Belloc leaves no doubt as to his incarnationism.

"Your business is not to catch men with show,
With homage to the perishable clay,
But lift them over it, ignore it all,
Make them forget there's such a thing as flesh.
Your business is to paint the souls of men—"
. . . .
Now, is this sense, I ask?
A fine way to paint soul, by painting body
So ill, the eye can't stop there, must go further
And can't fare worse! Thus, yellow does for white
When what you put for yellow's simply black,
And any sort of meaning looks intense
When all beside itself means and looks naught.
Why can't a painter lift each foot in turn,
Left foot and right foot, go a double step,
Make his flesh liker and his soul more like,
Both in their order?
—Robert Browning, "Fra Lippo Lippi"

Essaying and the Strain of Incarnational Thinking

G. K. Chesterton's "A Piece of Chalk"

G. K. CHESTERTON'S "A PIECE OF CHALK" is a strikingly beautiful essay, elegantly written and full of noble sentiments. Sentences and sententiae alike charm and beguile even jaded undergraduates. Who but can marvel at such craftsmanship as these words incarnate: "But though I could not with a crayon get the best out of the landscape, it does not follow that the landscape was not getting the best out of me"; "They ['the old poets who lived before Wordsworth'] preferred writing about great men to writing about great hills; but they sat on the great hills to write it. They gave out much less about Nature, but they drank in, perhaps, much more"; "The inspiration went in like sunbeams and came out like Apollo" (250).

I said that this essay beguiles, and that is apparent from the opening sentence, pleasantly in face of the essay's brevity (barely three pages in *The*

Art of the Personal Essay): "I remember one splendid morning, all blue and silver, in the summer holidays, when I reluctantly tore myself away from the task of doing nothing in particular, and put on a hat of some sort and picked up a walking-stick, and put six very bright-coloured chalks in my pocket" (249). What we subsequently get—are treated to—is about neither walking, a staple of essaying, nor Romantic experience in nature, which, in fact, it will criticize.

"A Piece of Chalk" becomes very nearly a paradigmatic essay: not merely, or even primarily, in its successful execution and highlighting of the power of sentences (of which, E. B. White allowed, *Walden* is made), a virtual demonstration of that love that Cynthia Ozick both discusses and embodies in the beautiful "The Seam of the Snail." In beginning with the ordinary and the mundane—pieces of chalk—and moving outward to large discussions of universal significance—the making of art, the relation of body and soul, even the nature and meaning of civilization—Chesterton's magnificent writing shows as well as embodies both the basic structure of the essay as form and its nearly defining indirectness of procedure. "By indirections find directions out," the old fool Polonius instructed Reynaldo in *Hamlet*. Perhaps it takes a fool, or an essayist, to have the patience—and the "stamina" that E. B. White spoke of—as well as the humility to make the commonplace, the small, and the apparently insignificant "liker" and the universally meaningful "more like / *Both in their order*" (Robert Browning, "Fra Lippo Lippi" 207–8; italics mine).

Chesterton begins slowly, as essayists are wont to do, "sneaking up" on large prey only in due course. The opening paragraph, one of seven, Chesterton devotes to the acquisition of the requisite brown paper on which he plans to practice his drawing. Having dealt with the requirement of paper on which to draw, and having described the difficulty of managing to convey some of his exact requirements to "a very square and sensible old woman in a Sussex village" (249) where he was staying, Chesterton proceeds to explain the necessity that the paper be brown, still trying to wrest the proper material from his host. The writing is enjoyable, in considerable part because of the character of the speaking voice: particular, somewhat eccentric, vulnerable, able to see himself clearly and to poke fun at both his foibles and his impossible ambitions. I hope I am not being merely indulgent in adducing the entire paragraph.

I then tried to explain the rather delicate logical shade, that I not only liked brown paper, but liked the quality of brownness in paper, just as I liked the quality of brownness in October woods, or in beer, or in the peat-streams of the North. Brown paper represents the primal twilight of the first toil of creation, and with a bright-coloured chalk or two you can pick out points of fire in it, sparks of gold, and blood-red, and sea-green, like the first fierce stars that sprang out of divine darkness. All this I said (in an off-hand way) to the old woman; and I put the brown paper in my pocket along with the chalks, and possibly other things. I suppose every one must have reflected how primeval and how poetical are the things that one carries in one's pocket; the pocket-knife, for instance, the type of all human tools, the infant of the sword. Once I planned to write a book of poems entirely about the things in my pocket. But I found it would be too long; and the age of the great epics is past. (249)

Here at the end appears, as elsewhere, the fondness, the almost-characteristic fondness, for paradox, which Hugh Kenner wrote brilliantly about as a Toronto undergraduate nearly sixty years ago.

Thus armed, Chesterton reports, he set out on to "the great downs," crawling across what he says expresses "the best quality of England, because they are at the same time soft and strong." (With such an amiable companion who indeed would not travel far and without quibble about direction? And who would not but applaud that English fondness for both/and?) The quest is for "a place to sit down and draw," hardly epic, but fraught with strain enough. Then comes this—in more than one sense, central—paragraph.

Do not, for heaven's sake, imagine I was going to sketch from Nature. I was going to draw devils and seraphim, and blind old gods that men worshipped before the dawn of right, and saints in robes of angry crimson, and seas of strange green, and all the sacred or monstrous symbols that look so well in bright colours on brown paper. They are much better worth drawing than Nature; also they are much easier to draw. When a cow came slouching by in the field next to me, a mere artist might have drawn it; but I always get wrong in the hind legs of quadrapeds. So I drew the soul of the cow; which I saw there plainly walking before me in the sunlight; and the soul was all purple and silver, and had seven horns and the mystery that belongs to all the beasts. But though I could not with a crayon get the best out of the landscape, it does not follow that the landscape was not getting the best out of me. And this, I think, is the mistake that people make about the old poets who lived before Wordsworth, and were supposed not to care very much about Nature, because they did not describe it much. (250)

Chesterton follows up with a paragraph-long paean to the "old poets," with their depiction of "holy virgins" and heraldic figures, drinking in, as he puts it, rather than painting Nature. Much of this is well said, and certainly beguiling, so much so that students, once charmed, decline to be critical.

Reading laterally, I think at this point of T. S. Eliot's *Four Quartets*, specifically the third, *The Dry Salvages*, which represents, differently, this issue of the relation of body and spirit, immanence and transcendence. Here the entire poem reaches a climax, for Eliot makes explicit the (name of the) pattern that he has been treating since at least "The Hollow Men" over fifteen years earlier. The climactic passage is this, having to do with "The point of intersection of the timeless / With time," the poem's consuming concern throughout:

> The hint half guessed, the gift half understood, is
>   Incarnation.
> Here the impossible union
> Of spheres of existence is actual,
> Here the past and future
> Are conquered, and reconciled . . .

The pattern, that which makes sense of our existence, is Incarnation, the paradigmatic instance of which is *the* Incarnation, God becoming man: spirit *embodied*.

Now, Chesterton was a devout Christian, a staunch Roman Catholic, and an able and prolific apologist for both his religion and his church. A hundred years later, his book *Orthodoxy* remains in print and respected. And yet in the central paragraph of "A Piece of Chalk" he evidently gets wrong the central Christian dogma—the paradox—for he would draw the soul without going in, through, and by means of the body. The point is subtle, but all-important. It is also only fair to acknowledge that Chesterton is by no means the only Christian to feel the strain of incarnational thinking, with its tension as a "middle way" (the hardest way of all to maintain, allowed Eliot, who was Anglo-Catholic) — the contemporary Anglican apologist C. H. Sisson springs to mind, author of, among countless other works, *Anglican Essays* and *The Discarnation.*

I am quite sure that Chesterton did not intend to call the Incarnation into question, nor to speak against it, let alone to flout it. He was, after all, writing only about drawing with chalk — and even then, drawing cows. Nevertheless what he wrote is essentially anti-Christian, specifically Gnostic, in its apparent belief that the soul may be reached directly, without mediation, without the intermediary that is the body, the flesh. According to this pattern, God may be reached without Christ's mediation. It is a kind of purity, or purism, that is clearly different from Christianity, orthodox or otherwise.

Equally (but differently) impure, and unorthodox, the painter Fra Lippo Lippi, in Robert Browning's famous poem, from which I have borrowed for my epigraph, confronts an artistic (and religious) establishment that would have him depict only the soul. He rightly refuses, or at least does so for the nonce, escaping from his quarters to join for a while a street party, attracted, as he should not be, by the sensual and the sensuous. His artistic values are presumably Browning's; they are, in any case, conventionally incarnational. He represents body and soul, flesh and spirit, in their proper "order." Although he might be mistaken for a materialist, Fra Lippo doubts that, for more than one reason, you can have body without also having soul. The perhaps greater danger is believing that you can have, treat, or deal with soul directly, without the byway of the body. Wars aplenty attest to the severe repercussions of such idealism.

I sometimes think that Chesterton was himself a bit uneasy with his anti-incarnational passage. Notice both what he says and how he says it, immediately afterwards: "But as I sat scrawling these silly figures on the brown paper, it began to dawn on me, *to my great disgust,* that I had left one chalk, and that a most exquisite and essential chalk, behind" (italics mine). He had, that is, no white, and white, he insists, is "positive and essential" for proper drawing on brown paper. Here he draws "a moral significance," writing that white "is a colour," "not a mere absence of colour," but something "shining and affirmative." This produces further reflection, and a rather dogmatic assertion, followed by writing that becomes, to my ear, moralistic and preachy.

> And one of the two or three defiant verities of *the best religious morality, of real Christianity,* for example, is exactly the same thing; the chief assertion of religious morality is that white is a colour. Virtue is not the absence of vices or the avoidance of moral dangers; virtue is a vivid and separate thing, like pain or a particular smell. Mercy does not mean being cruel or sparing people revenge or punishment; it means a plain and positive thing like the sun, which one has either seen or not seen. Chastity does not mean abstention from sexual wrong; it means something flaming, like Joan of Arc. In a word, God paints in many colours; but He never paints so gorgeously, I had almost said gaudily, as when He paints in white. (251; italics added)

Whether white be a color, I do not contest. I am certainly aware of its symbolic value in our culture. But with a positive view of *mixture,* deriving from Christ's very nature, a view that even a non-Christian like George Eliot would endorse (I am thinking of *Adam Bede* and Eliot's embrace of life as "a mixed, entangled affair"), I am much less smitten with whiteness (as well as purity). White smacks, for me, of the "thoroughgoing."

However that may be, Chesterton pushes too hard, having opted for a disembodied spiritualism. "A Piece of Chalk" comes close to turning into a sermon, rather than an essay. For the latter, as form, avoids the "thoroughgoing," indeed the positive. Instead the essay creates a space, opens a space—more, exists as a space (of welcome), a *site.* By this point in "A Piece of Chalk," I no longer feel welcome. Instead of a space open for me, I find that I must take the place Chesterton has created for me. The preachy, the sermon is too much, the delicacy that attends the essay violated, Chesterton unable to sustain the "*ondoyant et divers*" moderation that virtually defines the form Montaigne bequeathed to us. That my admittedly controversial reading carries some weight is indicated by Chesterton's open embrace of "the positive." He names and advocates, that is, that tendency he is enacting, defending and representing what the essay tends to avoid in its skepticism, indirectness, and negative way: impure art.

Chesterton, meanwhile, is sitting on a hill "in a sort of [very un-Christian] despair"—because he "could not find my chalk": "without white, my absurd little pictures," he writes, "would be as pointless as the world would be if there were no good people in it." Of course, "good" cannot be equated with "white," in any sense. Suddenly, Chesterton reports, he erupted in laughter, realizing that

> I was sitting on an immense warehouse of white chalk. The landscape was made entirely out of white chalk. White chalk was piled mere miles until it met the sky. I stooped and broke a piece off the rock I sat on: it did not mark so well as the shop chalks do; but it gave the effect. And I stood there in a trance of pleasure, realizing that this Southern England is not only a grand peninsula, and a tradition and a civilization; it is something even more admirable. It is a piece of chalk. (251–52)

Thus ends the essay.

The ending, too, is nicely said—another paradox, I reckon, certainly a charming and beguiling twist. In effect: the big is not contained in the little or ordinary. Rather the two are identical. In incarnational thinking, differently, identity is refused along with absolute difference. The *via media* is, indeed, difficult to maintain—look at Dryden—the history of the essay the drama of that strain.

I do not suggest, by any means, that "A Piece of Chalk" fails; indeed I do not wish to minimize its considerable achievement as a piece of writing. Moreover its form is brilliantly essayistic, as I trust I have made clear. That very form exists in uneasy tension with the ideas that Chesterton here represents.

I rejoice to concur with the common reader; for by the common sense of readers, uncorrupted by literary prejudices, after all the refinements of subtilty and the dogmatism of learning, must be finally decided all claim to poetical honours.

—Samuel Johnson, *The Life of Gray*

Homage to the Common Reader

Or How Should One Read Virginia Woolf's "The Death of the Moth"?

VIRGINIA WOOLF PRESENTS "God's plenty" of essays from which to choose for reading. A personal favorite is "The Death of the Moth." Tempting for less personal reasons is "The Moment," which stands contrast with Woolf's friend T. S. Eliot's poetic lucubrations on time, arguably the essayist's consuming subject. Not to be overlooked, of course, are the essays that make up *A Room of One's Own*. I did not, finally, feel confident about this possibility, partly because I am not sure which of the six parts I would have chosen, partly because, in fact, the whole is an essay, or so Woolf herself says. The right choice ultimately presented itself: for a book such as this, with its focus on reading, I could not but choose something from the most famous collections of Woolf's essays, *The Common Reader* or *The Common Reader*, Second Series. The reader can, in any case, rest assured that Woolf's masterstrokes as an essayist, some of which mark her technically brilliant fiction, are on display in these collections of critical writing as they are in other collections (e.g., *The Death of the Moth and Other Essays, The Moment and Other Essays*), where the focus is much more personal. Having taken that first step, I seemed fated to read "How Should One Read a Book?"

In *Virginia Woolf and the Essay*, a coedited collection of *articles* that focuses on *The Common Reader*, both series, little mention is made, despite the title, of Woolf's personal essays. That reveals, I reckon, a lingering academic bias. So why not, then, I at last concluded, attempt to combine the critical and the personal, as Woolf herself did so brilliantly, not least, of course, through the magisterial fictions of *A Room of One's Own*? In so doing, I would be following Alexander Pope's instruction in *An Essay on Criticism* to "read with the Spirit that its Author *writ*." My other choice became "The Death of the Moth" rather than "The Moment" simply because the latter is much more difficult, with its reflecting "angles of vision," and should probably await a first acquaintance with the other, short essay.

Twenty-first-century education has no more important object than the teaching of reading, and in this effort the idea of "the common reader," while seemingly antiquarian, may prove fundamental. Virginia Woolf would be crucial in this effort, renewing, as she does, Dr. Johnson's brief for "the common reader." Especially since the advent of theory and its insistence on critical-as-adversarial reading, this nonprofessional manner is of great importance.

Woolf thus writes in a brief section in the first collection of her mainly critical essays, expanding significantly on her predecessor whom she has just approvingly quoted:

> The common reader, as Dr. Johnson implies, differs from the critic and
> the scholar. He is worse educated, and nature has not gifted him so
> generously. He reads for his own pleasure rather than to impart knowledge
> or correct the opinions of others. Above all, he is guided by an instinct
> to create for himself, out of whatever odds and ends he can come by,
> some kind of whole—a portrait of a man, a sketch of an age, a theory of
> the art of writing. He never ceases, as he reads, to run up some rickety
> and ramshackle fabric which shall give him the temporary satisfaction of
> looking sufficiently like the real object to allow of affection, laughter, and
> argument. Hasty, inaccurate, and superficial, snatching now this poem,

now that scrap of old furniture without caring where he finds it or of what nature it may be so long as it serves his purpose and rounds his structure, his deficiencies as a critic are too obvious to be pointed out; but if he has, as Dr. Johnson maintained, some say in the final distribution of poetical honours, then, perhaps, it may be worth while to write down a few of the ideas and opinions which, insignificant in themselves, yet contribute to so mighty a result. (12)

The paragraph is beautifully done. But as relevant as I am maintaining Woolf's reflections are, they are very much rooted in her own time. I do not think that you can now believe that the reader of whom Woolf speaks, "the common reader" of 1925, was "worse educated" than today's critic or scholar, whose narrowness has been too well documented—and displayed—to require elaboration. We may all be, as readers, worse off than in Virginia Woolf's time, common and professional alike.

I cannot forbear noting that Woolf's terms for the act of "common" reading smack of the essay via its affiliation with that text(ile) known as the quilt—a point I made years ago in an essay in the *Kenyon Review* elaborately titled "In Other Words: Gardening for Love—The Work of the Essayist." Implicitly Woolf is aligning herself with a mode of responding to literature—criticism—that follows, rather than turns its back upon, that on which it comments. There is, she suggests without developing the point, an *essayistic reading*, which demands the essay form for the writing that constitutes the response to that reading.

What the essay as form celebrates, and treats, is what "common" reading entails. In a line from Dr. Johnson through Woolf, Clara Claiborne Park has recently developed the notion of this kind of reading. Buoyed by experiences teaching in a public two-year institution (before moving on to prestigious Williams College), Park seeks in *Rejoining the Common Reader* to focus in her teaching as well as in her writing on the personal issues, those that matter to ordinary people in their struggles with life and time. Reading, teaching, and writing about literature, she thus sees, with both Dr. Johnson and Virginia Woolf looking approvingly over her shoulder, not at all as a professional or academic matter but as a familiar and practical one. As her title indicates, Park is under no illusions about "being" or "becoming" the kind of reader that her predecessors envisaged; we bear, as Geoffrey Hartman would say, too many burdens of historical, cultural, and textual knowledge. We can, nevertheless, keep alive the "big"—the *essential*—questions, those nowadays too often sacrificed on the altar of "cultural studies," so-called theory, and such adversarial studies as those practiced in the current fad of race, gender, and class.

The opening paragraph of "How Should One Read a Book?" in *The Common Reader*, Second Series, stirs even today, with its defiant clarion call for self-reliance and independence, worthy of Emerson or Thoreau. I shall quote this important paragraph whole, in part to convey the clarity of Woolf's prose, in part to give a just introduction to her major themes here. Woolf is approachable, even accommodating.

> In the first place, I want to emphasise the note of interrogation at the end of my title. Even if I could answer the question for myself, the answer would apply only to me and not to you. The only advice, indeed, that one person can give another about reading is to take no advice, to follow your own instincts, to come to your own conclusions. If this is agreed between us, then I feel at liberty to put forward a few ideas and suggestions because you will not allow them to fetter that independence which is the most important quality that a reader can possess. After all, what laws can be laid down about books? The battle of Waterloo was certainly fought on a certain day; but is *Hamlet* a better play than *Lear*? Nobody can say. Each must decide that question for himself. To admit authorities, however heavily furred and gowned, into our libraries and let them tell us how to read, what to read, what value to place upon what we read, is to destroy the spirit of freedom which is the breath of those sanctuaries. Everywhere else we may be bound by laws and conventions—there we have none. (258)

Stirring these words are, and resonant, perhaps especially for an American. But they are also extreme. I mean, for one, the defeatist notion regarding literary quality: we *can* say that *Lear* is a better play than *Hamlet*, even though the latter more broadly touches modern sensibilities, that Woolf's novel *Mrs. Dalloway* is better than Michael Cunningham's recent adaptation-version of it.

A related problem occurs when, next, she attempts, fearlessly, to describe the reading process, dividing it into two separate phases, although writing brilliantly about each. Her first point is nearly "spot on," one today's students need to hear. Here, though, Woolf does not go quite far enough, for not to read sympathetically is tantamount to misreading, plain and simple. Still Woolf is right in her premise that so many of us bring agendas to our reading. I, however, would go—further—with, say, C. S. Lewis. Here is Woolf:

> If we could banish all such preconceptions when we read, that would be an admirable beginning. Do not dictate to your author; try to become him. Be his fellow-worker and accomplice. If you hang back, and reserve and criticise at first, you are preventing yourself from getting the fullest possible value from what you read. But if you open your mind as widely as possible, then signs and hints of almost imperceptible fineness, from the twist and turn of the first sentence, will bring you into the presence of a human being unlike any other. (259)

Only after some seven pages does Woolf finally turn to the second phase of the reading process, about which she writes more precisely and in greater detail.

> The first process, to receive impressions with the utmost understanding, is only half the process of reading; it must be completed, if we are to get the whole pleasure from a book, by another. We must pass judgment upon these multitudinous impressions; we must make of these fleeting shapes one that is hard and lasting. But not directly. Wait for the dust of reading to settle; for the conflict and the questioning to die down; walk, talk, pull the dead petals from a rose, or fall asleep. Then suddenly without our willing it, for it is thus that Nature undertakes these transitions, the book will return, but differently. It will float to the top of the mind as a whole. (266–67)

By "understanding," of course, Woolf means not comprehension but, rather, sympathetic engagement. Calling for patience and something of a respite, she recalls Wordsworth's revolutionary Romantic idea of poetry as emotion "recollected in tranquillity."

Woolf's description becomes the more valuable because the more subtle, penetrating, and daring; she is now *inside* what is clearly a multiform process.

And the book as a whole is different from the book received currently
in separate phrases [sic]. Details now fit themselves into their places. We
see the shape from start to finish; it is a barn, a pig-sty, or a cathedral.
Now then we can compare book with book as we compare building with
building. But this act of comparison means that our attitude has changed;
we are no longer the friends of the writer, but his judges; and just as
we cannot be too sympathetic as friends, so as judges we cannot be too
severe. (267)

I cannot but wonder if, in the first sentence, Woolf meant "phases" (but
the first edition of *The Common Reader*, Second Series, published by the
Woolfs' Hogarth Press, has "phrases"). In any case, I worry that Woolf may
have unduly complicated matters by blurring her focus on judgment with
her superior observations on comparison.

However that may be, her major problem—if I may be so bold as to
say—stems from the strict division of reading into two distinct phases,
or processes. Self-examination alone reveals that we do not read so neatly
or programmatically. I suspect Woolf caught a glimpse of this truth, for
there is the uneasy last part of the last sentence just above. The truth is,
you can be too sympathetic when you read, just as you can be too severely
judgmental. What comes to the rescue, preventing such extremism, is the
inseparability of the "phases" of the reading process: sympathy must always
be tempered with judgment. It does not come first, separate, and then await
later judgment; both are engaged simultaneously. Pope said it well in *An
Essay on Criticism*, discussing the relation of wit and judgment: wit *manages*
wit, judgment not being distinct from it but, rather, involved in it as an
inseparable part of the whole. Woolf's essay "The Moment," I suggest, may
be read as addressing precisely these issues.

"The Death of the Moth," the greatest instance I know of the familiar
estranged, stands, for this reason as well as others, comparison with G. K.
Chesterton's "A Piece of Chalk." I should say that I am not about to offer
some clever rhetorical or critical strategy such that this essay too takes on
the issues that we have been treating. This essay, little more than two pages
long, is, instead, lyrical in nature, but that lyricism is tightly controlled.
Woolf as essayist is in the picture, to be sure, scrupulously observing the

tiny and delicate moth, but the subject is that fragile instance of life. Here is an altogether fresh manner of treating the relation of small to large, mundane to universal.

Woolf begins head-on, with the moth, and not with description either: "Moths that fly by day are not properly to be called moths; they do not excite that pleasant sense of dark autumn nights and ivy-blossom which the commonest yellow-underwing asleep in the shadow of the curtain never fails to rouse in us." Distinction thus matters, getting it right. Moreover there is foreboding here, of something *not* pleasant, but something that will be aroused in us. These are, Woolf hastens to tell us, "hybrid creatures, neither gay like butterflies nor sombre like their own species," further complicating matters (231). Distinction may be necessary, but it is going to be hard to effect.

The difference between Woolf the observer and "the present specimen," this scrupulously observed moth, is not, however, at stake. Nor is there any sense in which, as in E. B. White's great essay "Death of a Pig," the observer becomes one with the observed. The relationship is more complicated.

Very soon Woolf moves out from statement to description, thence to world beyond. Comparison is at least implied as Woolf represents that outer world as dynamic, full of energy and motion: certainly different from the sense we have of the moth and the "mild, benignant" mid-September morning, on which the tiny moth "seemed to be content with life." But that life too is distinguished from the poor moth: "The same energy which inspired the rooks, the ploughmen, the horses, and even, it seemed, the lean bare-backed downs, sent the moth fluttering from side to side of his square window-pane." The energy that had at first seemed to us magnificent, thrilling, and entirely positive now appears destructive, or least capable of destruction. Our sympathies lurch quickly toward the moth; Woolf records "a queer feeling of pity for him." Small suddenly appears against enormous, the moth pitiable in his meanness, his mereness: "The possibilities of pleasure seemed that morning so enormous and so various that to have only a moth's part in life, and a day moth's at that, appeared a hard fate, and his zest in enjoying his meagre opportunities to the full, pathetic" (231). Our sympathies, or at least the essayist's, have veered from the moth: pathetic because his part in life is so minuscule—he hardly matters.

But then Woolf watches more intently as the moth flies from corner to corner to corner to corner of *his* world: "That was all he could do, in spite of the size of the downs, the width of the sky, the far-off smoke of houses, and the romantic voice, now and then, or a steamer out at sea." The contrast, utter, huge, and devastating, triumphs. Yet the moth continues: "What he could do he did." And now Woolf realizes a great truth: "Watching him, it seemed as if a fibre, very thin but pure, of the enormous energy of the world had been thrust into his frail and diminutive body. As often as he crossed the pane, I could fancy that a thread of vital light became visible. He was little or nothing but life" (231). The contrast has acquired greater complexity, taken a new turn.

The moth now becomes "marvellous as well as pathetic" (232). Woolf understands him as a simple "form of the energy that was rolling in at the open window and driving its way through so many narrow and intricate corridors in my own brain and in those of other human beings" (231–32). The moth has become—it does not stand for—pure life, embodied, *seen*:

> It was as if someone had taken a tiny bead of pure life and decking it as lightly as possible with down and feathers, had set it dancing and zigzagging to show us the true nature of life. Thus displayed one could not get over the strangeness of it. One is apt to forget all about life, seeing it humped and bossed and garnished and cumbered so that it has to move with the greatest circumspection and dignity. Again, the thought of all that life might have been had he been born in any other shape caused one to view his simple activities with a kind of pity. (232)

Following the central, climactic third paragraph, "The Death of the Moth" becomes more complex in perspective, "*ondoyant et divers.*" "One" morphs into "I," and we hear far more of and from this "I," who now shares the scene with the struggling moth. The observer oscillates between active and passive.

> After a time, tired by his dancing apparently, he settled on the window ledge in the sun, and, the queer spectacle being at an end, I forgot about him. Then, looking up, my eye was caught by him. He was trying to resume his dancing, but seemed either so stiff or so awkward that he could only flutter to the bottom of the window-pane; and when he tried to fly across it he failed. Being intent on other matters I watched these futile attempts for a time without thinking, unconsciously waiting for him to resume his flight, as one waits for a machine, that has

stopped momentarily, to start again without considering the reason of its
failure. (232)

Woolf thus records the break, the change, and in more than one respect.
Her metaphor now shifts to difference from life: the moth compared to
a machine. She herself now observes "without thinking," which makes us
realize, if we had not before, that she has been uniting thinking and observing, precisely thinking *through* observing.

As she continues, Woolf begins to move back and forth between observer and observed, finally to action that involves the former with the
latter, offering not sympathy but direct assistance.

> After perhaps a seventh attempt he slipped from the wooden ledge and
> fell, fluttering his wings, onto his back on the window sill. The help-
> lessness of his attitude roused me. It flashed upon me that he was in
> difficulties; he could no longer raise himself; his legs struggled vainly. But,
> as I stretched out a pencil, meaning to help him to right himself, it came
> over me that the failure and awkwardness were the approach of death. I
> laid the pencil down again. (232)

The repetition of the verb "rouse" is surely deliberate, especially as it resonates with "raise." Now, as the moth declines, the observer becomes inspired, keenly cognizant. Her final resignation, in the last sentence above,
prefigures the moth's. Woolf had evidently been reading rather than writing—she had earlier written only that "it was difficult to keep the eyes
strictly turned upon the book." Is it pushing too hard to suggest that reading or writing or both thus come to bear on the scene, on the moth in
particular, but prove ineffective, unhelpful?

The final paragraph is beautiful, moving, haunting—and disagreeable.
As the moth struggles, Woolf looks "as if for the enemy against which he
struggled." Naturally she turns to the outdoors, where both sameness and
difference appear immediately:

> Presumably it was midday, and work in the fields had stopped. Stillness
> and quiet had replaced the previous animation. The birds had taken them-
> selves off to feed in the brooks. The horses stood still. Yet the power was
> there all the same, massed outside indifferent, impersonal, not attending

to anything in particular. Somehow it was opposed to the little hay-coloured moth. (232)

Difference thus morphs into opposition, and Woolf participates, "roused" as the world-as-energy lies "indifferent, impersonal," inattentive and no more capable of being "raised" than the very moth.

Woolf now, darkly, comprehends why earlier she had laid the pencil down: "It was useless to try to do anything." The sentence devastates, especially if we recall the evident earlier evocation—and incapacity—of writing or reading or both. "One could only watch the extraordinary efforts made by those tiny legs against an oncoming doom which could, had it chosen, have submerged an entire city, not merely a city, but masses of human beings; nothing, I knew, had any chance against death" (232).

Thinking of Woolf's eventual suicide in the face of overwhelming depression adds to the poignancy. But it is not poignancy that I primarily feel—instead something near upon nausea, so powerful and so powerfully bleak has the picture turned. This little essay, tiny and delicate like its subject, with a short reading life, is doomed, as well. Like the moth, however, it does not quite despair, this proto-existentialist effort. The essay is simply under no illusion. The remainder is truly magnificent. Even if it does not completely relieve the bleakness, at least clarity of vision triumphs over impending despair. The first word is emphatic, the later "righting" charged with meaning: it resonates, of course, with "writing," and it strongly suggests "correcting."

> Nevertheless after a pause of exhaustion the legs fluttered again. It was superb this last protest, and so frantic that he succeeded at last in righting himself. One's sympathies, of course, were all on the side of life. Also, when there was nobody to care or to know, this gigantic effort on the part of an insignificant little moth, against a power of such magnitude, to retain what no one else valued or desired to keep, moved one strangely. (232)

"I" has morphed back to "one," "moved" replacing "roused."

The concluding sentences are more than magnificent—they are magisterial. Taking up her pencil again, Woolf too struggles on, not quite defeated, although not exactly inspired either. The penultimate sentence below beautifully returns us, with a difference, to both "righting" and "writing": composure is just the quality the essayist typically quests for, perhaps elusive, perhaps inseparable from literal composing.

> Again, somehow, one saw life, a pure bead. I lifted the pencil again, useless
> though I knew it to be. But even as I did so, the unmistakable tokens
> of death showed themselves. The body relaxed, and instantly grew stiff.
> The struggle was over. The insignificant little creature now knew death.
> As I looked at the dead moth, this minute wayside triumph of so great
> a force over so mean an antagonist filled me with wonder. Just as life
> had been strange a few minutes before, so death was now as strange. The
> moth having righted himself now lay most decently and uncomplainingly
> composed. O yes, he seemed to say, death is stronger than I am. (232–33)

Defeat and triumph converge, the last sentence an affirmation of death's strength.

"The Death of the Moth" may be a greater triumph, as essay, than even "Death of a Pig," if for no other reason than for its sure artistic control and restraint. It is a masterpiece of telling that is also showing. Woolf achieves something quite different from the ordinary essay—if there be such! Instead of reflection on experience, she gives us description as revelation (of universal significance). What matters, clearly, is the seen (scene). That counts more than the spectator-observer-essayist, although her eyes are present and matter. It is not, however, individual—certainly not personal—interpretation that emerges here: through Woolf's far-from-clinical eye we see the seen, and share in it. What that eye sees makes the point, that eye a medium. It is not that *it* sees that matters so much, but what it *sees*—which is there. This is Modernism, not Romanticism.

"The Death of the Moth" may fudge a little on the question of whether death triumphs. Certainly death defeats the moth, in the perhaps major sense. Yet the moth has the last word.

As I read and reread "The Death of the Moth," I remember T. S. Eliot's account of Lancelot Andrewes, the seventeenth-century Anglican divine. Woolf's essay is no sermon, of course, and Woolf seems about as far from Andrewes, if not also her friend Eliot, as one could imagine. Still these words resonate: "from beginning to end you are sure that he is wholly in his subject, . . . that his emotion grows as he penetrates more deeply into his subject, that he is finally [alone] . . . with the mystery which he is seeking to grasp more and more firmly." Shortly Eliot adds these applicable words: "Andrewes's emotion is purely contemplative; it is not personal, it is wholly evoked by the object of contemplation, to which it is adequate; his emotion is wholly contained in and explained by its object" (*Selected Essays* 351). Such, I think, helps us understand and appreciate Woolf's manner in "The Death of the Moth."

Death may be—and is—opposed to life, but life can be more complex. Woolf herself has suggested *in the essay* the pattern whereby differences rather than oppositions prevail, complicating the notion of either/or. Life need be no more opposed to death than sympathy is to judgment; the way to life, as to judgment, may lie precisely in, through, and by means of that which it seems to oppose.

The only way of expressing emotion in the form of art is by finding an "objective correlative"; in other words, a set of objects, a situation, a chain of events which shall be the formula of that *particular* such that when the external facts, which must terminate in sensory experience, are given, the emotion is immediately evoked.

—T. S. Eliot, "Hamlet and His Problems"

The Turning of the Essay

T. S. Eliot's "Tradition and the Individual Talent"

I INTRODUCE ELIOT'S GREAT, revolutionary essay "Tradition and the Individual Talent" indirectly, at least to undergraduates, by way and means of Hilaire Belloc's magnificent, and much more accommodating, "The Mowing of a Field." Those who have read this work and sympathetically considered the entire essay tradition may be somewhat less resistant to Eliot's anti-Romantic reinterpretation of tradition, individualism, the nature of poetry—and of the essay. Included in *The Sacred Wood* (1920), his essay is justly famous, although not eagerly taken up by either graduates or undergraduates, the latter of whom find it "tough sledding" while the former—these days—do not want to hear what Eliot has to say. It deserves the closest reading, itself dependent on sympathetic engagement and the very control of emotion that Eliot discusses. According to Graham Good, writing in *The Observing Self: Rediscovering the Essay*, "Tradition and the Individual Talent" "must be easily the most commented-on essay in English in the twentieth century" (137). Lydia Fakundiny includes it in *The Art of the Essay*, as I mentioned above, while Phillip Lopate excludes it from *The Art of the Personal Essay*. Good even surmises that Eliot's supreme values here, tradition and impersonality, "may have a lot to do with the low regard in which the essay genre has been held since the 1920s" (ibid.). It thus focuses, we might say, our concerns.

In a brilliant and controversial series of three essays titled "The Sacred Jungle," included in *Criticism in the Wilderness* (1980), Geoffrey H. Hartman blames Eliot for the influence he has had not so much on the essay as on criticism. In particular, Hartman, himself a scholar of Romanticism and Wordsworth's greatest critic, locates in Eliot "a critique of enthusiasm" (49). In this, he is surely right, for the essayist of "Tradition and the Individual Talent" keeps in mind the disastrous consequences of the Cromwellian revolution and the ascendancy of the unbridled "private spirit." As Hartman shrewdly notes (Tom Paulin has more recently made essentially the same point, writing about William Hazlitt):

> The issue of enthusiasm is not separable from that of religion, and could draw us into a complex analysis of the relation of literary style to religion and politics. The relation of enthusiasm to political fanaticism is a fearful reality that hovers over English history and the establishment of *via media* institutions from the reign of Elizabeth on. Literary criticism like everything else became a *via media* institution. Though the fear of enthusiasm gradually receded into the *angustiae* of the Gothic novel it was given a temporary renewal by the French Revolution with its regicide, its Reign of Terror, and its atheistic religion of reason. (49–50)

Exactly so, and Eliot opposes it all from the "present" perspective just as Dryden did, anticipating, aware of the implications of the Reformation and then the Puritan revolution.

Unfortunately Hartman gets exactly wrong the nature and texture of Eliot's anti-enthusiastic response, so interested is he in pursuing stylistic qualities and advancing the case for criticism as "intellectual poetry." According to Hartman, "Eliot's conservative Modernism identifies the poet's critical or intellectual ability mainly with that of purification, the filtering out of 'mere ideas' or technical terms not yet polished into poetic diction" (57). He is right, however, to read in Eliot a certain "distrust of 'ideas,' that is, excess baggage of a spiritual or intellectual kind" (ibid.). Distrustful of *disembodied* ideas, Eliot actually opposes, therefore, purification, committed to *via media* thinking and the tension that it necessarily entails.

If "Tradition and the Individual Talent" is the "most commented-on" essay, it is apparently not the most accessible; certainly it has elicited a variety of responses and even readings. Hartman, I am sorry to say, is unsympathetic to begin with, and so consigns Eliot to the netherworld of genteel talk, a "teatotalling" criticism ignorant of theory and deliberately isolated from needed European philosophical leavening. Eliot ultimately fails, in Hartman's Romantic assessment, because for him the critic, like the poet, is a medium but not in "the ghostly sense"; he is, in other words, no enthusiast. Good may have similar interests, but he manages for the most part to rein them in. He does not misuse Eliot, although he does misread him.

The place to start with this essay is not the beginning, but Eliot's overturning of Wordsworth's definition of poetry as "the spontaneous overflow of powerful feelings" (2:143). This comes, of course, from the preface to the *Lyrical Ballads*, Wordsworth's and his friend Samuel Taylor Coleridge's revolutionary poems heralding Romanticism. Wordsworth says further of what he calls the "short essays" (144) composing that volume and of poetry in general that "it takes its origin from emotion recollected in tranquillity: the emotion is contemplated till by a species of reaction the tranquillity gradually disappears, and an emotion, kindred to that which was before the subject of contemplation, is gradually produced, and does itself actually exist in the mind" (151). What Wordsworth is talking about sounds, indeed, very much like the essay—and what Eliot *attacks* and seeks to replace smacks of the same form, for the focus Wordsworth and Coleridge inaugurate is expressive of the personality and emotion of the writer, based in recollection and reflection. Defending his own practice as a poet, just as Wordsworth does, while advancing the cause of a new interpretation of poetry and the poet, Eliot seeks what "Prufrock" embodies: observation instead of reflection, elucidation rather than either judgment or the expression of the writer's personality.

As soon developed in the essay "The Metaphysical Poets," Eliot's point is that the later seventeenth-century "dissociation of sensibility" produced "reflective" (instead of "intellectual") poets: "The poets revolted against the ratiocinative, the descriptive; they thought and felt by fits, unbalanced;

they reflected" (*Selected Essays* 288; italics added). Although Wordsworth, like Eliot, emphasizes contemplation, the object for him of that act is the poet's own emotion, not an external "thing." In "Tradition and the Individual Talent," Eliot sets about defining, the job of historical explanation due later. He writes, here, that " 'emotion recollected in tranquillity' " is an inexact formula; in fact, says Eliot, Wordsworth thus got it wrong on all counts: "For it is neither emotion, nor recollection, nor, without distortion of meaning, tranquillity." Wordsworth was not the first by any means, but he was perhaps the primary spokesman for and exponent of poetry as reflection. Not at all "the expression of personality," poetry, according to the Modernist Eliot,

> is a concentration, and a new thing resulting from the concentration, of a very great number of experiences which to the practical and active person would not seem to be experiences at all; it is a concentration which does not happen consciously or of deliberation. These experiences are not "recollected," and they finally unite in an atmosphere which is "tranquil" only in that it is a passive attending upon the event. (21)

Those readers who complain of Eliot's difficulty are right. He *is* difficult, and the reason why is his precision.

The essential point, for our purposes at the moment, is Eliot's positing of an "Impersonal theory of poetry," one thus based not on reflection but on observation. As he puts it, "The business of the poet is not to find new emotions, but to use the ordinary ones and, in working them up into poetry, to express feelings which are not in actual emotions at all" (21). In other words, the poet does not express *his* personality or *his* emotions, although he may well present a character expressing his personality and his emotions, J. Alfred Prufrock being a famous case in point. Always secondary, the critic, likewise, following suit, "must not coerce, and he must not make judgments of worse and better. He must simply elucidate: the reader will form the correct judgment for himself" ("The Perfect Critic," in *The Sacred Wood* 10). Neither the critic, whose form is the essay, after all, nor the poet reflects, but rather presents, leaving the reader free to share in the observation. The stress must follow, Eliot everywhere insists, on the thing made, the work of art: "For it is not the 'greatness,' the intensity, of the emotions [of the writer], the components, but the intensity of the artistic process, the pressure, so to speak, under which the fusion takes place, that counts" (*Selected Essays* 19).

Rightly (of course), Eliot calls his points "observations." The point of view that he is "struggling to attack," he says, is "perhaps related to the metaphysical theory of the substantial unity of the soul." He goes on:

> my meaning is, that the poet has, not a "personality" to express, but a
> particular medium, which is only a medium and not a personality, in
> which impressions and experiences combine in particular and unexpected
> ways. Impressions and experiences which are important for the man
> may take no place in the poetry, and those which become important in
> the poetry may play quite a negligible part in the man, the personality.
> (19–20)

Eliot's precision, here and elsewhere, is born of the most exacting and scrupulous discrimination.

For Graham Good, "Tradition and the Individual Talent" is *too* personal and autobiographical. He writes: "The whole essay is a personal confession disguised as impersonal doctrine. It is a piece of ventriloquy: the suffering poet speaks through the mouth of the doctrinal critic, impersonating his impersonality" (139). While extremely suggestive, very clever, and nearly brilliant, this reading is, as I hope you are beginning to understand, improbable. In the first place, Eliot bore witness, but he never made a personal confession, perhaps the closest he came being the still-reserved 1948 *Sermon*. To be sure, Eliot frequently impersonated, but the style, manner, mode, and texture in this essay are those found elsewhere in his critical essays, indeed everywhere in and characteristic of them.

Most disturbing is that Good reads Eliot as, behind the disguise, highly individualistic and advancing a private program or agenda.

> Both in the form and the content of the "Tradition" essay we confront the
> paradox of personal impersonality. Eliot's tone is one of aloof authority
> and doctrinal pronouncement. But what is he "authoritative" about? The
> process by which experiences become poems. How can anyone pronounce
> on this other than from personal experience? What grounds can he have
> for contradicting Wordsworth's formula for poetic creation, "emotion
> recollected in tranquillity," other than the fact that it does not correspond
> to his own experience of composition? (139)

Even if the answers to these questions be wrong, the questions are of immense value, taking us to the very heart of the matter of Eliot and the essay. Is Eliot's appeal ultimately to his own, private experience? Perhaps in spite of himself, is he, in the final analysis, an individualist, like Wordsworth, Thoreau, and latter-day Romantics and Transcendentalists, whose name is Legion? Or to come to the overweening question, whence authority? And so, where does Eliot stand vis-à-vis the essay *tradition*?

Although Graham Good is surely right to distinguish Eliot from his friend and sometime publisher Virginia Woolf, he is just as clearly wrong to contrast them severely. Although as he writes, Eliot may lack a certain flexibility, such as we find in both Woolf's critical and her familiar essays, there is an abundant, related, and indeed central quality that Good mistakes. Close to flexibility is a quality of the writing mind that Eliot shares with "the father of the essay," Michel de Montaigne, whose skepticism Eliot, of course, writes against, particularly in the important essay on Pascal's *Pensées*. I refer to the frequently cited honorific "*ondoyant et divers*," which Montaigne employs in writing of Seneca and Plutarch. To be sure, Eliot's prose is neither undulating nor diverse; on the contrary, it appears remarkably of a piece, from the essays collected in *The Sacred Wood* through the lectures that compose *After Strange Gods, The Idea of a Christian Society*, and *Notes Towards the Definition of Culture*, on to *A Sermon* and *On Poets and Poetry*. And yet the writing, like the mind that produced it, is certainly not inflexible or stiff. It partakes instead of erudition, not pedantry, nor narrow or academic professionalism. It assumes both intelligence and knowledge, derived from wide reading. We might call it civilized, if that term were not an opprobrium. I mean to say that Eliot's style displays an agility, rather than an elasticity, of mind, a capacity for movement that Good may glimpse but mistakes. It bears some kinship to the wit that Eliot prizes (as does Alexander Pope). Less a play of mind than scrupulosity, that particular quality may best be seen both negatively (in opposition to the thoroughgoing and a refusal to reduce) and positively (as a meticulous insistence on both/and that follows from acute analysis). As a result of such *work*, Eliot appears sure of himself, but that certainty is always earned and so is, *pace* Graham Good, not at all doctrinaire. Good ascribes the virtues of both/and thinking to Virginia Woolf and, incredibly enough, finds Eliot to body forth either/or, which, as it happens, is precisely what Eliot opposes. I know of no other writer, in essay form or other, who embodies quite these qualities—and so makes of the essay something "new under the sun," at once belonging to the tradition that stems from Montaigne and altering it. "Tradition and the Individual Talent" may or may not be the "paradigmatic" Eliot essay (as Good claims), but it clearly addresses, embodies, and dramatizes the issues at stake in consideration of T. S. Eliot and the essay.

Appropriately perhaps (or necessarily?), we cannot adequately consider "Tradition and the Individual Talent" without relating it to another essay of Eliot. Any number of relations might be adduced, for this essay is like a wheel with spokes extending out variously, the most resonant of all of Eliot's essays. Our focus here being Eliot's particular contributions to the essay as form, I find more to be said about his moving away from reflection to observation. To help us grasp the nature and significance of this move, I want to take a look, however brief, at the important essay on the seminal seventeenth-century divine, Bishop Lancelot Andrewes, which I have cited several times already in this book.

Eliot's essay, titled simply "Lancelot Andrewes," constitutes the lead in his 1928 collection *For Lancelot Andrewes: Essays on Style and Order*. A keen and deep exercise in *recovery*, this essay represents precisely the sort of immersion in the object that is essential for responsible reading; the essay is itself built on the foundation of comparison and analysis. Eliot constructs his "elucidation" of Bishop Andrewes by means of comparison with John Donne, the more modern writer, "dangerous only for those who find in his sermons an indulgence of their [dissociated] sensibility, or for those who, fascinated by 'personality' in the romantic sense of the word—for those who find in 'personality' an ultimate value—forget that in the spiritual hierarchy there are places higher than that of Donne" (352). The resonances with "Tradition and the Individual Talent" not only loom large but point to further elucidation of the value of observation as different from reflection and its basis in "personality."

The following passage from "Lancelot Andrewes," which I have quoted before, makes the point clearly—by means of the embraced observation rather than reflection, Eliot himself immersed in his subject just the way, he says, Bishop Andrewes was—the passage is simply crucial for understanding Eliot, both his poetry and his prose. (Think, as well, of what Eliot famously says about *Hamlet* and Hamlet, in another essay included in *The Sacred Wood*, illustrative of what he coined as the "objective correlative.")

> When Andrewes begins his sermon, from beginning to end you are sure that he is wholly in his subject, unaware of anything else, that his emotion grows as he penetrates more deeply into his subject, that he is finally "alone with the Alone," with the mystery which he is seeking to grasp more and more firmly. . . . Andrewes's emotion is purely contemplative; it is not personal, it is wholly evoked by the object of contemplation, to which it is adequate; his emotions wholly contained in and explained by its object. But with Donne there is always the something else, the "baffling." . . . Donne is a "personality" in a sense in which Andrewes is not: his sermons, one feels, are a "means of self-expression." He is constantly finding an object which shall be adequate to his feelings; Andrewes is wholly absorbed in the object and therefore responds with the adequate emotion. Andrewes has the *goût pour la vie spirituelle*, which is not native to Donne.

"Andrewes," Eliot concludes, "is the more mediaeval, because he is the more pure," and his bond is "with tradition." Donne, on the other hand, who "is primarily interested in man, . . . is much less traditional" (351–52).

It is precisely the necessity for and the making of distinctions, the work of comparing, that is, that stands out in the first section of "Tradition and the Individual Talent," which treats the dualism there announced. Here, too, is sounded a clarion call for subordination of the individual, for surrender of personality. That argument is manifest in the tone and manner of Eliot's own presentation, which leads many, students and others alike, to mistake the point of it all. Eliot is neither dry nor unfeeling, although his essay reflects none of his personality, his own emotion, or his opinions. It is, then, a very different kind of essay from Michel de Montaigne's.

Of Montaigne, by the way, Eliot spoke appreciatively, even admiringly, but also critically, warning that "a fog, a gas, a fluid, insidious element," he is "one of the least destructible" authors (409–10). For, writes Eliot in an essay on Pascal and his *Pensées*, he "does not reason, he insinuates, charms, and influences; or if he reasons, you must be prepared for his having some other design upon you than to convince you by his argument." He is, in other words, the father of the essay, sneaky like the form he practically

invented, and indirect. He may be "the most essential author to know"—
Shakespeare knew him, and was influenced by him, as *Hamlet* for one
shows—but in any case, "by the time a man knew Montaigne well enough
to attack him, he would already be thoroughly infected by him." And that
infection, Eliot makes clear, is "of the original and independent solitary
'personality'" (*Selected Essays* 410).

Opposite, or very nearly so, stands the sense of tradition that Eliot both
defines and defends in his most famous essay. With at least as much ap-
plicability today as eighty-five years ago, Eliot writes that "seldom" does
the word "tradition" "appear except in a phrase of censure. If otherwise, it
is vaguely approbative, with the implication, as to the work approved, of
some pleasing archaeological reconstruction" (13). Such writing, already in
the essay's first paragraph, with its firmness and assurance, leads some to
mistake for dogmatism what is knowledge. Nowhere, perhaps, is Eliot's undogmatic manner clearer than when he turns to the difficult task of defining
tradition, a page or so in. Most apparent is the work of distinction, here
performed in the service of deconstructing a facile but prevalent sense of
tradition.

The qualities that make Eliot both traditional and unique in the history
of essay writing appear as early as the third paragraph of "Tradition and the
Individual Talent." Already he has made clear that, counter to the times, he
will represent tradition in a positive light; "we" typically dwell "upon the
poet's difference from his predecessors" (14). This Eliot calls "prejudice";
without it, he has said, suggesting both the main point of his argument
and his own manner of proceeding, "we shall often find that not only the
best, but the most individual parts of his work may be those in which the
dead poets, his ancestors, assert their immortality most vigorously" (ibid.).
The way is thus prepared: Eliot undertakes to complicate, to interimplicate,
and so to oppose simple and reductive thinking. To employ the language I
have introduced above, Eliot will oppose the "thoroughgoing."

And so the third paragraph of "Tradition and the Individual Talent"
immediately follows, opening with a clarification, and deepening, of what
has preceded regarding the force and attractiveness of tradition.

Yet if the only form of tradition, of handing down, consisted in following
the ways of the immediate generation before us in a blind or timid adher-

ence to its successes, "tradition" should positively be discouraged. We have seen many such simple currents soon lost in the sand; and novelty is better than repetition. (14)

This we might not have expected, given the opening positive treatment of tradition. What else might one hope for, though, from the author of "Prufrock" and soon *The Waste Land,* work that, in the words of the later *Ash-Wednesday* applied to other matters, "restor[es] / With a new verse the ancient rhyme"? In any case, Eliot is about distinctions, and clarity, uninterested in either currying favor or mindless retention.

> Tradition is a matter of much wider significance. It cannot be inherited, and if you want it you must obtain it by great labour. It involves, in the first place, the historical sense, which we may call nearly indispensable to anyone who would continue to be a poet beyond his twenty-fifth year; and the historical sense involves a perception, not only of the pastness of the past, but of its presence; the historical sense compels a man to write not merely with his own generation in his bones, but with a feeling that the whole of the literature of Europe from Homer and within it the whole of the literature of his own country has a simultaneous existence and composes a simultaneous order. This historical sense, which is a sense of the timeless as well as of the temporal and of the timeless and of the temporal together, is what makes a writer traditional. And it is at the same time what makes a writer most acutely conscious of his place in time, of his own contemporaneity. (14)

The conjunction of the timeless with time that impels *Four Quartets* already forms a central theme and a central concern for Eliot. It is, of course, in terms of uniting time and the timeless that Eliot offers his crucial account of Incarnation in *The Dry Salvages,* the third poem of *Four Quartets* (which I consider also an essay): "The hint half guessed, the gift half understood," pointing, for example, to the thinking in binaries that results in getting but "half" the truth.

The *whole* truth, to return directly to "Tradition and the Individual Talent," is that "no poet, no artist of any kind, has his complete meaning alone." He is dependent upon that of which he is, willy-nilly, a part. There is a "*whole* existing order" that is itself altered, "if ever so slightly," by the advent of the new work. This means, among other things, that the poet "must inevitably be judged by the standards of the past" (15). As ever, Eliot is precise, as well as insistent.

He thus argues "the necessity that [the poet] shall conform, that he shall cohere," and he knows that this is not only controversial but perhaps counterintuitive. So Eliot immediately adds that that necessity "is not onesided," proceeding to claim that the "ideal order" made of "existing monuments" is itself "modified by the introduction of the new (the really new) work of art among them" (15). This position appears analogous to the situation of the Church of England, and so of what became, thanks, says Eliot elsewhere, to Elizabeth, the established church and the *via media*. Anglicanism, too, occupied the position of the individual striving first against tradition and then within it, becoming, in fact, *Anglo*-Catholicism, thus modifying, or altering, the Church of Rome and emerging *thereby* as something really new. As Eliot puts it, continuing, "The existing order is complete before the new work arrives"—art or church, I conclude—"for order to persist after the supervention of novelty, the *whole* existing order must be, if ever so slightly, altered; and so the relations, proportions, values of each work of art toward the whole are readjusted; and this is conformity between the old and the new" (15).

Having said so, Eliot moves then to clarify what he means by "conform." The "standards of the past," inevitably invoked, will judge, but not "amputate." Entailed is, precisely, "a judgment, a comparison, in which two things are measured by each other" (15)—an apt description of his own characteristic critical procedure. This last is a particularly important point, for Eliot considers analysis and comparison the tools of criticism ("Imperfect Critics," included in *The Sacred Wood*). Moreover, in treating dualisms, as he characteristically does, Eliot engages in precise comparison: thus tradition and the individual are *compared*, measured by each other, neither totally separable from the other, neither complete in and of itself, apart from the other. Eliot's eye remains steadfastly on the whole, although he knows full well that the way to the whole lies in, through, and by means of the part.

These points emerge in what Eliot adds: "To conform *merely* would be for the new work not really to conform at all; it would not be new, and would therefore not be a work of art. And we do not quite say," he allows, "that the new is more valuable because it fits in; but its fitting in is a test of its value" (*Selected Essays* 15; italics added). *Pace* Graham Good, Eliot pointedly argues against an either/or: "We say: [the work of art] appears to conform, and is perhaps individual, or it appears individual, and may conform; but we are *hardly likely to find that it is one and not the other*" (15–16; italics added).

On the main matter of the individual versus tradition, Eliot is quite clear: "the mind of Europe—the mind of [one's] own country" is, simply, "more important than his own private mind," to emphasize which, since the Renaissance and the Reformation, through the English Civil War, and into and beyond Romanticism, has wreaked havoc, creating unmitigated disasters, one after another, politically, religiously, culturally. Still, no *mere* conservative, no *mere* anything, Eliot recognizes and accepts change; and the change he welcomes "is a development which abandons nothing *en route*, which does not superannuate either Shakespeare, or Homer, or the rock drawing of the Magdalenian draughtsmen. . . . [T]his development, refinement perhaps, complication certainly, is not, from the point of view of the artist, any improvement" (16). The kind of *relation* between dualisms that Eliot endorses is indeed clear; there is *no transcendence* of the prior— and no march of easy progress. Eliot thus "complicates." He might best be called, if a label be required, a pre-servative. In fact the poet and the critic may, differently, keep alive, but neither can rightly be said to make something live. Eliot is much more humble, as the last sentence of "Tradition and the Individual Talent" illustrates: the poet, he writes, "is not likely to know what is to be done unless he lives in what is not merely the present, but the present moment of the past, unless he is conscious, not of what is dead, but of what *is already living*" (22; italics added).

About the relation of the poet to the past, Eliot has more to say still, offering his following statements modestly as an essay toward "a more intelligible exposition," the critic far from being "doctrinaire." Like the poet, the critic must respond to complications, intricacies, and complexities. Change is inevitable, says this defender of tradition, but that defense is far from simple or "thoroughgoing." The poet, in fact, "must be quite aware of the obvious fact that art never improves, but that the material of art is never quite the same"—a statement that describes *The Waste Land.* The mind thus changes, that of Europe, that of his own country, itself "more important than his own private mind." Importantly this change does not result in a transcendence of the past; it is instead, as already noted, "a development which abandons nothing *en route*, which does not superannuate either Shakespeare, or Homer, or the rock drawing of the Magdalenian draughtsmen" (16). Approaching a conclusion to the first of the essay's three marked sections, Eliot offers these striking sentences, so oft quoted as to have grown very nearly too familiar: "What happens is a continual surrender of himself as he is at the moment to something which is more valuable. The progress of an artist is a continual self-sacrifice, a continual extinction of personality" (17).

In the second section of the essay, Eliot further elaborates on "this Impersonal theory of poetry," now considering the relation of the poem to the poet. "By an analogy," he writes, he has suggested that "the mind of the mature poet differs from that of the immature one not precisely in any valuation of 'personality,' not being necessarily more interesting, or having 'more to say,' but rather by being a more finely perfected medium in which special, or very varied, feelings are at liberty to enter into new combinations" (18). With this, Eliot seems as far as imaginable from the founding desires and character of the essay, where personality and individuality reign like tyrants. Drawing on the chemical notion of the catalyst, Eliot explains that "the poet has, not a 'personality' to express, but a particular medium, which is only a medium and not a personality, in which impressions and experiences combine in peculiar and unexpected ways" (19–20).

Clearly the pattern operative in the relation of individual to tradition mirrors that of the poet to the poem; Eliot continues, in other words, to discuss the new and the changed and changing. He is interested, above all, in the emotion that the literary work entails, better, incarnates, emotion not indebted to the poet's feelings but, rather, the result of the internal action of the poem and deriving from what he elsewhere defines as an "objective correlative" *in* the work of art: "One error, in fact, of eccentricity in poetry is to seek for new human emotions to express; and in this search for novelty in the wrong place it discovers the perverse. The business of the poet," instead, "is not to find new emotions, but to use the ordinary ones and, in working them up into poetry, to express feelings which are not in actual emotions at all" (21). Key is the working up into poetry. In the event, tradition and "the ordinary" are not traduced, or transcended, but modified, altered if ever so slightly.

As elsewhere, so in "Tradition and the Individual Talent" Eliot works out relations—or, rather, the precise nature of the relation that obtains. In this (early) essay, Eliot, I feel, struggles some, his subject so huge by analogy that it takes in virtually everything he would ever be at pains to elucidate. I'm not sure that it is quite irony that is at play here. It is not so much, as

Georg Lukács would have it, that Eliot "appears" to be discussing only pictures and books and even then only their surfaces and superfluities. Instead analogy is at work, the relation of the individual to tradition mirroring as it partakes of other relations. In that case, pattern or structure emerges as most important, and Eliot will spend his career honoring that sense of the nature of that prevailing and revealing pattern. More than a hint appears here, already in 1920—that is, a half dozen years or so before his formal embrace of Christianity in general and Anglo-Catholicism in particular—of Incarnation as that pattern.

The poems culminating in *Four Quartets* most elaborately and fully work out the nature of relation that Incarnation explains. This last, great poem is itself, I argue, an essay, or a series of essays. In the prose of the 1930s, in works more traditionally essayistic, Eliot clarifies, if he does not quite develop, what "Tradition and the Individual Talent" is on the way to knowing. That essay, at the very least, intuited what the lectures published as *After Strange Gods, The Idea of a Christian Society*, and *Notes Towards the Definition of Culture* notably found a name for.

As I read him, over time Eliot becomes clearer and clearer about the pattern structuring existence and already intuited (at least) in "Tradition and the Individual Talent," a pattern that bears directly on his understanding of and intentions for the essay as form. At the close of the third essay in *The Idea of a Christian Society*, he describes this structure, pointing to the tension that inevitably defines it:

> even in a Christian society as well organised as we can conceive possible in
> this world, the limit would be that our temporal and spiritual life should
> be harmonised: the temporal and spiritual would never be identified.
> There would always remain a dual allegiance, to the State and to the
> Church, to one's countrymen and to one's fellow-Christians everywhere,
> and the latter would always have the primacy. There would always be a
> tension; and this tension is essential to the idea of a Christian society, and
> is a distinguishing mark between a Christian and a pagan society. (56)

That tension is also, I add, essential to the idea of Christianity and is a distinguishing mark between it and all other forms of religion. It matters so much because it lies at the very heart of reality, the nature of which Christianity reveals paradigmatically. Harmony is the goal rather than identity, with difference, and thus tension, kept in play instead of transcendence, duality never overcome.

In *Notes Towards the Definition of Culture* sixteen years later, Eliot makes the same point in somewhat different terms, the issue here "the theory of religion and culture" (31). Specifically, at the end of the first essay, he writes, even more tellingly I find, clearly indicating that the pattern of which he speaks is Incarnation:

> we have to avoid the two alternative errors: that of regarding religion and culture as two separate things between which there is a *relation*, and that of *identifying* religion and culture. I spoke at one point of the culture of a people as an *incarnation* of its religion; and while I am aware of the temerity of employing such an exalted term, I cannot think of any other which would convey so well the intention to avoid *relation* on the one hand and *identification* on the other. (31–32)

Thus Eliot defines Incarnation. He then adds: "The truth, partial truth, or falsity of a religion neither consists in the cultural achievements of the peoples professing that religion, nor submits to being exactly tested by them. For what a people may be said to believe, as shown by its behaviour, is, as I have said, always a great deal more and a great deal less than its professed faith in its purity" (32).

The third essay here, "Unity and Diversity: The Region," reiterates the central points, Eliot repeating "a recurrent theme of this essay, that a people should be neither too united nor too divided, if its culture is to flourish" (*Notes* 49). To return to the term he used in *After Strange Gods*, to be avoided is the "thoroughgoing." In *Notes Towards the Definition of Culture*, Eliot reiterates: "Excess of unity may be due to barbarism and may lead to tyranny; excess of division may be due to decadence and may also lead to tyranny: either excess will prevent further development in culture" (ibid.).

As he proceeds in this third essay, Eliot introduces "a new notion," reminiscent of Pope: "that of the vital importance for a society of *friction* between its parts" (58). He very carefully works out the meaning and significance of this new term, these paragraphs among the most important in the book. Therefore I must quote extensively.

> Accustomed as we are to think in figures of speech taken from machinery, we assume that a society, like a machine, should be as well oiled as pos-

sible, provided with ball bearings of the best steel. We think of friction as waste of energy. I shall not attempt to substitute any other imagery: perhaps at this point the less we think in analogies the better. . . . I now suggest that both class and region, by dividing the inhabitants of a country into two different kinds of groups, lead to a conflict favourable to creativeness and progress. And . . . these are only two of an indefinite number of conflicts and jealousies which should be profitable to society. Indeed, the more the better: so that everyone should be an ally of everyone else in some respects, and an opponent in several others, and no one conflict, envy or fear will dominate. (58–59)

Eliot here also echoes René Girard, whose notions of "sacred difference" derive in part from Ulysses' famous speech in Shakespeare's *Troilus and Cressida* on order and the necessity of distinction.

At this point Eliot turns to the individual and contends that the same pattern of tension, or friction, is healthy and productive, and once again he speaks, albeit indirectly, against any transcendence of one position so as to achieve some putative purity.

As individuals, we find that our development depends upon the people whom we meet in the course of our lives. (These people include the authors whose books we read, and characters in works of fiction and history.) The benefit of these meetings is due as much to the differences as to the resemblances; to the conflict, as well as the sympathy, between persons. Fortunate the man who, at the right moment, meets the right friend; fortunate also the man who at the right moment meets the right enemy. I do not approve the extermination of the enemy: the policy of exterminating or, as is barbarously said, liquidating enemies, is one of the most alarming developments of modern war and peace, from the point of view of those who desire the survival of culture. One needs the enemy. So, within limits, the friction, not only between individuals but between groups, seems to me quite necessary for civilisation. The universality of irritation is the best assurance of peace. A country within which the divisions have gone too far is a danger to itself: a country which is too well united—whether by nature or by device, by honest purpose or by fraud and oppression—is a menace to others. (59)

Brief reflection follows on the troubles accruing to Germany and Italy as a result of their lack of this balance.

In the following essay in *Notes Towards the Definition of Culture*, titled "Unity and Diversity: Sect and Cult," Eliot acknowledges that he may appear to be contradicting himself: "The reader may have difficulty in reconciling [just preceding assertions] with the point of view set forth in my first chapter, according to which there is always, even in the most conscious and highly developed societies that we know, an aspect of identity between the religion and the culture" (68). He then elaborates, openly embracing both/and and proceeding to the clearest account I believe he ever gave of the character and implications of this prized *tension*, which includes a pointed rejection of "mere" or pure transcendence. I quote the rest of this crucial and fundamental paragraph, which grows in importance as Eliot proceeds to think down the page.

> I wish to maintain *both* these points of view. We do not leave the earlier stage of development behind us: it is that upon which we build [as with the individual and tradition, or, in Swift's terms, Moderns and Ancients]. The identity of religion and culture remains on the unconscious level, upon which we have superimposed a conscious structure wherein religion and culture are contrasted and can be opposed. The *meaning* of the terms "religion" and "culture" is of course altered between these two levels. To the unconscious level we constantly tend to revert, as we find consciousness an excessive burden; and the tendency toward reversion may explain the powerful attraction which totalitarian philosophy and practice can exert upon humanity. Totalitarianism appeals to the desire to return to the womb. The contrast between religion and culture imposes a strain: we escape from this strain by attempting to revert to an identity of religion and culture which prevailed at a more primitive stage; as when we indulge in alcohol as an anodyne, we consciously seek unconsciousness. It is only by unremitting effort that we can persist in being individuals in a society, instead of merely members of a disciplined crowd. Yet we remain members of the crowd even when we succeed in being individuals. Hence, for the purposes of this essay, I am obliged to maintain two contradictory propositions: that religion and culture are aspects of one unity. and that they are two different and contrasted things. (68–69)

Here, of course, the essayist has moved close to philosophy, the reasoning both precise and studied.

What Eliot has done, to return directly now to "Tradition and the Individual Talent," is to inch the essay, sometimes, it appears, ever so slightly, toward the philosophical and the general, thus countering the individualist, experiential, and personal mode that would to him smack of the values he reprobated in the seventeenth century and saw as characteristic of modernity. To put the matter more baldly: *in* "Tradition and the Individual Talent," Eliot offers a counterstatement and gives a counterturn *to* the essay. Clearly he recognizes the triumph of individualism as well as of "personality," and as we have read, he proposes nothing so simple as either rejection or mere return; that would be "thoroughgoing." Instead Eliot considers what to do *from within* this condition, which no amount of wishing or lamenting will change. There is, then, to his way of thinking, to be neither rabid opposition nor unthinking acceptance and resignation. The solution he proposes, if that term be allowed with its connotations of perhaps more definition and finality than Eliot would allow, is to write, say, a poem in the modern manner that (yet) teaches a quite traditional (and Ancient) lesson.

And to write an essay that forswears mindless clutching to the past as it declines to acquiesce before all things new: to be both philosophical and familiar. To establish tension at its very heart. To write an essay in which *the individual* finds that the way to his own voice leads through the earned victories of *tradition*. Such an *essay*, as practiced by Eliot, looks and feels different from the way it did in the hands of Thoreau and Emerson, say. At the same time it looks significantly the way it did in the hands of Dryden and Swift and Pope—and does in Eliot's time, despite obvious differences, in his friend Virginia Woolf's magnificent and capacious instances of the form.

Tradition and the individual are not opposed; immersion in the fires of the former purge the latter of self, allowing the "new creature" then successfully to "alter" tradition. Tradition, though, Eliot insists, in the final, great sentence of his critical essay, needs not the individual to survive: the poet, he writes there, "is not likely to know what is to be done unless he lives in what is not merely the present, but the present moment of the past, unless he is conscious, not of what is dead, but of what *is already living*" (*Selected Essays* 22; italics added). Eliot thus incarnates, we might say, the surrender he describes as necessary in the poet.

As an essay, "Tradition and the Individual Talent" does not reflect Eliot's "personality." As essayist, he has succeeded in extinguishing *that*. Yet the essay hardly appears the work of a machine—there is a sense of a *person* here, even if the writing reflects no *personality*—nor does it much resemble the article that was then in the process of replacing the essay as the medium of critical writing. Unlike the characters in *The Waste Land*, the voice we hear—and voice there is, occasionally using the first-person plural and even the second person—does not seem imprisoned in its ego. It is not, in other words, the private self. No hint appears, either, of insight deriving from a private light or spirit. What *does* appear is, rather than the absorption of the self in something outside and grander, a connection, a relation, to others, to tradition. The voice I hear in "Tradition and the Individual Talent" derives its meaning, even its very being, from its relations—it is, fundamentally, mediated by its knowledge of and subordination to tradition. Eliot's argument here mirrors the situation of the essay, accepting the bequest of Montaigne but in no thoroughgoing way.

> To me, calling it an essay means that it's not just a story but reflection
> on that story, which is also a way of making it less personal or not
> only personal.
> —Anne Carson, interview in *Poets & Writers*

A Site to Behold

Richard Selzer's "A Worm from My Notebook"

THESE "THOUGHTS WERE BRED / BY READING," of course (I
quote John Dryden's *Religio Laici or A Laymans Faith* 226–27). First
of all, surgeon-teacher-writer Richard Selzer's essay "A Worm from My
Notebook." But also, frankly, Lydia Fakundiny's comments on an earlier version of the present essay, on which I feed heartily, parasitical. She,
however, incurs no responsibility for whatever "crude"-ness (Dryden's self-
characterization) I have shown in moving with her observations. She says,
rightly, that I did Selzer's deceptively complex essay a considerable disser-
vice in "under-reading" it. A lesson attends, I reckon—for all of us.

"A Worm from My Notebook" may or may not be Selzer's best essay. More
representative of his artistry as a wordsmith is "An Absence of Windows,"
with its description of the stethoscope as "the ever-asking Y." That essay
succeeds, too, because of its layers of meaning and significance and its dramatic self-criticism of the medical profession and of Selzer himself as surgeon. His generosity of spirit and capacity for human sympathy endear—
and never fail to send my students in search of more of his essays.

I choose, however, to read "A Worm from My Notebook" *because* it appears less subtle. As it consists of strong story and narrative, it points to the quality and depth of Selzer's imaginative writing—a recent book, *The Whistlers' Image*, bears the subtitle *Stories and Essays*. "A Worm from My Notebook" precisely foregrounds questions, which students always and rightly ask, about the relation between the essay and the short story and in so doing sheds important light on the essay as form.

Essays frequently, of course, enfold stories—Sam Pickering is a current master at incorporating "tall tales" into his essays. Stories *worm* their way easily and often seamlessly in and out of essays, and essays not infrequently do the same in fiction. To invoke again a central contention of the present book, Selzer's essay "A Worm from My Notebook" is a *site* where fiction and reflection, writer and reader, essay and story—and more: host and parasite, life and death—meet and confront one another, soliciting us to "measure two things by each other." In more than one telling way, Selzer literalizes *site*.

Now most of Selzer's essay is a story, presented as fiction, concerning a poor Zairean farmer (that country being unabashedly chosen "[f]or the beauty of the name")—perhaps as close to a true "other" as could reasonably be imagined. The story is simple, a "Romance," Selzer calls it: the man Ibrahim contracts and then heroically fights the dreaded infestation that will eventually take his life. The drama consists in Ibrahim's struggle with the worm that enters his body with the very water that sustains him, the site a watering hole at the edge of the hot, desiccated desert, to which he must lead his small herd of barely alive cattle. "It is a fated moment," writes Selzer. "For this is no mere water, but water inhabited by the tiny crustacean Cyclops, a microscopic crab with a large and median eye" (435)—the worm's very name ironic and just hinting that "worm" might be capitalized. In any case, Ibrahim drinks his death.

The worm grows and grows, soon extending more than two feet in length and having "the thickness of a piece of twine." Ibrahim now feels it—and Selzer feels it, too, differently to be sure, but you can feel his respect, his own patience, his *love*: "One day, while [he] is squatting by his resting herd, his idle finger perceives the worm as a long undulating ridge just beneath the skin of his abdomen." With the hand of an artist, the eye of a surgeon, and the heart of an *amateur*, Selzer adds: "Again and again he runs his finger up and down the awful ridge, feeling the creature respond with slow pruritic vermiculation." A year passes, and the worm morphs into "a tube filled with embryos. Then comes the day when an instinct, more, a diabolical urge, tells Dracunculus that the hour of its destiny has arrived; it must migrate to the foot of the man." Everything then changes, for worm and man, and man's struggle begins in earnest. Ibrahim "shudders, for it is with horror that you acknowledge the presence within your body of another creature that has a purpose and a will all its own, that eats your flesh, that you can *feel*. Feel moving!" (436; italics added). The creature has thus wormed its way into us, the readers, who are at the same time para-sites ourselves, feeding alongside (on this story, this essay-story).

So far, the story has been related movingly, lovingly, the writer's humanity capacious and readily apparent. Like its host, the parasite requires water to sustain itself, but Ibrahim does not know "that only when water covers the hole in his foot will the worm stick out its head"—that fearsome Cyclopean head—"and spew the liquid that contains the many thousands of its get," this last word perhaps unexpected and startling and powerful. It happens, and so the "milky fluid" from Ibrahim's submerged foot, at the watering hole at the edge of the desert, contaminates the same water that the man immediately slurps: opposites united by the water that both sustains and kills—"death by water," the title of Eliot's brief fourth section of another work representing a desert, *The Waste Land*. Ibrahim slurps "palmsful of Cyclops and larvae. The cycle begins again" (436).

Up to this point, writes Selzer, interrupting and briefly entering the narrative, Ibrahim "has had the patience of the desert; now, he will have the heroism of the leopard." The farmer has already fashioned a notched twig for the battle to come, his only material weapon.

> At last he sees that an inch or two of the preoccupied worm is protruding from his still submerged foot. Darting, he grasps with thumb and forefinger, capturing, and, with all the grace and deftness of a surgeon litigating an artery, he ties the head of the worm in a knot around the notched end of the twig, ties it so that the worm cannot wriggle free.

With patience as well as stealth, Ibrahim abides: "There is no room for rashness." After a little more than a fortnight, "the whole of the worm is wrapped around the twig. It is dead. Ibrahim is healed" (437).

His story is far from over, however. Remember the "palmsful of Cyclops and larvae" he had slurped at the watering hole? Cycle names truth, not progress, or if progress, only temporary at best.

Ibrahim now turns his cattle toward the village, where in three days a feast will be held in face of old men's predictions of impending catastrophe: "the rite of circumcision when the young boys are taken into the adult life of the tribe." Hearing the announcing and preparatory "drums and the singing of the women," Ibrahim quickens his pace, hurrying his few cattle along— for there be always a time and a rhythm, even in the undifferentiating and indifferent desert. Selzer understands time and rhythm, embodying them in his respectful and appropriate tale-telling, fleshing out details so that we too come to care about Ibrahim as his creator *loves* him. Is the writer here a God-like figure, as the surgeon differently is, Zaire a desert Eden? In any case, Selzer writes directly and fearlessly of his character, addressing *him* in his care and concern and love, fiction twining itself around life, burrowing into it:

> He has been away for three full moons. The smells of his village come out
> to the desert to grab him by the nose, to pull him toward home. Hurry,
> hurry, Ibrahim! On and on he walks and all the while the space within
> him where the worm had been was filling up with the music of the feast
> until now Ibrahim is brimful of it. And he has a moment of intoxication
> during which he feels the sun pounding him like a drum, and he feels
> his blood seeping out of the still unhealed hole in his foot to dance about
> his footsteps in the sand. Then, something stirs in Ibrahim, something,
> like a sunken branch long trapped beneath the water, bobs to the surface
> with considerable force. At that moment, Ibrahim decides to take a wife.
> (437–38)

A remarkable passage! That something stirring inside Ibrahim, which leads to his taking a wife, recalls the worm; his own blood "dances" on the sand; he himself, under the relentless sun, is like the drums whose music has drawn him home, drawn him out. Differences thus blur, apparent opposites meet—in the site that is the Zairean farmer Ibrahim—and change places. Noticing such things means that the reader is worming his or her way into the story—not going deeper and deeper, though, for you need not try to dig deeply since there is not so much depth as plain but charged meaning.

Directly the essay worms *its* way into the story.

Selzer is both a writer and a surgeon, his pen, he once said, also his scalpel. He could, if he wished, simply proceed with his story, his character one that we care about, the action sustaining our interest, the plot dramatic and brimful of tension.

But instead of continuing the tale, Selzer pauses, interrupts the story, addresses the reader directly. The reflection with which this essay begins — about which much more shortly — is not transcended, or left behind; instead Selzer returns to it, takes up that reflection again: "Such, such are the plots are parasitology. Ah, but you are hooked, aren't you? I have caught you, then? You want me to go on, to write the story of Ibrahim? Well. Where should the story go from here?" (436). The reader *is* hooked — as the writer is, even as the parasite insinuates its way into the host. So hooked is the reader that Selzer aims to make me not just host but also parasite too, for I too worm.

So where *would* the story go, from this point? Selzer writes it, sensuously, sensually, albeit with some pretense of doubt — or, more likely, humility: he is clearly in love with his story.

> First to the village, I think, where Ibrahim would join the feast, find a woman with good hands and abundant breasts and make love to her. They would be married. I should like very much to describe the ritual circumcision, the ordeal of the young boys in the jungle, how they are wrapped in the skins of three animals and put in a pit for nine days from which they emerge reborn as men. I should like to render for you the passion of Ibrahim for Ntanga, his new wife, who each night lifts her throat to him for whatever he might wish to do to it; then tell of how, in time, he must once again take his little herd away from the village in search of forage. (438)

Returning to the narrative, Selzer turns it, seamlessly. Time has slipped by — many days, many nights have, as it seems, flown by. Doom now impends, and the play, the tension, between inside and outside, worm and flesh, host and parasite, what sustains and what destroys, moves inexorably toward a conclusion that even Ibrahim's heroism can do little to prevent or forestall. Writing here, Selzer sculpts his prose, with his scalpel-pen, as he enters directly his character's consciousness.

> But now the terrible drought *has* come, the famine as predicted by the men at the wateringhole the year before. The desert itself is undulant, looking most like the water it craves. Ibrahim's skin and hair are soon white with the dust kicked up by the starving cows. He watches the cloud of sand rise and slowly descend. Even the desert wants to leave this place, he thinks. The knives of the sun have split one of his cows in two so that it falls apart before his eyes. Another, the sun has turned into metal. Ibrahim's fingers burst into flames as he grasps a bronze horn to ease the creature's last stumble. (438)

This romance is also a modern *Metamorphosis.*

Man and beast are locked in a fierce, fated struggle, not against each other, of course, nor against a common enemy, but intertwined. *Dracunculus medinensis,* the tiny but lethal Guinea worm, is very nearly forgotten. Site is once again rendered literal, for as Ibrahim returns to the watering hole, death meets him, already little more than a beast of burden himself.

> Ibrahim staggers on to the wateringhole—three hundred yards, yet a whole day's trek. It is a dry ditch, the bottom fissured. Sinking to his knees, he lowers his head like a cow and licks the clay. Kneeling there alone, his tongue stuck to the baked basin of the hole, Ibrahim hears a muffled clamoring as of a herd far off. A lamentation of hoofbeats and mooing swirls about him. Then all is still. The life cycle of the parasite is broken at last. (438–39)

Restraint of statement, of expression, is matched in Selzer by his giving to character, his complete lack of ego, his love.

So ends the story of Ibrahim. And so ends Selzer's essay. But the story of that essay has not yet been finished, in my account, because I have not yet treated the opening paragraph.

Selzer's language is charged with meaning. "Were I a professor of writing," he begins. As it happens, he was a professor at Yale of both surgery and writing. The subjunctive, suggesting what is not the case, points to the mixture of fact and fiction that will follow and constitute this remarkable piece of writing. We begin with the "I," that is, Selzer himself, because, as he will say directly, the essayist writes about and from what he or she knows. You always begin, moreover, with the concrete and the particular, and you never leave that behind, or transcend it.

In fact Selzer begins his brief excursus on writing by animadverting against any kind of transcendence in writing. No matter how attractive or apparently important they are, the "big issues" are not directly approachable; the writer cannot forgo the concrete and the particular, cannot leap over them, and confront "ideas" head-on; above all, the writer must not write about abstractions:

> Were I a professor of the art of writing, I would coax my students to eschew all great and noble concepts—politics, women's liberation or any of the matters that affect society as a whole. There are no "great" subjects for the creative writer; there are only the singular details of a single human life.

The person is central, and fundamental. Send off your imaginations, then, Selzer would instruct his charges, to seek out "the exceptional and the mysterious." In this respect, "A doctor/writer is especially blessed in that he walks about all day in the middle of a short story" (434). Selzer proceeds to give a short story inside an essay.

"Fine writing," he asserts, "can spring from the most surprising sources." Here, too, he practices what he teaches, incarnating the very values he espouses and describes, textual description matching declaration perfectly.

> Take parasitology, for instance. There is no more compelling drama than the life cycle of *Dracunculus medinensis,* the Guinea worm. Only to tell the story of its life and death is to peel away layers of obscurity, to shed light upon the earth and all of its creatures. That some fifty million of us are even now infested with this worm is of no literary interest whatsoever. Always, it is the affliction of one human being that captures the imagination. So it was with the passion of Jesus Christ; so it is with the infestation of a single African man. (434–35)

By his own admission, Selzer is not a conventionally or particularly religious person, and yet he clearly recognizes the gift of *the* Incarnation, which, for Christians at least, affirms the irreducibility of the person, educing love of a person, not of an idea or an ideology.

"Shall we write the story together?" he asks of his reader, now also his student, inviting us in and thus initiating a whole fundamental series of complications, mixes, and exchanges, his essay a brilliant site where contending forces meet—and feed, side by side. We are now inside Selzer the writer; he allows us to see what otherwise we would be blind to.

> A Romance of Parasitology? Let me tell you how it goes thus far. I will give you a peek into my notebook where you will see me struggling to set words down on a blank piece of paper. At first whimsically, capriciously, even insincerely. Later, in dead earnest. You will see at precisely what moment the writer ceases to think of his character as an instrument to be manipulated and think of him as someone with whom he has fallen in love. For it is always, must always be, a matter of love. (435)

Reflection absent story—or, better, "the singular details of a single human life"—runs the risk of being sterile, abstract, and productive of something far different from shared love. Story without reflection, on the other hand, may be experience absent meaning. We have, nowadays perhaps more than ever before, too little of the quiet and capacious artistry that makes of "A Worm from My Notebook" a magisterial essay.

If you have built castles in the air, your work need not be lost; that is where they should be. Now put the foundations under them.
—Henry David Thoreau, *Walden*

Yet what we think is less, for sure,
Than what we are, and that is flesh.
  Its fresh
Bloom is the best we know. Its dure
  Descent
The hardest way that we are sent.
—C. H. Sisson, *The Discarnation*

The Discarnate Word

Scott Russell Sanders's "Silence"

OVER THE PAST TWENTY YEARS, roughly, Scott Russell Sanders has published some half dozen collections of essays, including the prize-winning *The Paradise of Bombs* (1985), and continuing through his latest, *The Force of Spirit*. Hailed as a nature writer and social critic, Sanders surely derives from Thoreau, but is far less prickly. Perhaps most apparent in Sanders is a deep and broad sympathy. There is, at the same time, a clear rootedness and an abiding appreciation of place, in Sanders's case stemming from his youth in the limestone country of southern Ohio and, for thirty-some years, Bloomington, Indiana. Sanders's voice may not (yet) be unmistakable, but it is readily identifiable: warm though not self-effacing, conscientious and caring, particularist and yet universal, questing but by no means restless. When you read his familiar account of the essayist in his important apologia "The Singular First Person," you cannot but apply the description to Sanders himself. His is, then, a voice to be contended with.

If the fine essays in *Secrets of the Universe: Scenes from the Journey Home*, including the much-anthologized "Under the Influence," first published in *Harper's*, herald the overarching themes of Sanders's work, elaboration and refinement occur in the subsequent volumes *Staying Put* and *Writing from the Center*. An academic (he teaches at Indiana University), Sanders was trained as a literary scholar—he has a PhD from Cambridge and wrote his dissertation, eventually published, on D. H. Lawrence. That background figures in his work, which still shows academic hesitation, many institutional and political values, and a style that appears neither so wild as Thoreau's nor as polished as, say, E. B. White's. He seems a bit unsure of his status: whether he belongs among the critics and scholars or the writers. Sanders is learned, impressively so, not least in the ways of physics, knowledge of which figures prominently in his coming-to-grips with the world. His is a world in which religion has long been suspect, if not reviled and dismissed. It is also a world in which feeling has been undervalued and downright misunderstood. Sanders has recovered the latter and is on the way to rediscovering the former.

Sanders thus contends with the big questions, those that matter to the so-called common reader and therefore to the essayist. In the introduction to *The Force of Spirit*, Sanders mentions some recent events that have made him keenly aware "of time passing," perhaps the quintessential essay subject (we are given, however, no window onto these struggles, Sanders being as ever personal but not confessional, wary still as an academic of the "I" in spite of his artistic commitments).

> In struggling with these questions, I have come to appreciate more fully why the remarkable sixteenth-century French writer Michel de Montaigne chose to call this literary form he invented an *essai*, by which he meant a trial or experiment, an effort at making sense. The deeper I go into my days, the more I'm convinced that living itself is an experiment. Life keeps confronting me with puzzles that I can neither ignore nor easily solve. I am moved to write essays not because I understand so much but because I understand so little. (2)

This is well said, and thoroughly Montaignian. The tone changes as Sanders continues:

> The world appears to be a vast whirl of bits and pieces, yet scientists operate on the belief that behind this dazzling variety there is a single set of laws, and a single energy, at play in the universe. Religion makes the same assumption, although it offers quite different explanations for those laws, tells quite different stories about that energy. The word *religion*

derives from *re-* plus *ligare*, meaning to bind back together, as if things have been scattered and now must be gathered again. That is the rhythm of my days—a scattering and gathering, scattering and gathering. The writing of essays allows me to gather what is essential in my life, and by pondering these things perhaps to discover something essential to the lives of others. (2–3)

Sanders thus writes to understand himself and his world and the relation between them. A process of discovery, essaying amounts, admirably enough, to thinking down the page. Reflection plays a key role in this "pondering." Moreover "scattering" and "gathering" appear as distinct activities, or efforts, unmarked, evidently, by the tension that Sanders misses. The matter at stake here is even clearer in the preface to *Secrets of the Universe* when Sanders "reflect[s] on that encompassing mystery we call the universe. The movement outward to greater and greater circles," he writes, forging an identity where difference remains, "is also a movement inward, ever closer to the center from which creation springs" (x). As Alexander Pope, for one, recognized, you proceed to the whole only in, through, and by means of the part. The name of *that* pattern is Incarnation.

"Silence" is the last, and concluding, essay in *The Force of Spirit*, toward which you cannot but feel the whole book moves. Aside from his just-published memoir, *A Private History of Awe*, this essay constitutes Sanders's most substantial attempt to come to terms with that which he calls "spirit." Indeed, in the book's first, and titular, essay, he struggles to name the ineffable that he is sure somehow exists. It is, he believes, "magnificent energy," and he supposes that whether we call it "Spirit or Tao, Creator or God, Allah or Atman or some other holy name, or no name at all makes little difference so long as we honor it" (16).

Sanders struggles to describe this "magnificent" something that both draws and sustains him. In "The Force of Spirit," he explains: among other reasons, "I want a name for the force that binds me to Ruth [his wife], to her parents, to my parents, to our children, to neighbors and friends, to the land and all its creatures." I cannot but think, then, of pantheism as well as Thoreauvian Transcendentalism.

This power is larger than life, although it contains life. It's tougher than love, although it contains love. It's akin to the power I sense in lambs

nudging the teats of their dams to bring down milk, in the raucous tumult
of crows high in trees, in the splendor of leaves gorging on sun. I recognize
this force at work in children puzzling over a new fact, in grown-ups
welcoming strangers, in our capacity, young and old, for laughter and
kindness, for mercy and imagination. (15)

For autobiographical reasons treated elsewhere having to do with his father,
Scott Sanders wishes to avoid offending, a point made clear in his following sentences, which explain his unease, academically fueled and liberal in
orientation. He would avoid offense to all parties, the religious and the
nonreligious alike.

No name is large enough to hold this power, but of all the inadequate
names, the one that comes to me now is spirit. I know the risks of using
such a churchy word. Believers may find me blasphemous for speaking of
the wind that blows through all things without tracing the breath to God.
Nonbelievers may find me superstitious for invoking any force beyond
gravity, electromagnetism, and the binding energy of atoms. But I must
run those risks, for I cannot understand the world, cannot understand my
life, without appealing to the force of spirit. (15)

I certainly applaud Scott Sanders for his (perhaps belated) recognition of
the force of religious yearning, and I rather suspect that his spirit-ualism
will appeal to a great many. A question that Sanders's understanding raises
is important: what to make of this emphasis on spirit, disembodied and
discarnate, particularly in relation to the essay's formal incarnationism?

"Silence" is a narrative essay, a sub-form that Annie Dillard in 1988 pre-
dicted would be the future. That seems not to have come to pass, and
frankly, I for one find Sanders more effective when he foregrounds his
thematic interest rather than story. This particular essay is, in any case,
powerful, especially as it concludes *The Force of Spirit*, making a whole
that is somewhat more than the mere sum of its parts (in the classroom,
I have found, this book works particularly well, raising all sorts of crucial
questions about essaying).

On a snowy Sunday morning in January, in Indianapolis, perhaps point-
edly away from home, Sanders finds himself driving around looking for a
Quaker meetinghouse (as the British poet Basil Bunting always called the
Northumbrian worship place of his youth—and perhaps beyond). Sanders

never explains exactly why, only that he had worshipped "with Quakers off and on for thirty years, beginning when I was a graduate student in England." The opening is characteristically auspicious, thematically burdened as well as inviting:

> Finding a traditional Quaker meeting in Indianapolis would not be easy. No steeple would loom above the meetinghouse, no bell tower, no neon cross. No billboard out front would name the preacher or proclaim the sermon topic or tell sinners how to save their souls. No crowd of nattily dressed churchgoers would stream toward the entrance from a vast parking lot filled with late-model cars. No bleat and moan of organ music would roll from the sanctuary doors. (151)

I say "inviting," but inviting (only) to those who are like-minded, those who embrace Sanders's values as they have been expressed and embodied in all his essays — those who, I might say, embrace the Montaignian essay's take on the simple life and the plain style, shorn of doctrine and dogma, a no-nonsense and no-frills approach to worship as to life generally. Sanders here plays on difference, erecting an "us" and "them," these latter associated — somewhat subtly — with loaded terms: "neon cross," "nattily dressed," "vast parking lot," "late-model cars," "bleat and moan of organ music."

Although I did not know this before I read "Silence," I can see a definite affinity in Sanders's essays all along with Quakers, whose "position" he well describes here in terms that cement the shared nature of their views, what he calls "a steady article of faith." It is based on silence, itself the instrument through which God would speak to the individual soul: "I tried stilling my thoughts, tried hushing my own inner monologue, in hopes of hearing the voice of God." Sanders then offers a valuable account of Quaker belief, a passage that deserves full quotation.

> They recite no creed, and they have little use for theology, but they do believe that every person may experience direct contact with God. They also believe we are most likely to achieve that contact in stillness, either alone or in the gathered meeting, which is why they use no ministers or music, no readings or formal prayers, no script at all, but merely wait in silence for inward promptings. Quakers are mystics, in other words, but homely and practical ones, less concerned with escaping to heaven than with living responsibly on earth. (155)

The last sentence here is clearly loaded, Sanders having erected a straw man (reading cannot, and must not, mean separation from evaluation and judgment, even though sympathetic engagement is the prior commitment, and I cannot begin a Sanders essay with anything other than sympathy because Scott Sanders is my friend, to whom I am much indebted). Further, the "inward promptings" that he sets opposite dogma, music, formal prayer, and the like recall, to my mind at least, Swift's exposure of "enthusiasm," canting, and the perversions to which the "inner spirit" is famously subject (see, on this account, Donald Davie's 1978 asseverations in his autobiography *These the Companions*). Finally the expectation that one "*may* experience direct contact with God" certainly differs from the incarnational understanding that one *can* approach God only indirectly and through mediation. Still, Sanders follows the founder of Quakerism, George Fox, who "journeyed around England amid civil and ecclesiastical wars, searching for true religion." He found that "within his own depths" (155). Precisely that new orientation, which Quakers shared willy-nilly with various sects, fueled those very wars. The essay came to be as a *via media* between such individualism—for that is the name of the fundament here—and passé authoritarianism. Even so, this essay is a matter of relation and so of lateral movement, rather than depth.

I would be doing Sanders a serious injustice if I left you with the sense that "Silence" is only about a visit to a Quaker meetinghouse swaddled in heavy intellectual or thematic raiment. What else is here appears before we reach the meetinghouse. As Sanders seeks directions at a diner, he catches a glimpse of a homeless man outside, on the street, "slouching past":

> He wore a knit hat encrusted with leaves, a jacket torn at the elbows to
> reveal several dingy layers of cloth underneath, baggy trousers held up
> with a belt of rope, and broken leather shoes wrapped with silver duct
> tape. His face was the color of dust. He carried a bulging gray sack over
> his shoulder, like a grim Santa Claus. Pausing at a trash can, he bent down
> to retrieve something, stuffed the prize in his bag, then shuffled north . . .
> into the slant of snow.

Sanders finds it "odd" that none of the diners was affected enough by the sight to bring the man in for a hot meal. Of course, neither was he: "I only stood there feeling pangs of guilt, an ache as familiar as heartburn. What held me back? Wouldn't the Jesus whom I try to follow in my own muddled way have chosen to feed that man instead of searching for a prayer meeting?" (152). Why, though, I am inclined to ask, must it be one or the other, rather than both?

Further reflection leads Sanders to conclude that fear, of various sorts, led him to inaction. In any case, guilt remains. Inside the meetinghouse finally arrived at, Sanders reflects: "The homeless man shuffled past the House of Pancakes with his trash bag, right down the main street of my brain" (155–56). Soon his mind is on the service, if such it be called, Sanders waiting with the handful of others present for "the Spirit of God" to descend upon them. The picture is alluring.

> When the refreshing comes, when the Spirit stirs within, one is supposed
> to rise in the meeting and proclaim what God has whispered or roared.
> It might be a prayer, a few lines from the Bible or another holy book, a
> testimony about suffering in the world, a moral concern, or a vision. If the
> words are truly spoken, they are understood to flow not from the person
> but from the divine source that upholds and unites all of Creation. (157)

Outside *is*, indeed, inside in this vision, creation capitalized as virtually one with God, the "divine source" being spirit.

As Sanders continues to reflect, in the writing, that is, he becomes more oppositional than earlier, in largely repeating his earlier asseveration.

> Quakerism itself arose in reaction to a lackluster Church of England, just
> as the Protestant Reformation challenged a corrupt and listless Catholic
> Church, just as Jesus challenged the hidebound Judaism of his day. It
> seems to be the fate of religious movements to lose energy over time,
> as direct encounters with the Spirit give way to secondhand rituals and
> creeds, as prophets give way to priests, as living insight hardens into words
> and glass and stone. (158)

I understand and sympathize with Sanders's desire, one I long shared. The charges readily pile up: "lackluster," "listless," "hidebound," "secondhand," "hardened"—versus energy, freshness, directness. And yet what if, as T. S. Eliot once put it, "the spirit killeth, but the letter giveth life" (*Essays Ancient and Modern* 66n)?

Reflection leads Sanders, finally, to another opposition, this between "silent meetings" and "'programmed' Quaker churches." That particular Sunday morning, he reports, baring the individualist bent that appears in his moving description of the essay in "The Singular First Person": "I was in no mood to sit through anybody's program, no matter how artful or uplifting it might be":

> What I craved was silence—not absolute silence, for I welcomed the ruckus of doves and finches, but rather the absence of human noise. I spend nearly all of my waking hours immersed in language, bound to machines, following streets, obeying schedules, seeing and hearing and touching only what my clever species has made. I often yearn, as I did that morning, to withdraw from all our schemes and formulas, to escape from the obsessive human story, to slip out of my own small self and meet the great Self, the nameless mystery at the core of being. (*The Force of Spirit* 159)

I think of Pope, who, in *The Dunciad*, represents the return of Darkness and Old Night as that impending reductiveness (of the whole to the part) that reflects "a God like Thee: / Wrapt up in Self" (4.484–85). If it seems strange to acknowledge and worship Self, however figured, the following lines do little to relieve my anxiety, Sanders offering a direct and stinging criticism of more traditional Sunday services:

> It's no wonder that most religions put on a show, anything to fence in the wandering mind and fence out the terror. It's no wonder that only a dozen people would seek out this Quaker meeting on a Sunday morning, while tens of thousands were sitting through scripted performances in other churches all across Indianapolis. (159)

Of course, as Sanders has made clear, what he is attending is no church.

Upon leaving the meeting, Sanders remains tormented, still guilt ridden, with no hint of absolution or forgiveness in sight.

> To go home, I should have turned south on Meridian, but instead I turned north. I drove slowly, peering into alleys and doorways, looking for the man in the torn jacket with the bulging gray sack over his shoulder. I never saw him, and I did not know what I would have done if I had seen him. Give him a few dollars? Offer him a meal at the International House of Pancakes? Take him home? (163)

Sanders offers no answers. Instead, "Silence" winds toward a close, with a further, Wordsworthian lament that "the accelerating pace of technology, the flood of information, the proliferation of noise, all combine to keep us from that inward stillness where meaning is to be found." Driving back toward Bloomington, Sanders encounters blowing snow, approaching whiteout conditions. He ends with these resonant words, which I quote entire:

> By the time I reached the highway outside of Indianapolis, snow was falling steadily and blowing lustily, whiting out the way ahead. Headlights did no good. I should have pulled over until the sky cleared, as the more sensible drivers did. Rolling on into the whiteness, I lost all sense of motion, lost awareness of road and car. I seemed to be floating in the whirl of flakes, caught up in silence, alone yet not alone, as though I had slipped by accident into the state that a medieval mystic had called the cloud of unknowing. Memory fled, words flew away, and there was only the brightness, here and everywhere. (164)

The word "state" makes *me* think of Swiftian enthusiasm, but Sanders means it entirely positively, of course, a prelude to perhaps an ultimate revelation, afforded—maybe—by Grace.

The tone and texture of "Silence" reappears in Sanders's memoir *A Private History of Awe*. Thus picking up the notion of the brightness that appeared amid the January Sunday snow and regarding it as one of his life's significant "openings," a kind of moment-in-the-rose-garden markedly different from the representation in *Four Quartets* of Incarnation, by means of which *every* moment "burns" with meaning:

> Saints and bodhisattvas may achieve what Christians call mystical union or Buddhists call satori—a perpetual awareness of the force at the heart of things. For these enlightened few, the world is always lit. For the rest of us, such clarity comes only fitfully, in sudden glimpses or slow revelations. Quakers refer to these insights as "openings." When I first heard the term from a Friend in England who was counseling me about my resistance to the Vietnam War, I thought of how, on an overcast day, sunlight pours through a break in the clouds. After the clouds drift on, eclipsing the sun, the sun keeps shining behind the veil, and the memory of its light shines on in the mind.

Writes Sanders, never more an essayist: "The enlightenment I wish .to describe is ordinary, earthy, within reach of anyone who pays attention" (4).

My differences with Sanders's individualism and indeed Romanticism do not qualify my admiration for his accomplishments. Grant his particular understanding of and focus on "spirit," and you have a clear and generally effective account—with reflection—of an unexpected and significant experience. "Silence" *is* a personal, as well as a narrative, essay, Montaignian and Romantic.

Although never exactly confessional, Sanders is thoroughly autobiographical. More than that, and impressively so, he is honest. Indeed, I feel, in every essay of his that I have read, scrupulous and unstinting honesty; the man simply cannot lie. He has, I suspect, fewer imperfections than he is able to acknowledge. In short, Scott Sanders *embodies* the essayistic as bequeathed by Montaigne. In E. B. White, who is more personal than autobiographical, I feel throughout his essays the presence of a persona, partially White himself, partially made for the occasion of the writing, albeit consistent. In Sanders, differently, there is no persona; there is Scott Russell Sanders himself, plain—like a Quaker—though hardly simple. White seems most himself when he is most literary, employing fictional and other devices; when Sanders waxes allusive, or tries for literary effect, he is not always successful—as in the last paragraph, noted above, of "Silence."

In essays, I am tempted to conclude, honesty, perhaps the "basic ingredient," appeals most and best when it is represented rather than presented, when there is artful mediation. The hand of the writer inevitably appears, and when we have not been prepared for it, when it comes as a surprise, unexpected and uninvited, we feel the jar and the jolt. Its manner and mode indirect, the essay is an impure thing. Scott Sanders's "Silence" is impure too, certainly in the way that its "*embodied* truth" exists alongside and in tension with a brief for discarnation.

But to apprehend
The point of the intersection of the timeless
With time, is an occupation for the saint—
No occupation either, but something given
And taken, in a lifetime's death in love,
Ardour and selflessness and self-surrender.

. . .

The hint half guessed, the gift half understood, is Incarnation.
Here the impossible union
Of spheres of existence is actual,
Here the past and future
Are conquered, and reconciled,
Where action were otherwise movement—
Of that which is only moved
And has in it no source of movement—
Driven by daemonic, chthonic
Powers.

—T. S. Eliot, *The Dry Salvages* in *Four Quartets*

"Love Came to Us Incarnate"

Annie Dillard's "God in the Doorway"

WHENEVER I READ these climactic lines in *Four Quartets*, which I take to be an essay, I cannot but picture Annie Dillard, poet, author of *Pilgrim at Tinker Creek* (which won the Pulitzer Prize in 1974), critic, memoirist, essayist, and mystical seeker after the Infinite. *For the Time Being*—unclassifiable, it seems to me—represents the turns her seeking has taken, including Hasidism and Buddhism, Hinduism, and medieval Christian mysticism. Her writing—notably, I think, in *The Writing Life*—is a secular saint's life: writing as monastic, mystical to the core, also essayistic in its probing of the line of the words, in its indirectness (chopping, you aim not at the wood but past it), in its basis in and extreme love of sentences. The book—really, a volume of linked essays—should be required reading of all writers (and readers).

Her only denominated book of essays—so far, at least—is *Teaching a Stone to Talk*, which bears the subtitle *Expeditions and Encounters*. There are fourteen essays in all, which, in "Author's Note," Dillard refers to as simply "these," going on to aver: "At any rate, this is not a collection of occasional pieces, such as a writer brings out to supplement his real work; instead this is my real work, such as it is." Her fondness for, belief in, and commitment to the essay as form reappears in her 1988 introduction to *The Best American Essays*, where she boldly predicts that, in light of the current sorry state of both fiction and poetry, the (narrative) essay will become the genre of preference.

I have chosen here to read one of the slighter essays in *Teaching a Stone to Talk* — slighter in size, at least: "God in the Doorway." It takes up less than three pages, and it serves as an inviting introduction to this incomparable writer, whose longer essays would require more space than I can afford to provide at the moment. "God in the Doorway" is certainly not slight. Better than any other essay or chapter of hers, "God in the Doorway" whets the appetite and prepares it for the feast available to the reader willing to make an effort perhaps involving nothing less than "prayer, observance, discipline, thought and action."

Like the Advent sermons of Lancelot Andrewes, the seventeenth-century Anglican divine so important to T. S. Eliot, this essay has to do with Christmas. It is no sermon, of course, nor a homily, but instead a narrative, a *story*, with some of the mystical power of the journey of the Magi and of the Christmas story itself, as Bishop Andrewes "squeezed" it for its sustenance.

Dillard's story too begins conventionally, rather unpromisingly, quite ordinarily, in fact: "One cold Christmas Eve I was up unnaturally late because we had all gone out to dinner" (139). Food — sustenance — is precisely the matter. The simple adverb "unnaturally" alerts us to the eruption of the Extraordinary in the ordinary.

Dillard sets the scene: the stockings "drooped" from the mantel, and "beside them, a special table *bore* a bottle of ginger ale and a plate of cookies" (italics added). Suddenly "a commotion at the front door; it opened, and cold wind blew around my dress." What it was, was "whom I never — ever — wanted to meet. Santa Claus was looming in the doorway and looking around for me" (139–40). Dillard ran upstairs. The simplicity — nigh on to starkness — of her prose matches the story perfectly. As she explains it, "Like everyone in his right mind, I feared Santa Claus, thinking he was God." She describes herself then as "still thoughtless and brute, reactive."

She knew, she says, right from wrong but "had barely tested the possibility of shaping my own behavior, and then only from fear, and not yet from love" (140).

Back, then, to the story: Despite both parents' encouragement and pleading, Dillard refused to return downstairs. She nevertheless stole glimpses of Santa Claus, still standing in the doorway "monstrous and bright, powerless, ringing a loud bell and repeating Merry Christmas, Merry Christmas." She never came down. "I don't know who ate the cookies," she says (140).

Dillard next tells us that "for so many years now" she has known that Santa was actually a neighbor, Miss White, from across the street. In her mind, Santa, God, and Miss White get mixed up, mixed together, forming, she writes, "an awesome, vulnerable trinity." The story she now tells, she says, is "really a story about Miss White." As important as the word "trinity" is "vulnerable," which resonates suggestively with the earlier "powerless" to describe Santa as he stood waiting in the doorway (140).

To Miss White, Dillard now turns, describing her only as old and living in a "big house across the street." She writes of her, as follows:

> She liked having me around; she plied me with cookies, taught me things about the world, and tried to interest me in finger painting, in which she herself took great pleasure. She would set up easels in her kitchen, tack enormous slick soaking papers to their frames, and paint undulating undersea scenes: horizontal smears of color sparked by occasional vertical streaks which were understood to be fixed kelp. I liked her.

"She meant no harm on earth," and still, Dillard confesses, "half a year after her failed visit as Santa Claus, I ran from her again" (140–41).

This is no allegory, of course, nothing so simple or so elaborate. Likable herself, companionable, and meaning no harm, Miss White is not merely powerless or vulnerable; she also fails.

Dillard's second telltale response she then recounts, the season the virtual opposite. This scene occurs outdoors, instead of within.

> That day, a day of the following summer, Miss White and I knelt in her yard while she showed me a magnifying glass. It was a large, strong hand lens. She lifted my hand and, holding it very still, focused a dab of sunshine on my palm. The glowing crescent wobbled, spread, and finally contracted to a point. It burned; I was burned; I ripped my hand away

DILLARD'S "GOD IN THE DOORWAY" { 179 }

and ran home crying. Miss White called after me, sorry, explaining, but I didn't look back. (141)

If Dillard mixes together Santa Claus, God, and Miss White, the reader — or at least I do — mixes together God and light and truth: too much we — or at least I — cannot bear. It also burns, hurts — but, writes Eliot in *East Coker*, "the healer's art" derives from "sharp compassion," with the result that "Our only health is the disease."

In any case, Dillard separates Miss White out from God: "Even now," time having brought no full revelation (or is it epiphany?), "I wonder: if I meet God, will he take and hold my bare hand in his, and focus his eye on my palm, and kindle that spot and let me burn?" (141). Will He be like Miss White, in other words, she His possible embodiment?

Suddenly a turn, sharp, self-critical, Dillard herself now focused, under the lens, rather than God, or Miss White. Her response is, after all, what matters, what Santa Claus meant, what Miss White was after.

But no. It is I who misunderstood everything and let everybody down. Miss White, God, I am sorry I ran from you. I am still running, running from that knowledge, that eye, that love from which there is no refuge. For you meant only love, and love, and I felt only fear, and pain. So once in Israel love came to us incarnate, stood in the doorway between two worlds, and we were all afraid. (141)

Indeed, sore afraid. There remains what Eliot calls, in *East Coker*, in his brief, lyrical allegory of the human situation, "the absolute paternal care / That will not leave us, but prevents us everywhere."

The knowledge that Dillard still runs from is, apparently, that of gift, the gift that is love freely given. It could not be more important that that love is *incarnate*, made flesh, appearing in person. Incarnation itself is precisely the pattern that reveals the in-betweenness that functions to fuse apparent opposites: two worlds, inside and outside, experience and meaning, flesh and spirit, God and Miss White, standing in the doorway, "looking around for me" (140).

> But mostly his [Orwell's] essays are full of the apprehension that the essay world is vanishing, that the world of doctrine has almost reconquered it. . . . For him, the essayistic attitude, the offering of independent views based on individual thought and experience, came to have an immense *political* significance.
>
> —Graham Good, *The Observing Self: Rediscovering the Essay*

"A Free Intelligence"

George Orwell, the Essay, and

"Reflections on Gandhi"

GEORGE ORWELL IS SUDDENLY "IN," owing only partially to the pundit and author Christopher Hitchens's interest in and recent book on him. Perhaps the rabid sectarianism and party spirit now dominating the American political scene, at least, accounts for this rediscovery. Certainly it is for his politics, rather than his significant contributions to the essay form, that Orwell is now receiving widespread attention. The danger remains of appropriation, as in the past, by exponents of the Left and the Right alike—despite Orwell's declared and demonstrated embrace of what he once attributed to Charles Dickens: a "free intelligence," with its echoes of Matthew Arnold and, more important, Edmund Burke. (That succinct phrase, by the way, Orwell also uses in his wildly mistaken essay on *Gulliver's Travels*, denying Swift the capacity he lauded in Dickens.)

George Orwell, born Eric Blair, was an avowed Socialist, and yet he was also what Alexander Pope celebrated—and claimed he himself was—

in *An Essay on Man*: "Slave to no sect" (4.331). Pope, however, went on to complete the description, asserting a traditionalism as well as religious faith alien to Orwell: "who takes no private road, / But looks thro' Nature, up to Nature's God" (331–32). While it would be inaccurate to call Orwell Janus-faced, it is the case, undeniably, that he defies easy labeling, a complex figure, his intelligence perhaps as free as he thought Dickens's to be.

I have chosen to read Orwell's very last essay, "Reflections on Gandhi." I do so with some regret, stemming from the recognition that other essays are better: the widely reprinted "Shooting of an Elephant," for example, also "Such, Such Were the Joys" and the famous essay on the English language, to bring the list up short. Still Lydia Fakundiny chose the Gandhi essay to represent Orwell in her important anthology *The Art of the Essay*. She in fact writes, introducing the essay, that Orwell here confronts the totalitarianism that not only threatens "the political order" but is also, "and most dangerously, a bondage of the intellect." In Orwell, she writes finely, we see here "a whole mind revealing its energetic complexity, one mind resisting the conventional, the orthodox, the reductive views of its subject, a mind capacious and supple enough to honor the political achievements of a man whose basic values it dismantles and rejects" (297). Here Orwell thus offers a supreme instance of essaying.

"Reflections on Gandhi" initially appears as if a book review, but it is actually an essay originally published in *Partisan Review*, in 1948, as Orwell was completing his novel *Nineteen Eighty-Four*. When he writes, in the essay's opening paragraph, of "this partial autobiography," I am inclined to expect a review; what I get is more capacious and more telling, the famous and lionized Indian figure starkly revealed as more narrow and limited than we thought. The true hero here is not Gandhi but the essayist himself, although Orwell pulls that off without a hint of either arrogance or presumption.

Reading Gandhi's *The Story of My Experiments with Truth* has bred these "reflections." (I think of Dryden's great essay-poem *Religio Laici*, itself "bred" by the reading of a book, or so the author claims.) Perhaps the consuming issue for Orwell *is* truth, and so he opens the essay with a bold declaration signaling his intention to get at the truth, no matter how unpleasant or radical, about his subject: "Saints should always be judged guilty until they are proved innocent." As daring as bold, this direct statement, uncharacteristic of the essay, opens the way to the extended reflections on "the saint, or near-saint." Before one is canonized, or proved innocent, such explicit questions as the following need be answered: "to what extent was Gandhi moved by vanity—by the consciousness of himself as a humble, naked old man, sitting on a praying mat and shaking empires by sheer spiritual power—and to what extent did he compromise his own principles by entering politics, which of their nature are inseparable from coercion and fraud?" (298). Orwell's voice thus rings true and, more, determined to find nothing less than the truth, to which Gandhi's own book may have (inadvertently) called him. The voice is strong and clear and forthright, the light of its intelligence perfectly reflected in the crystalline prose.

That voice—the essayistic voice, I venture—is also practical, not cynical but skeptical, and certainly critical. Early on, Orwell reports, he was wary of Gandhi; he found his "home-spun cloth, 'soul-forces' and vegetarianism . . . unappealing"; moreover, Orwell thought, perhaps rashly, that "his medievalist program was obviously not viable in a backward, starving, over-populated country." In any case, Orwell was sure, Gandhi was being used by the all-powerful British: "at any rate, the gentleness with which he was nearly always handled was due partly to the feeling that he was useful. The British Conservatives only became really angry with him when, as in 1942, he was in effect turning his non-violence against a different conqueror" (298). Orwell the British citizen is an arch-anticolonialist.

Of Gandhi he speaks well, acknowledging some of his extraordinary gifts and virtues and declaring him free of corruption, ambition "in any vulgar way," fear, and malice. From his autobiography, Orwell gathers that Gandhi was indeed naturally courageous, a fact apparent in the manner of his death. He was also free, writes Orwell, of "that maniacal suspiciousness which, as E. M. Forster rightly says in *A Passage to India*, is the besetting Indian vice, as hypocrisy is the British vice." Nor can Orwell adduce evidence of envy or a sense of inferiority, certainly no racism or "color feeling." He did not, moreover, "lack European friends," and although he was "shrewd enough" to detect dishonesty, "he seems wherever possible to have believed that other people were acting in good faith and had a better nature through which they could be approached" (299).

Not enough, not nearly, to make a saint. Indeed, says Orwell, "he was not one of those saints who are marked out by their phenomenal piety from childhood onwards, nor one of the other kind who forsake the world after

sensational debaucheries" (299). With continued reference to the autobiography he has recently been reading, after first encountering him years
before "in the ill-printed pages of some Indian newspaper" (298), Orwell
notes Gandhi's "full confession of the misdeeds of his youth," although
"there is not much to confess." Nor did he have much in the way of material
possessions at the time of his death: "The whole outfit could be purchased
for about" five pounds. As to Gandhi's sins,

> at least his fleshly sins . . . would make the same sort of appearance
> if placed all in one heap. A few cigarettes, a few mouthfuls of meat, a
> few annas pilfered in childhood from the maidservant, two visits to a
> brothel (on each occasion he got away without "doing anything"), one
> narrowly escaped lapse with his landlady in Plymouth, one outburst of
> temper—that is about the whole collection. (299–300)

Earnestness had always marked Gandhi, ethical in nature rather than
religious until around age thirty. Orwell surmises that Gandhi would have
succeeded as a lawyer, had he been so inclined; he was certainly "a hard-
headed political organizer." "His character," concludes Orwell, "was an extraordinarily mixed one," one that might indeed have appealed deeply to
the essayist's insistence on complexity; "but there was almost nothing in it
that you can put your finger on and call bad"—and that may just put him
out of reach of ordinary humanity. Still, writes Orwell, not at all grudgingly,

> I believe that even Gandhi's worst enemies would admit that he was an
> interesting and unusual man who enriched the world simply by being
> alive. Whether he was also a lovable man, and whether his teachings can
> have much value for those who do not accept the religious beliefs on
> which they are founded, I have never felt fully certain. (300)

Here, we approach the heart of this essay. It is important to note, with Lydia
Fakundiny, that the last words above point "not a question of ambivalence
towards a revered leader; Orwell is not indecisively of two minds about
Gandhi" (297).

What has been said of Gandhi, which Orwell proceeds to describe, applies to the essayist himself, with some due acknowledgment of differences,
of course:

> Of late years it has been the fashion to talk about Gandhi as though he
> were not only sympathetic to the Western Left-wing movement, but were

integrally part of it. Anarchists and pacifists, in particular, have claimed him for their own, noticing only that he was opposed to centralism and State violence and ignoring the other-worldly, anti-humanist tendency of his doctrines. (300)

I cannot but recall Eliot's similar disapproval of the "thoroughgoing."

Orwell's rejection of totalitarianism in favor of the critical and capacious intelligence that F. Scott Fitzgerald heralds in "The Crack-Up" as "the ability to hold two opposed ideas in the mind at the same time, and still retain the ability to function" (in Lopate 520) certainly thrives on comparison, if it does not actually call for it, encourage it, and perhaps require it. Not only Fitzgerald and Eliot spring to mind, but so do many others, as we have seen. Orwell's *difference*—from Gandhi as well as from so many of the essayists we are reading—appears with striking clarity when he proceeds to write that

> Gandhi's teachings cannot be squared with the belief that Man is the measure of all things and that our job is to make life worth living here on this earth, which is the only earth we have. They make sense only on the assumption that God exists and that the world of solid objects is an illusion to be escaped from. (300)

With such a view, tenaciously held, individualism triumphs, the essay as inaugurated by Montaigne having perhaps reached its destined end. It does, after all, root us in "the world of solid objects," a largely secular form skeptical that, if God exists, He has not much if anything at all to do with our daily living, which it believes should receive all our attention.

Orwell is surely right to emphasize the things we take for granted in our quotidian existence—although I question that they cannot coexist with religious belief, which, in fact, I would contend, depends upon them and grows precisely out of them. Orwell takes the negative path, describing what Gandhi's principles, and "disciplines," rule out: much that the flesh finds appealing and even sustaining; the issue concerns man (not "Man") as a fleshly creature and not merely a spiritual one.

> First of all, no meat-eating, and if possible no animal food in any form. (Gandhi himself, for the sake of his health, had to compromise on milk, but seems to have felt this to be a backsliding.) No alcohol or tobacco, and no spices or condiments even of a vegetable kind, since food should be taken not for its own sake but solely in order to preserve one's strength.

Secondly, if possible, no sexual intercourse. If sexual intercourse must happen, then it should be for the sole purpose of begetting children and presumably at long intervals. . . . And finally—this is the cardinal point—for the seeker after goodness there must be no close friendships and no exclusive loves whatever. (300–301)

Saintliness is thus being defined along puritanical lines.

Puritanism is no great friend of inclusiveness, of course, but Orwell opposes the inclusive as he does the puritanical. Some of his strongest writing comes in the long paragraph in which he treats the point that he had reached at the end of the previous one. Orwell now, in other words, not only rejects sainthood but denounces it as essentially inhuman. I must quote the paragraph entire. But first: Orwell reckons that Gandhi calls for us all to be saints like him. Sainthood may be, however, a far more special and extraordinary state and condition than Orwell appears to suggest. To accept "the things of the world" by no means obligates you to reject the spiritual—only to realize that the path to the latter leads through, and by means of, the former. Unfortunately Orwell seems unaware of that particular complexity. Now Orwell on Gandhi, friendship, and love:

> Close friendships, Gandhi says, are dangerous, because "friends react on one another" and through loyalty to a friend one can be led into wrong-doing. This is unquestionably true. Moreover, if one is to love God, or to love humanity as a whole, one cannot give one's preference to any individual person. This again is true, and it marks the point at which the humanistic and the religious attitude cease to be reconcilable. To an ordinary human being, love means nothing if it does not mean loving some people more than others. (301)

From universal reflection Orwell moves on to particular reference, returning to Gandhi's autobiography and the testimony there to the type of love that he practiced toward those whom he would be expected, by contract as it were, to love. Gandhi's inhumanity appears in full bloom, although it is not quite totalitarian or without nuance:

> The autobiography leaves it uncertain whether Gandhi behaved in an inconsiderate way to his wife and children, but at any rate it makes clear that on three occasions he was willing to let his wife or a child die rather than administer the animal food prescribed by the doctor. It is true that

the threatened death never actually occurred, and also that Gandhi—with, one gathers, a good deal of moral pressure in the opposite direction— always gave the patient the choice of staying alive at the price of committing a sin: still, if the decision had been solely his own, he would have forbidden the animal food, whatever the risks might be. There must, he says, be some limit to what we will do in order to remain alive, and the limit is well on this side of chicken broth. This attitude is perhaps a noble one, but, in the sense which—I think—most people would give to the word, it is inhuman. (301)

Having reached this stirring point, Orwell modulates into reflection on just what makes a human being human.

The essence of being human is that one does not seek perfection, that one *is* sometimes willing to commit sins for the sake of loyalty, that one does not push asceticism to the point where it makes friendly intercourse impossible, and that one is prepared in the end to be defeated and broken up by life, which is the inevitable price of fastening one's love upon other human individuals. (301)

The pattern called Incarnation promotes an *understanding*, rather than resignation.

At this point in the paragraph, Orwell broadens his animadversions on sainthood, surely right in rejecting "non-attachment" and asceticism (the very first "choice of life" that the young seeker Siddhartha must refuse, in Hermann Hesse's essay-novel of that name):

No doubt alcohol, tobacco, and so forth, are things that a saint must avoid, but sainthood is also a thing that human beings must avoid. There is an obvious retort to this, but one should be wary about making it. In this yogi-ridden age, it is too easily assumed that "non-attachment" is not only better than a full acceptance of earthly life, but that the ordinary man only rejects it because it is too difficult: in other words, that the average human being is a failed saint. It is doubtful whether this is true. Many people genuinely do not wish to be saints, and it is probable that some who achieve or aspire to sainthood have never felt much temptation to be human beings. If one could follow it to its psychological roots, one would, I believe, find that the main motive for "non-attachment" is a desire to escape from the pain of living, and above all from love, which, sexual or non-sexual, is hard work. But it is not necessary here to argue whether the otherworldly or the humanistic idea is "higher." The point is that they are incompatible. One must choose between God and Man, and all "radicals" and "progressives," from the mildest Liberal to the most extreme Anarchist, have in effect chosen Man. (301–2)

The choice is a false one, just as is that between "otherworldly" and the "humanistic." The latter may rightly be contrasted with the Christian, which refuses to limit its concerns to any duality, including the "otherworldly" and the worldly. Accordingly the choice is not between Man and God, for in this case we have revealed that "full life," including "here below," consists, say Christians, in recognizing that "God in the Doorway," to invoke Annie Dillard: that is, Love Incarnate, God and man at-oned.

In the remainder of "Reflections on Gandhi," Orwell turns, somewhat anticlimactically, to the controverted matter of pacifism. Rightly Orwell poses the most difficult question, having acknowledged that Gandhi's famous version was practiced in a limited struggle for national independence. "What about the Jews?," though, Orwell wants to know. Is a pacifist "prepared to see them exterminated? If not, how do you propose to save them without resorting to war?" (302). Orwell surmises that Gandhi, born in 1869, "did not understand the nature of totalitarianism and saw everything in terms of his own struggle against the British government." As a consequence, Orwell suggests, Gandhi's form of pacifism is simply impractical, including in contemporary Russia, where the "masses could only practice civil obedience if the same idea happened to occur to all of them simultaneously, and even then . . . it would make no difference." In short, "applied to foreign politics, pacifism either stops being pacifist or becomes appeasement." There is this, too: "the assumption, which served Gandhi so well in dealing with individuals, that all human beings are more or less approachable and will respond to a generous gesture, needs to be seriously questioned. It is not necessarily true, for example, when you are dealing with lunatics," among whom count not just Hitler and Stalin but also radical Islamic terrorists of our own time (303).

For all his doubts, Orwell can still write—one feels with complete genuineness—that "it is at least thinkable that the way out lies through nonviolence." The following is, in fact, fair and beautifully balanced. "One feels of him [Gandhi] that there was much that he did not understand," writes Orwell, "but not that there was anything that he was frightened of saying or thinking" (303–4). Still and all, Orwell declares, "I have never been able to feel much liking for Gandhi." And yet, so complicated a figure and a man was he, Orwell can go on immediately to say, that "I do not feel sure that as a political thinker he was wrong in the main, nor do I believe that his life was a failure." The remainder of the paragraph consists of more balancing, one "on the other hand" followed immediately by another. And then these final, careful, respectful words, Orwell readily giving the (alleged) saint his due:

> One may feel, as I do, a sort of aesthetic distaste for Gandhi, one may reject the claims of sainthood made on his behalf (he never made any such claim himself, by the way), one may also reject sainthood as an ideal and therefore feel that Gandhi's basic aims were anti-human and reactionary; but regarded simply as a politician, and compared with the other leading political figures of our time, how clean a smell he has managed to leave behind! (304)

Upon leaving "Reflections on Gandhi," I for one feel that at the end Orwell's essayistic attitude counts for a great deal. As Graham Good has written in *The Observing Self* about another of Orwell's essays, "he does not adopt the *method* of Marxism, but rather the method (or non-method) of the essay" (154). The reading practiced by Orwell is "individualist" (160). He may transcend party differences, showing no particular allegiance, itself "a characteristically essayistic viewpoint" (157), yet Orwell speaks for "humanity," for "Man." That may be essayistic as well, but it is not in the final analysis catholic and so is limited by its puritanism.

It is probably no harder to eat a woodchuck than to construct a
sentence that lasts a hundred years.
—E. B. White, "A Slight Sound at Evening"

Perfectionism pervades . . . the efforts and the ideals implied in
deeds done flawlessly, with poise and elegance, as great gifts to
deserving recipients.
—David Morowitz, introduction to *Trifles Make Perfection:*
   The Selected Essays of Joseph Wechsberg

Where "Trifles Rule Like Tyrants"

Cynthia Ozick's "The Seam of the Snail"

NO SLOUCH HIMSELF when it comes to composing them, E. B.
White once praised Thoreau's *Walden* as made of sentences. That "hair-
shirt of a man" (241), says White, "tended to write in sentences, a feat not
every writer is capable of, and *Walden* is, rhetorically speaking, a collection
of certified sentences, some of them, it would now appear [he was writing
on the centennial of its publication], as indestructible as they are errant."
The "off-beat prose that Thoreau was master of," according to his admirer,
was "at once strictly disciplined and wildly abandoned"; indeed, "a copy-
desk man would get a double hernia trying to clean up" some of *Walden's*
more eccentric sentences—that nevertheless befit their maker (239). Anyway, Thoreau, concludes White, managed to construct more than a few
sentences that last "a hundred years" (238).

It was sentences that first drew me to the essay, some twenty years ago,
just as its renaissance was getting underway. I read Bacon, Richard Selzer,
Cynthia Ozick, and White himself, and was smitten. More than in any
other kind of writing, I believe, in essays sentences matter; they are the

building blocks, of course, in fact the "pack mules," someone has said. In essays, sentences do more: they stand out, often being sculpted, an epitome of the maker's craft and artistry; they constitute his or her art. The essayist takes pride in them, become, as "the core of the affair," "the thing with which you work"; when "you treat it honourably and in a manner that makes it recognize its service," the sentence thinks for you (Belloc, "The Mowing of a Field" 202).

No one's sentences are better, more majestic, than Cynthia Ozick's, for instance in "The Seam of the Snail," which first appeared in *Ms.* under the title "Excellence." Here they *express* her point, embodying the very qualities and virtues she considers as excellence.

The essay is brilliantly brief, little more than three pages in the major collection *Metaphor and Memory* (1989). It first seems a memoir, as Ozick's essays often do, but she has a unique way of moving from autobiography to reflection and generalizable point(s). The opening paragraph is, of course, carefully crafted, although we won't fully appreciate it until its thematic promise is fulfilled in time. The time here is the Depression, Ozick's childhood, and the mundane matter of her mother's sewing, her cousin Sarah's competitiveness, and the contrast between the two styles these seamstresses represent: "My mother's sewing had elegant outsides, but there was something catch-as-catch-can about the insides. Sarah's sewing, by contrast, was as impeccably finished inside as out; not one stray thread dangled" (107). Thus ends the opening paragraph.

The next paragraph opens with a shift to Uncle Jake, a perfectionist at clock building. He serves as further contrast with the essayist's mother, who built "serviceable" objects, like radiator covers, cabinets, and bookcases, and who repaired sewer pipes, painted ceilings, and reupholstered chairs. With her, "nothing was perfect. There was always some clear flaw, never visible head-on." With Cynthia Ozick the essayist, everything *is* perfect, her next sentence returning to her title and cousin Sarah: "You had to look underneath, where the seams were." Then, having said that her mother once "planted a whole yard of tall corn," she ends the paragraph with this pair of abutting sentences, the second surely as majestic as anything Thoreau could make: "The corn thrived, though not in rows. The stalks elbowed one another like gossips in a dense little village" (107–8). Uncle Jake would surely be proud.

As would "Miss Brrrroooobaker," as her mother called Ozick's high-school English teacher, mocking her and invoking her name "as an emblem of raging finical obsession." Ozick admits that her mother's voice "hoots at me down the years, as I go on casting and recasting sentences in a tiny hand-writing on monomaniacally uniform paper," just as she had been taught in school. The subject of the essay is not, of course, the essayist, far from it. Nor is it her mother, although she receives great attention—and obvious reverence. The contrast with her, in any case, continues, Ozick edging ever closer to the essay's center.

> The loops of my mother's handwriting—it was the Palmer Method—were as big as soup bowls, spilling generous splashy ebullience. She could pull off, at five minutes' notice, a satisfying dinner for ten concocted out of nothing more than originality and panache. But the napkin would be folded a little off center, and the spoon might be on the wrong side of the knife. She was an optimist who ignored trifles; for her, God was not in the details but in the intent. (108)

The implications ring out—likely beyond even those Ozick herself was aware of. Indeed the last sentence here marks Ozick as Jewish, a commitment she embraces and describes in "stiff-necked" fashion in "The Riddle of the Ordinary," in *Art and Ardor*, her first collection, as well as in other essays in *Metaphor and Memory*.

What Ozick does in "The Seam of the Snail" is deceptively brilliant. It looks easy, but looks notoriously deceive—part, but only a part, of her point. She moves seamlessly (if you will) between details and the reflection that produces meaning and significance. She also lavishes praise on both her mother and her mother's almost Mother Earth–type fecundity—even as she will finally distinguish herself from them. Here, note: "Lavish: my mother was as lavish as nature. She woke early and saturated the hours with work and inventiveness, and read late into the night. She was all profusion, abundance, fabrication" (108). There is more, and Ozick may appear to struggle to get this character sketch of her abundant mother down right, but she certainly succeeds with this distinguishing paragraph, which just precedes her pyrotechnical display with her mother's opposite, with the trifles that are sentences:

> Despite the gargantuan Palmer loops (or possibly because of them), I
> have always known that my mother's was a life of—intricately abashing

word!—excellence: insofar as excellence means ripe generosity. She bur-
geoned, she proliferated; she was endlessly leafy and flowering. She wore
red hats, and called herself a gypsy. In her girlhood she marched with the
suffragettes and for Margaret Sanger and called herself a Red. She made
me laugh, she was so varied: like a tree on which lemons, pomegranates,
and prickly pears absurdly all hang together. She had the comedy of
prodigality. (109)

In Montaigne's terms, certainly "*divers*" (perhaps as well as "*ondoyant*").
With her admiring representation, her daughter reveals her own generosity.

Difference reigns supreme, however, if generously so. Only now does
the essayist actually focus on herself, although even here the point transcends autobiography. The sentences are as *expressive* as the young Alexander Pope's, then perhaps twenty-one or so, writing in *An Essay on Criticism*
and making his verses *do*—that is, *embody*—his point. No extravagance appears in Ozick, in any case; what she succeeds in doing, intentionally or not,
is to show profusion, abundance, fabrication, prodigality (and excellence)
in the narrow strait of the sentence—Henry James, or Jane Austen, perhaps,
to her mother's Dickens, or Shakespeare. In her terms, she makes sentences
both "comely and muscular," in other words, beautiful *and* strong, feminine *and* masculine. Structure, syntax, image, diction, tone—they all, and
more, work together, weaving a tapestry magnificent in texture, resonant
and forthright. The paragraph also beautifully instances how the essayist
herself functions, in this glorious form, as a window through which others
may look. I must quote liberally, Ozick's language just about as fresh as any
human can effect.

My own way is a thousand times more confined. I am a pinched perfectionist, the ultimate fruition of Miss Brubaker; I attend to crabbed
minutiae and am self-trammeled through taking pains. I am a kind of
human snail, locked in and condemned by my own nature. The ancients
believed that the moist track left by the snail as it crept was the snail's own
essence, depleting its body little by little; the farther the snail toiled, the
smaller it became, until it finally rubbed itself out. That is how perfection-
ists are. Say to us Excellence, and we will show you how we use up our
substance and wear ourselves away, while making scarcely any progress
at all. The fact that I am an exacting perfectionist in a narrow strait only,
and nowhere else, is hardly to the point, since nothing matters to me so
much as a comely and muscular sentence. It is my narrow strait, this snail's

road; the track of the sentence I am writing now; and when I have eked out the wet substance, ink or blood, that is its mark, I will begin the next sentence. (109–10)

The power of the prose is so great that I have to pause, even in quoting; I want to absorb the sentences, etch them in memory, and have in fact done so, so many times have I shared the passage with students. I must pause so to prepare myself for what I know is to come, what is, if anything, even better than what has gone before. My commentary would, besides, be not only superfluous but condemned to second- or third-rate status. Now to continue, in the same paragraph:

> Only in treading out sentences am I perfectionist; but then there is noth-
> ing else I know how to do, or take much interest in. I miter every pair
> of abutting sentences as scrupulously as Uncle Jake fitted one strip of
> rosewood against another. My mother's worldly and bountiful hand has
> escaped me. The sentence I am writing is my cabin and my shell, compact,
> self-sufficient. It is the burnished horizon—a merciless planet where
> flawlessness is the single standard, where even the inmost seams, however
> hidden from a laxer eye, must meet perfection. Here "excellence" is not
> strewn casually from a tipped cornucopia, here disorder does not account
> for charm, here trifles rule like tyrants. (110)

I marvel at—and revere—the way Ozick, with seeming effortlessness, pulls and weaves together the threads of the tapestry on which she has been working since the essay's first words. I marvel too that in perfection the tone matches the pitch.

But she is not done—what great writer ever stops where a lesser would rest content? Abundance and exuberance she is not without. Ozick makes two more paragraphs, each less intense than the previous, as if sympathetic to the heightened state in which she knows we cannot long exist. Like every other great essayist, Ozick takes pains to ensure that we not think her egoistical (White confronts the charge often leveled at essayists by claiming, rather than admitting, that he is nothing else). Here, then, is the penultimate paragraph of "The Seam of the Snail," the last I shall quote:

> I measure my life in sentences pressed out, line by line, like the lustrous
> ooze on the underside of the snail, the snail's secret open seam, its wound,
> leaking attar. My mother was too mettlesome to feel the force of a comma.

She scorned minutiae. She measured her life according to what poured from the horn of plenty, which was her own seamless, ample, cascading, elastic, susceptible, inexact heart. My narrower heart rides between the tiny twin horns of the snail, dwindling as it goes. (110)

I won't quote the final, shorter paragraph, partly because I want to leave something for you when you take up this wondrous essay. I *will* say that "The Seam of the Snail" ends as many of Ozick's essays do, on a note that unsettles, not jarring but leaving us with a question. Whether that works against or toward perfection, I find myself unable to say.

Among the sadder and smaller pleasures of this world I count this pleasure: the pleasure of taking up one's pen. . . . I will tell you frankly with what I am writing. I am writing with a Waterman's Ideal Fountain Pen. . . . Well then, the pen is of pure gold, a pen that runs straight away like a willing horse, or a jolly little ship; indeed, it is a pen so excellent that it reminds me of my subject: the pleasure of taking up one's pen.

—Hilaire Belloc, "On the Pleasure of Taking Up One's Pen,"
　　On Nothing and Kindred Subjects

Essaying and Pen Passion

Anne Fadiman as Common Reader

in "Eternal Ink"

PEN PASSION IS A MIGHTY PASSION. Writers have long testified so, from Sir Walter Scott to John Grisham, Virginia Woolf to Edmund White, Roland Barthes to Barry Hannah. For some, the passion takes the form of collecting, for the lucky ones, both collecting and writing. The latter of us suppose we cannot write with anything else—certainly cannot write so well. We practically crave the pen, eagerly await the return to it in the morning, happy only when pen and person are in sync, instrument become appendage. Little I know approaches in pleasure that of a flexible nib caressing the page and issuing words and sentences, maybe even paragraphs, that seek to be worthy of that which allows them, participates in their making.

In a couple of essays published a few years ago in *JAC* (formerly *Journal of Advanced Composition*), I went so far—impassioned by my own Sailor and also my Dunhill—as to claim a connection not just between pen use and good writing but also between using a fountain pen and essaying. Then computer illiterate, I wrote that "the pen is the instrument by which writing is best made" (77); in support, I cited a number of writers past and present. And then I went on, perhaps not cautiously enough, to say this:

> You don't have to write with a pen to make such an essay [as Joseph Epstein describes in his note to the title of his collection of familiar essays *A Line Out for a Walk*], but it helps. Essay-writing and pen-writing: double first-cousins. Michel de Montaigne, acknowledged progenitor of the essay, famously declared for writing "*ondoyant et divers*," and pen fancier Barry Hannah believes that a fountain pen promotes a cognate "mental hygiene. It will make you have a more athletic and supple mind."

I approached conclusion with these (increasingly melodramatic) words:

> They share a line-age, essay-writing and pen-writing. The capaciousness I have elsewhere ascribed to the essay—which I have characterized, borrowing from Cynthia Ozick, as prompting, indeed requiring us "to envision the stranger's heart"—that capaciousness, or a similar one, I have felt in the use of the fountain pen. It has literally opened up worlds to me, enriching, layering, expanding. (83)

Key here, the thread common to essaying and penning, as well as reading as "the common reader," may well be *slowing down*, as I suggested in my second *JAC* essay, "Art and Anger—Upon Taking Up the Pen Again." Writing with a fountain pen, I then claimed, bears an important analogy to essaying: related events need time to accumulate meaning. You therefore have to slow down, respect time, take a line out for a walk or a saunter. In a hurry, a writer fails to explore, to give the mind time and space to reflect, to savor a thought, extend and pursue it, follow its mazy and unpredictable ways. The computer, on the other hand, I then wrote from inexperience and ignorance, increases the speed of communication, evidently breeding haste. With the pen, you cannot write fast. For one thing, you have to stop occasionally to refill with ink; for another, with a good pen you simply want to do your best, respecting and honoring the instrument with which you work, that appendage. (Some years later now, and somewhat chastened by direct experience of the "glorious" computer, I realize the difference between physical slowing down and mental. To be sure, haste breeds problems, impatience more; but I find that I can both put words on the screen faster than I can put them on paper and, at the same time, savor and develop thoughts and feelings. One kind of speed does not necessarily entail the other.)

Like Hilaire Belloc a century earlier, Anne Fadiman has confessed her passion for an "easy pen" (Belloc, "The Mowing of a Field"). Former editor of *The American Scholar*, and the scion of a famous intellectual family (her father was the renowned Clifton Fadiman, himself an essayist as well as columnist), Fadiman wrote a number of essays for the Smithsonian periodical *Civilization* and then in 1998 collected these familiar essays in a volume titled *Ex Libris*. On the dust jacket, Adam Gopnik described her book as a return to "a dusty literary form—the bookish essay about books"; these essays are, as Cynthia Ozick has there allowed, "literary reflections," "enchanting [writing] on letters and life."

"Eternal Ink" is one of the most charming of the eighteen shortish essays. Here Fadiman writes an *essay* about her own *pen passion*, which is pointedly addressed to "the common reader"—thus she adds a dimension hitherto absent in the linkage of essaying and penning. In fact, Fadiman subtitles her book *Confessions of a Common Reader*, and in her preface she acknowledges her predecessors Dr. Johnson and Virginia Woolf, the latter of whom borrowed from the former the phrase as title for her two volumes of mainly critical essays. Fadiman also describes there what she finely calls "the heart of reading: not whether we wish to purchase a new book but how we maintain our connections with our old books, the ones we have lived with for years, the ones whose textures and colors and smells have become as familiar to us as our children's skin" (x). More recently, and appropriately, by the way, Fadiman has edited a volume of essays called *Re-Readings*. Precisely because the essays in *Ex Libris* are intended for "the common reader," that person increasingly hard to find, they are important for the student— of all ages and inclinations. You could learn more about both reading and writing—and their connection—from spending time with this book than from a whole course in Advanced Composition, which too often now treats everything but writing, or from a course in literature, which likewise today treats not reading but "transcendent" ideas and political agendas.

After opening with a detailed and loving description of her "ideal" pen, notably "a gift from my fifth-grade boyfriend," Fadiman reflects on the particular qualities that it came to embody. "Muses are fickle," she writes, with earned wisdom,

> and many a writer, peering into the void, has escaped paralysis by ascribing the creative responsibility to a talisman: a lucky charm, a brand of paper, but most often a writing instrument. Am I writing well? Thank my pen. Am I writing badly? Don't blame me, blame my pen. By such displacements does the fearful imagination defend itself. (88)

Having so enunciated, Fadiman follows with illustrations from Woolf, Goethe, Kipling, and Sir Walter Scott. Then she turns autobiographical, completing the mixture, cementing the impurity—the writing is charming, witty, clever, finely balanced, intelligent, sensitive, all the while ringing true to a genuine lover of the pen (although I would emphasize the smoothness of the flow, rather than the width of the line made):

> I know how Kipling felt. Pen-bereavement is a serious matter. Ten years ago, my pen disappeared into thin air. Like a jealous lover, I never took it out of the house, so I have always believed that in rebellion against its purdah it rolled into a hidden crack in my desk. A thousand times have I been tempted to tear the desk apart; a thousand times have I resisted, fearing that the pen would not be there after all and that I would have to admit it was gone forever. For a time I haunted shops that sold secondhand pens, pathetically clutching an old writing sample and saying, "This is the width of the line I want." I might as well have carried a photograph of a dead lover and said, "Find me another just like this." Along the way I learned that my pen had been a Parker 51, circa 1945. Eventually I found one that matched mine not only in vintage but in color. But after this parvenu came home with me, it swung wantonly from scratching to spattering, unable, despite a series of expensive repairs, to find the silken mean its predecessor had so effortlessly achieved. Alas, it was not the reincarnation of my former love; it was a contemptible doppelgänger. Of course, I continued to write, but ever after, the feat of conjuring the first word, the first sentence, the first paragraph, has seemed more like work and less like magic. (89–90)

The silken mean effortlessly achieved—the way of an "easy pen," the way alike of the essay, truly understood. Such phrasing, such a paragraph, alerts us to the *familiar* mode of essaying that Fadiman is following; only she, Joseph Epstein, and Sam Pickering seem to be working effectively there. Love marks her account of pen passion, the same kind of response that I long ago described as marking the essayist's work—and that is by definition characteristic of such an *amateur*, notably including "the common reader."

Appropriately Fadiman emphasizes "the physical act of writing." She speculates on how it felt to write, in the eighteenth century, say, with a feather "(preferably the second or third follicle from a bird's left wing, which curved away from a right-handed writer)" (90). Then she writes, developing the love metaphor that marks this "perennial" (for another, striking instance of the metaphor, see the novelist-memoirist Edmund White):

> For those who consider writing a form of romance, a Parker 51 can't hold a candle to a crow's feather, but it sure beats a cartridge pen, a ballpoint, a felt-tip, or a roller-ball, especially those disposable models that proclaim, "Don't get too attached, I'm only a one-night stand." Pencils are fine in their way, but I prefer the immutability of ink. . . . Richard Selzer, the surgeon-essayist, fills his fountain pen from a lacquered Chinese inkwell with a bronze dragon on its lid. To feed the genie that he says dwells therein, he mixes, from an old recipe, his own version of Higgins Eternal Ink, the brand he used when he learned to write sixty years ago. Eternal! To what other medium could that word possibly be applied? (91)

Not even a typewriter, she argues—for all her writer-mother's devotion to a near-ancient Underwood. But, Fadiman confesses (these *are*, according to her subtitle, "confessions"), she has adapted, neither the first nor the last to succumb to a siren's song—note the implicit acknowledgment of the needed compatibility of form and instrument:

> These days I use a computer. I am using it to write this essay, even though I should really be using a hand-whittled crow's feather. It is, as many writers have noted, unparalleled for revision. Because it makes resequencing so easy, it enables me to recognize structural flaws that once would have been invisible, blocked from my imagination by the effort and violence of the old cut-and-paste method. (92)

That last sentence makes for the strongest argument for the computer that I know, capturing precisely the heart of my own experience. Fadiman continues, so balanced as to achieve that "silken mean" she has brilliantly described, and never minimizing the intimate, ineluctable relation between writing and reading:

> I am surprised by how much I like my computer, but I will never love it. I have used several; they seem indistinguishable. When you've seen one pixel you've seen them all. As a reader, I often feel I can detect the spoor of word processing in books, particularly long ones. The writers, no longer slowed by having to change their typewriter ribbons, fill their fountain pens, or sharpen their quills, tend to be prolix. I am especially suspicious of word-processed letters, which smell of boilerplate. Word-processed addresses are even worse. What a pleasure it is to open one's mailbox and find a letter from an old friend whose handwriting on the envelope is as instantly recognizable as a face! (93)

Fadiman concludes "Eternal Ink" with a paragraph extending the points just above. She writes of having recently finished a book whose first sentence she made with a pen on her birthday in 1991. Since then, she has "transitioned" to the word processor, and she says of the effects:

> I had planned to write the last page of the book in longhand, partly for the sake of sentiment, partly because I thought a pen might decelerate my prose and make me especially careful where it counted most. But when the morning finally arrived after a furious all-nighter, and I realized I was only an hour from the end, I could no more halt my pell-mell rush than a marathoner could be persuaded to sniff the roses that lined the last hundred yards of the racecourse. It was too late. My old pen may be buried somewhere in my desk, but my Daemon, who surely would never take up residence in a Compaq Deskpro 4/25 Model 120, has either fled the premises or is now—I've got my fingers crossed—living inside me. (93–94)

A tale written against arrogance, "Eternal Ink": against the hubris of technophilia and the smugness of technophobia alike—"silken mean."

Vigorous writing is concise. A sentence should contain no unnecessary words, a paragraph no unnecessary sentences, for the same reason that a drawing should have no unnecessary lines and a machine no unnecessary parts. This requires not that the writer make all his sentences short, or that he avoid all detail and treat his subjects only in outline, but that every word tell.
—Will Strunk, quoted by E. B. White, *The Elements of Style*

To compose our character is our duty, not to compose books, and to win, not battles and provinces, but order and tranquillity in our conduct. Our great and glorious masterpiece is to live appropriately.
—Montaigne, "On Experience"

Acts of Simplifying

Sense and Sentences in Sam Pickering's "Composing a Life"

SAM PICKERING MAY STILL BE BETTER KNOWN as the teacher on whom *Dead Poets Society* is based than as an essayist. Robin Williams's portrayal of John Keating, dedicated prep-school teacher, engaged millions; Pickering's volumes of personal and familiar essays also engage and endear for many of the same reasons. The movie is truthful to the character of the teacher-essayist, for years now professor of English at the University of Connecticut. That character is a definite persona, closely related although not identical to the man.

Of all of Pickering's essays, I have chosen to read here the last in *A Continuing Education*, published in 1985 and still in my judgment his best collection (I do very much admire his recent book *Letters to a Teacher*). "Composing a Life" lacks the home-spun yarns and local color of Pickering's later essays as well as the indulgent preoccupation with mundane details of a man's life—all to the good. It is a fine piece of writing, at times reminiscent of his predecessors, with its quintessentially essayistic notion of the ultimate value of sentences, shared with the likes of Annie Dillard, Cynthia Ozick, and E. B. White, who once allowed that *Walden* is made of sentences, "a collection of certified sentences," sometimes errant but all of them "indestructible" (239).

The humor is more raucous than White's, sometimes a bit coarse, the self-effacement not as delicate. The humor nevertheless recalls the master, along with the characterizations, especially that of Vicki, Pickering's deadpan wife, the daughter of a Princeton English professor, with whom Pickering once taught. (Pickering also taught at Dartmouth and published a proper academic book or two before moving to UConn.) More so, much more so than White, Pickering makes essays out of his own writing. The humor is both prominent and foregrounded, the part to which I sometimes feel the whole is subordinate (never the case in White).

In "Composing a Life," with no stated reference to an even greater predecessor, the inimitable Michel de Montaigne, "father" of the essay, Pickering links meanings of the word "compose." "For fifteen years," he writes,

> I have taught writing. For ten of these years writing has taught me, and
> I have labored not so much to compose sentences as to compose my life.
> Hours at the desk and countless erasures have brought success. I haven't
> committed a comma blunder in almost five years, certainly not since I
> married my second wife. Happily I have forgotten what participles and
> gerunds are, but then I have forgotten most things: books, loves, and most
> of my identities. At my dining room table, dangling modifiers are not
> mentioned, and I ignore all question marks as my days are composed, not
> of lurid prose and purple moments, but of calm of mind and forthright,
> workaday sentences. (157–58)

By this point a third sense of "compose" has emerged, resonating with Montaigne's that a composed life is one of internal and external "order and tranquillity." I am not sure, however, that Pickering quite manages to earn the epithet that Montaigne applied to Seneca: "*ondoyant et divers.*" There is a great deal of cleverness in Pickering, who strives for effect, more so certainly than White, whose prose appears—although it wasn't—effortless. I sense more ego than in White, despite the latter's "confession" of self-centeredness and egoism in the foreword to the 1977 *Essays*.

"Composing a Life" focuses, perhaps too narrowly, on the relation between the simple life and the simple sentence. As an opportunity—or an excuse—to describe the folk of his essays, set in the South and redolent with quaintness, Pickering writes that "rarely do I use a complex sentence, and even more rarely do I live with complexity. In a simple style," he says, "I write about simple people, people born before the first infinitive was split and the wrath of grammarians fell upon mankind." But it is not simply that Pickering *writes* about simple folk and simple living; he also lives—imitates, perhaps—such a life himself (158). "In my seven years in eastern Connecticut," he vows, "I have lived simply, rarely traveling to Hartford thirty miles away. Years ago," however, before his sea change, "simplicity held little attraction for me, and I traveled far afield seeking the confusion of mixed metaphors and long, run-on sentences"—for example, Syria. "When I began to write," he writes, "I was taught to vary my style."

> "Use different sentence structure; be different people," teachers told me.
> And for a while I did that, meandering along slowly then darting forward
> only to turn back abruptly. . . . Here I would insert a compound sentence,
> there a noun clause, here a grey man of mystery, there a colorful eccentric.
> For years experimenting was good, and although I didn't publish much, I
> had many styles and identities. Now the older and simpler me stays home,
> and as my car is a family station wagon—an American made Plymouth
> Reliant—I have only one style, the solid, economical, fifty-thousand mile
> warranteed reliable style of the short declarative sentence. (159)

Of course, his own sentences *now* do not quite bear out Pickering's claim. Still, it is an affecting image of the writer (of essays) as a middle-aged man, settling, an embrace of the old-fashioned. Sam Pickering is nothing if not conservative.

Perhaps, better, libertarian. For such politically incorrect stances, Pickering is too often dismissed, unread. That is a shame, if not also a disgrace, but certainly a loss. What he says may appear merely quaint, even contrived, but it is worthy of the attention of writers and teachers of composing alike. He strikes a serious note in writing:

> Other kinds of sentences offend me and seem unsound and unsettling.
> Words, rules, and life confuse people. The simple style orders confusion,
> at first producing the illusion of control and then, after time, the reality.

When pressure makes a person bear down so hard that he or his pencil breaks, he should struggle to write simply. By doing so one can regain composure. (159–60)

It is not so much, here and elsewhere, that humor relieves the seriousness as that seriousness leavens the humor.

Pickering maintains that "thoughts about writing never fail to contribute to my composure," but he adds, almost immediately, "I am not always successful in composing things." He adduces, by way of illustration, the following extended account of such a difficulty, dramatized in the first sentence here, with its display of wit based on an obvious double entendre:

Sometimes words get out of hand and carrying me beyond the fullstops I plan spill over into the tentative world of the colon and expose parts of life that ought to remain buried. Some time ago I decided to write about my summers in Virginia. The essay didn't turn out to be the hymn to golden days that I envisioned. When it appeared in print, I read it and was disturbed. None of my periods worked. "Good country people," the essay began, "scare the hell out of me. Once I liked the country and thought that the closer a person was to the soil, the nearer he was to God. I know better now. The closer a person is to the soil, the dirtier he is." The essay bothered me until I read a note a boy handed in with a story he wrote as an assignment for a course I teach in children's literature. The students were told to write cheerful stories with positive endings. "I am sorry this is such a terrible story," the boy explained, "but I just couldn't think of a good one. They all kept coming out the other way around with Evil triumphing. I am a very disobedient person by nature." All people and sentences are disobedient; and after reading the note, I realized that words like human beings occasionally violated the best outlines. All one could do was erase, rewrite, and hope that evil would not triumph in the final draft. (160–61)

It is a good story, *story*, in fact, being Pickering's larger point, for in his essays the stories carry the thematic burden.

Writing and living again consort, and so Pickering reckons that one "has to revise life" also. By way of illustration, he cites his own growing ability to "master simple thoughts," a result of age accompanied by a growing tendency to "violate rules of grammar" (e.g., "When I first began to teach,

I railed against the error [confusing *it's* and *its*], attributing ignorance about the possessive to a left-wing conspiracy that was sweeping the nation and undermining the concept of private property") (161–62). Over forty now, he lacks the energy of his greener years. Urged to use the active rather than the passive voice, Pickering accepts that he lives "in the passive," consigning to the young the "attempt to manage lively active verbs and do all sorts of creative things to predicates." "For my part," he writes, with evident resignation, "I am content to be acted upon. Occasionally I ponder taking a forceful part in life but the fit passes. As one grows older, material goods become less important; as one learns the virtues of the oblique approach, direct objects disappear from life" (162). The "character" is studied and carefully constructed; carefully *constructed* as well is the wit that links ways of writing, parts of speech, and grammar to both larger issues of writing and the art of living.

From the last sentence I have quoted follows immediately the topic sentence of a new paragraph, Pickering carrying over the linguistic wit. The anecdote is one of his best, yielding a point not merely linguistic or simply witty, despite the dangling modifier of the fourth sentence.

> Age has taught me the value of a familiar, relaxed style and life, beyond direct objects. On weekends I run races. My goal is never to complete a race in the first fifty percent of the finishers. Unlike top road racers, my performance never disappoints me. Sometimes I am tempted to thrust ahead but I always resist. Last weekend as I trotted down a street, a young woman yelled, "you are so cute." To be honest, after hearing that I heisted up my legs a bit and pranced for a while, but then as soon as I was around the corner and out of sight, I settled back into a slow, comfortable rhythm and let a crowd of younger active runners rush by, chasing celebrity and trophies. (162)

What Pickering writes about grammar, its inevitable violation by the aging and its alleged ultimate unimportance, strikes me as finally untenable, well below the level of his following account of writing, despite the exaggeration and the linguistic high jinks:

> Like a good essay, the composed life has a beginning, middle, and definite ending. Youth can dream about the future and imagine a multitude of endings, and as a result usually can't write well. After forty, dreams stop and one buys life insurance. Instead of invoking visions of idyllic

pleasure, the ellipsis that looms ahead leads only to an erasure and an empty notebook. For the writer beyond forty the end is clear and nothing can change it. In contrast the past is infinitely malleable, and I often write about it, trying to give shape to fragments that cling to memory. In classes I tell students to write about the small things in the first paragraph of life and not worry about the conclusion. It will take care of itself. All writers should avoid shadowlands where things are not clear and simple. (163)

But Pickering is careful to acknowledge that there is at least one significant downside to the life made compatible with "a passive, simple style," at least for the essayist, even though compensation occurs:

A problem arises after one turns life into a series of balanced, short declarative sentences. Well-placed modifiers and proper subordination do not lend themselves to startling essays. The run-on life, like the sentence, breaks through propriety and occasionally stumbles into interesting constructions. I wondered if I would be able to write once my sentences were under control and my life simple. I should not have worried. Almost every day the postman brings me matter for essays. (165)

This typically takes the form of response from readers to his published work—which here he inexplicably refers to as "articles," not once but twice. Some of this response he records, ending the essay on a story.

I thus leave "Composing a Life" with various, sometimes conflicting impressions. The wit and the ingenuity never fail to impress; they are, of course, inseparable from the humor that I delight in. A reader new to essays may well be smitten—or turned off—by the perceived egotism and self-centeredness; both such readers will miss the value available to the seasoned reader, familiar with the form and read in its many incarnations.

Pickering's is clearly a *familiar* essay, marked by a lightness of tone, in his case exaggerated. One might be tempted to over-read: that is, to suppose Pickering's wilder moments are hyperbolic, even ironic. Perhaps on occasion, although I think him, especially in more recent essays, indulgent rather than sneaky. A Pickering essay is, in any case, an old-fashioned thing, little interested in confession, indeed reluctant to reveal or even acknowledge the darkness of full humanity. Hints will do, guesses accepted as inevitable. Of primary concern is the creation of an amiable yet crotchety character—both a persona and a personality. He must be interesting, and quirkiness is sure to interest, never mind how "real" or true to the author. The world of the Pickering essay is often thoroughgoing, thoroughly fictional: from the representation of the "speaker," to the idealization of wife Vicki, the patterns of response described, to the anecdotes that take that fictionality to another dimension.

In the opening essay in his following collection, *The Right Distance* (1987), Pickering expatiates on the familiar essay and the way "familiar essays have changed the way I live." The main influence he sees as on his academic career. Still what he writes in "Being Familiar" helps us to understand what he conceives of as his writing project:

> Scholarly writing and the familiar essay are very different. Instead of driving hard to prove a point, the essay saunters, letting the writer follow the vagaries of his own willful curiosity. Instead of reaching conclusions, the essay ruminates and wonders. Rather than being right or informative, it is thoughtful. Instead of being serious, it is often lighthearted, pondering subjects like the breeding habits of beetles and, alas, of people. Of course as a person ages it becomes increasingly difficult to be scholarly or definitive. Truth seems beside the point, or at least amid the many doings of a day it seems to have progressively less to do with living. Being definitive, and perhaps even clever, is an activity for youth. Certainly it was in my case. . . . I now have trouble reaching conclusions. Instead of cudgeling stray dogs along the route I travel, . . . I stop and pet them. (9)

This is, I think, in a way admirable, and well said, and yet finally ineffective. Pickering gives too much away, supposing age forty a watershed, with life thereafter nothing much to speak of, certainly on a downward slide toward nothingness. At that age, moreover, or any other, truth is hardly "beside the point"; on the contrary, I would argue, at age sixty-something, truth is ever more to the point. And truth, simply, is not simple, but beautifully complex—and still comprehensible for all its complexity. That Pickering would almost certainly deny that he has any truck with truth, that his essay is light and even frivolous, a thing to be enjoyed rather than analyzed—such I find beside the point. We are free to discuss underlying values.

More remains to be said, focusing on the essay "Composing a Life," where three levels of representation join and sometimes vie. Consider: there is the declaration, the statement, the theme, the reflections, directly stated;

also the usually self-effacing autobiographical references; and finally the humorous anecdotes. Now, as I read his essay, I find the reflection separate from the stories, either the autobiographical or the anecdotal (and sometimes these two unite). The importance of this separation lies just here, and is by no means negligible: Pickering adds story in order to illustrate. Point is, then, not so much within the story as outside it, which it comes to augment. Story performs the essentially reflective function, serving as illustration rather than as source or inspiration.

Furthermore: most of the changes that Pickering details in his "composings" stem from a change in the form or kind of sentences he makes. Short, declarative sentences lead to a simple style and ultimately the essay as form, and that in turn produces some simplification in his life off the page. There are crucial differences here from the project of Michel de Montaigne, as Lydia Fakundiny has brilliantly described it. For Montaigne, she shows, "the doing, the writing itself, is both a path *to* knowing and a path *of* knowing" (678); as I write, says Montaigne, I am "forming my life," and that is "the greatest task of all" (qtd. in ibid.). For him, then, the essay becomes "a medium for the art of living" (ibid.).

For Pickering, contrariwise, I suggest, the primary and principal "self-fashioning" occurs on the page, for the sake of the essay. Those changes in sentences, from the complex to the simple, delivered in a voice more passive than active, with few if any conclusions in mind or available, affect the persona of the occasion, the personality of the writer as he appears on the page. The self is not, then, fashioned, or composed, only a fictionalized representation of that self.

The change even in that adopted persona comes about not as a direct result of a process of recognition. Change is represented not as occurring in the process but, rather, as added, afterward. We do not, in other words, apprehend a growth in understanding, only a certain adaptation that *parallels* and is analogous to the requirements of grammatical and linguistic adoption.

Every so often I make an attempt to simplify my life, burning my
books behind me, selling the occasional chair, discarding the
accumulated miscellany. I have noticed, though, that these
purifications of mine—to which my wife submits with cautious
grace—have usually led to even greater complexity in the long pull.
—E. B. White, *The Points of My Compass*

All through *The Elements of Style* one finds evidences of the author's
deep sympathy for the reader. Will felt that the reader was in serious
trouble most of the time, a man floundering in a swamp, and that it
was the duty of anyone attempting to write English to drain this
swamp quickly and get his man up on high ground, or at least throw
him a rope.
—E. B. White, "Will Strunk," later the introduction to
The Elements of Style

Caged Lions and Sustained Sibilants

E. B. White as "Recording Secretary" in
"The Ring of Time"

FOR THE READER NEW TO Elwyn Brooks White and the essay,
the oft-anthologized "The Ring of Time" may seem problematical, falling
abruptly and precipitously into two rather distinct parts and punctuated
with a three-paragraph postscript. For the reader familiar with White and
versed in the essay, "The Ring of Time" appears layered, carefully crafted,
and deeply resonant. For the college or university student, like some others acquainted with the author and conversant with the form of which
he was a master, this particular essay may seem characteristically wise, in
places very nearly brilliant, and a good "read"—even if it lacks the depth
of engagement of "Death of a Pig," about which I have written extensively
in *Tracing the Essay*, with its rich narrative, memorable characters, humor,
and wit, and the poignancy and power of "Once More to the Lake," with
its linguistic and structural successes. "The Ring of Time" *is* language and
form charged with meaning, to borrow from Ezra Pound, although not "to
the utmost possible degree."

"The Ring of Time," I find, invites just this sort of distinction, the recognition of such difference. Indeed difference plays at the very heart of this essay, thematically as well as structurally. At the same time, the essay begs comparison with those other essays of White that I have mentioned above.

Inescapable early in "The Ring of Time" is the essay's self-consciousness, perhaps off-putting to some readers, problematic to others. In fact, White begins his third paragraph with surprising if pregnant words—he refers to the scene that has captivated him, observing a circus rehearsal:

> In attempting to recapture this mild spectacle, I am merely acting as recording secretary for one of the oldest societies—the society of those who, at one time or another, have surrendered, without even a show of resistance, to the bedazzlement of a circus rider. As a writing man, or secretary, I have always felt charged with the safekeeping of all unexpected items of worldly or unworldly enchantment, as though I might be held personally responsible if even a small one were to be lost. But it is not easy to communicate anything of this nature. (143)

Note, first, that White admits to attempting to *re*capture the impressionable scene, carefully termed a "mild spectacle." Further, White describes his work as that of preservation. As a "secretary," his job, he understands, is (merely, modestly) to *record*.

To take such a task seriously is to go beyond, or, rather, to reshape and reconceive of the essay as form. For the essay, we have seen, is centrally reflective. In "The Ring of Time" White assumes a *declared* position less Romantic than Modernist. In "Death of a Pig," differently, invoking the idea of tragedy, farce, and performance to describe events, White says that he feels obligated to "do the accounting," repeating the essay's opening, where "I feel driven to account for" the days and nights spent with and devoted to his dying pig (17). At the end, following realizations owing to reflection, White concludes: "I have written this account in penitence and in grief, as a man who failed to raise his pig, and to explain my deviation from the classic course of so many raised pigs" (24). Guilt figures in this admission, this public confession of failure, textured as it is with sympathy and compassion born of clear-sighted understanding of man and pig's shared fate. "Account" may carry just the faintest hint of ledger books and profit-and-loss, but White's "account" transcends commerce, in an embodiment of warmth and humanity.

Such reflection as I am describing in "Death of a Pig" also occurs in "The Ring of Time"; and that means that, contrary to his claim, White is different from and more than a "recording secretary" here. He does not merely record; he also reflects, weighing experience, mining for meaning, which he then applies both to himself and the current political and social situation. What he records, is, in fact, *both* the events beginning with that warm afternoon in Florida, *and* his interpretation of the meaning and significance of the experience undergone (reflection plays an even greater role in the essay's second section, on the coming of integration to the South).

I must adduce a long account of the essayist's struggle with his form's true subject, time, here foregrounded.

> As I watched with the others, our jaws adroop, our eyes alight, I became painfully conscious of the element of time. Everything in the hideous old building seemed to take the shape of a circle, conforming to the course of the horse. The rider's gaze, as she peered straight ahead, seemed to be circular, as though bent by force of circumstance; then time itself began running in circles, and so the beginning was where the end was, and the two were the same, and one thing ran into the next and time went round and around and got nowhere. (144)

Immediately, though, White recognizes that truth lies elsewhere. The girl who has so entranced him "was too young to know that time does not really move in a circle at all." The mind realizes difference, itself also indebted to age (although "age" itself is a product of difference). White overtly records his "thought," even his (thinking) mind different from "himself":

> I thought: "She will never be as beautiful as this again"—a thought that made me acutely unhappy—and in a flash my mind (which is too much of a busybody to suit me) had projected her twenty-five years ahead, and she was now in the center of the ring, on foot, wearing a conical hat and high-heeled shoes, the image of the older woman, holding the long rein, caught in the treadmill of an afternoon long in the future. (145)

Here difference is represented—whether fully understood—as inseparable from similarity, for the girl exists as a repetition of her mother.

> "She is at that enviable moment in life [I thought] when she believes she can go once around the ring, make one complete circuit, and at the end be exactly the same age as at the start." Everything in her movements, her

expression, told you that for her the ring of time was perfectly formed, changeless, predictable, without beginning or end, like the ring in which she was traveling at this moment with the horse that wallowed under her. (145)

The literal ring having engendered these reflections on "the ring of time," White now—again—returns to his reverie, the fantasized made the foundation of the essay, reflection or thought offering the only *escape* from enchantment. Literal and metaphorical are mixed, confused, and exchange places: "And then I slipped back into my trance, and time was circular again—time, pausing quietly with the rest of us, so as not to disturb the balance of a performer" (145).

Balance may just be the issue, and so a lack of disturbance, public and private. Indeed, just before the essay breaks, White deftly links the circus performer(s) and the writer, both engaged in a delicate performance whose outcome may be just as portentous as, or more so than, that represented in "Death of a Pig." Here White turns again to the situation of writing and his assumed responsibilities. Writing and performing in a circus both take their power—their "light"—and their originality from within the individual performer/writer. Whereas rehearsal or practice is primary for the performer, for the writer reflection is a re-presenting that proves inadequate. In other words, observation—the presentation—*should* in and of itself reveal enough and all. Writing *is* a performing, White engaged here in a difficult and demanding "stunt" perhaps:

It has been ambitious and plucky of me to attempt to describe what is indescribable, and I have failed, as I knew I would. But I have discharged my duty to my society; and besides, a writer, like an acrobat, must occasionally try a stunt that is too much for him. At any rate, it is worth reporting that long before the circus comes to town, its most notable performances have already been given. Under the bright lights of the finished show, a performer need only *reflect* the electric candle power that is directed upon him; but in the dark and dirty old training rings and in the makeshift cages, whatever light is generated, whatever excitement, whatever beauty, must come from original sources—from internal fires of professional hunger and delight, from the exuberance and gravity of youth. It is the difference between planetary light and the combustion of stars. (145; italic added)

It is a difference, too, that for the writer consists in what he or she brings to the experience, reflection more valuable, White allows, than (mere) observation.

White had begun "The Ring of Time" with this sentence, this description: "After the lions had returned to their cages, creeping angrily through the chutes, a little bunch of us drifted away and into an open doorway nearby, where we stood for a while in semidarkness, watching a big brown circus horse go harumphing around the practice ring" (142). The essay thus opens in (semi)darkness, and the first section closes with "light." Moreover the lions mentioned in the very first phrase reappear, with a vengeance, in the first paragraph of the next, quite different, section—of course, "cages" have just been mentioned in the passage quoted above. Words are indeed now the matter.

And White starts off, unaccountably to some, with words, sounds, even letters. He is every bit as expressive as the young poet Alexander Pope, in *An Essay on Criticism*, exuberant, exorbitant, indulgent in showing how—and that—"The *Sound* must seem an *Eccho* to the *Sense*" (365):

> The South is the land of the sustained sibilant. Everywhere, for the appreciative visitor, the letter "s" insinuates itself in the scene: in the sound of sea and sand, in the singing shell, in the heat of sun and sky, in the sultriness of the gentle hours, in the siesta, in the stir of birds and insects. (145–46)

There is, however, something more, and different, and White may be seen as admitting upfront a difference within his essay between manner and matter and between the essay and its parts. He is about to complicate and mitigate this difference with the return to lions, mentioned in the essay's opening phrase (see Robert L. Root Jr.'s interpretation in his recent, quite valuable study *E. B. White: The Emergence of an Essayist*). That first sentence, incidentally, enacts what its says, the sibilants contrasted with the sharpness of the sounds in the main clause:

> In contrast to the softness of its music, the South is also cruel and hard and prickly. A little striped lizard, flattened along the sharp green bayonet of a yucca, wears in its tiny face and watchful eyes the pure look of death and violence. And all over the place, hidden at the bottom of their small

sandy craters, the ant lions lie in wait for the ant that will stumble into their trap.

The following parenthesis expatiates on, while distinguishing, the types of lions prominent in the South. With the human sort, the issue of segregation is broached, which literalizes, as it legalized, difference.

> (There are three kinds of lions in this region: the lions of the circus,
> the ant lions, and the Lions of the Tampa Lions Club, who roared their
> approval of segregation at a meeting the other day—all except one, a Lion
> named Monty Gurwit, who declined to roar and thereby got his picture in
> the paper.) (146)

With this paragraph, especially through the return to and expansion upon the word and idea "lions," White has taken a substantial step toward *integrating* the separate (but unequal?) parts of "The Ring of Time" (a perception inspired by my student Nedra Rogers, herself a poet and an essayist).

A visitor from the North, of course (see his poignant account of difference in "What Do Our Hearts Treasure?"), White first observes how things take their time in the South: "The Southern dawn," he begins, "is a pale affair, usually, quite different from our northern daybreak. It is a triumph of gradualism; night turns to day imperceptibly, softly, with no theatrics. It is subtle and undisturbing" (146). As a Southerner myself, with nearly forty years spent in the Midwest, I can attest to the truth of White's characterization. He seems to have learned a little something from the South, for he introduces integration gradually, softly—indeed the first section of the essay may be seen as an indirect way to this, perhaps his true subject in this essay. In fact, not until nearly a page after the mention of segregation does White utter the word "integration." He has slyly returned to the opening section by mentioning again the young circus rider, pretty much in passing. Now he edges up on the political and social issue, thus:

> On many days, the dampness of the air pervades all life, all living.
> Matches refuse to strike. The towel, hung to dry, grows wetter by the hour.
> The newspaper, with its headlines about integration, wilts in your hand
> and falls limply into the coffee and the egg. Envelopes seal themselves.
> Postage stamps mate with one another as shamelessly as grasshoppers. But
> most of the time the days are models of beauty and wonder and comfort,
> with the kind sea stroking the back of the warm sand. (146–47)

Via the active voice, White reveals the South's passivity, his own manner nevertheless indirect.

With the description—in 1956—of his status as "a beachcomber from the North," White takes up directly for the first time the difficult issue, apparently impervious to the weight of his own surname. To such a person as himself, he says, ingenuously I think, "the race problem has no pertinence, no immediacy." As a reconstructed Southerner, I find this frankly offensive, for he suggests that the North is exempt from racial discrimination— patently nonsense. Moreover "the race problem," itself a distancing phrase, is *everybody*'s problem! White's explanation, or excuse, for his noninvolvement, or disengagement, is equally shallow and disingenuous, as well as vaguely contradictory: "As a guest, I mind my manners and do not criticize the customs of my hosts. It gives me a queer feeling, though, to be at the center of the greatest social crisis of my time and see hardly a sign of it. Yet," he continues, "the very absence of signs seems to increase one's awareness." Here, he concludes, "I have had only two small encounters with 'color' " (147). One was with a "colored" laundry woman, who, in a show of much more than manners, "showed up one day with some laundry of ours that she had consented to do for us, and with the bundle she brought a bunch of nasturtiums." The Whites, with whatever graciousness, accepted the flowers and then asked the woman about her daughter, who, they learned, "was at Kentucky State College, studying voice"—voice *is* the issue, whether or not sufficiently noted by the essayist (ibid.).

The other encounter makes White look a bit less self-satisfied, and yet, or so it seems some fifty years later and in a different world altogether, he remains complicitous:

> The other encounter was when I was explaining to our cook, who is from Finland, the mysteries of bus travel in the American Southland. I showed her the bus stop, armed her with a timetable, and then, as a matter of duty, mentioned the customs of the Romans. "When you get on the bus," I said, "I think you'd better sit in one of the front seats—the seats in back are for colored people." A look of great weariness came into her face, as it does when we use too many dishes, and she replied, "Oh, I know—isn't it silly!"

Her remark, White reckons, probably correctly, is telling, for "people are, if anything, more touchy about being thought silly than they are about being thought unjust" (147).

The time, again, is 1956, the year of the Supreme Court's monumental decision in *Brown vs. Board of Education* outlawing segregation in public schools. White now takes (mild and politic) exception to "the recent manifesto of Southern Congressmen in support of the doctrine of 'separate but equal,' " which, they claimed, was "founded on 'common sense' " (147–48). The essayist then homes in, focusing the discussion by turning it from segregation to integration and, more particularly, the relation of the latter to acceptance of such change as his previous reflections affirmed as inevitable. Nowhere is White's historical relativism clearer—this alongside now-undeniable sensitivity and compassion:

> The sense that is common to one generation is uncommon to the next. Probably the first slave ship, with Negroes lying in chains on its deck, seemed commonsensical to the owners who operated it and to the planters who patronized it. But such a vessel would not be in the realm of common sense today. The only sense that is common, in the long run, is the sense of change—and we all instinctively avoid it, and object to the passage of time, and would rather have none of it.

Yet the South especially feels impervious to change, attractively so, White admits. You are tempted here, in fact, "to duck the passage of time" (148).

White concludes the essay "proper" on this note, circling back to its beginning. Now, though, at least White is undeluded.

> Lying in warm comfort by the sea, you receive gratefully the gift of the sun, the gift of the South. This is true seduction. The day is a circle— morning, afternoon, and night. After a few days I was clearly enjoying the same delusion as the girl on the horse—that I could ride clear around the ring of day, guarded by wind and sun and sea and sand, and be not a moment older. (148)

Oh those sustained sibilants, among them "seduction." White suggests that he has been "seduced" into the manners that keep him from objecting to segregation.

Not for the first time in his essays, White adds a postscript, dated April 1962. The practice is neither quite common nor indeed unusual, the *Essays* of 1977 showing five other instances ("Home-Coming," incidentally dated the same; "Coon Tree," dated the previous month; "Bedfellows," June of that year; "Sootfall and Fallout," May 1962; and "The Railroad," the same month and year). At least with regard to the essay presently under consideration, we can say that adding a postscript seems entirely appropriate, perhaps even necessary, for in updating White accentuates change and with it the movement of time that has been his theme.

The postscript is relatively short, consisting of three paragraphs. White begins with precisely the changes to Fiddler Bayou in the intervening six years; these are mainly the result of "development." "But despite man's encroachment," he writes, "Nature manages to hold her own and assert her authority." In fact, "the birds and the crabs accommodate themselves quite readily to the changes that have taken place" (148). As to men and women, whom White links to the animals:

> The Ringling circus has quit Sarasota and gone elsewhere for its hibernation. A few circus families still own homes in the town, and every spring the students at the high school put on a circus, to let off steam, work off physical requirements, and provide a promotional spectacle for Sarasota. At the drugstore you can buy a postcard showing the bed John Ringling slept in. *Time has not stood still for anybody but the dead,* and even the dead must be able to hear the acceleration of little sports cars and know that *things have changed.* (148–49; italics added)

White ends the postscript, and thus the essay (for the postscript *belongs* with and constitutes an *integral* part of it), brilliantly. He directly connects creature and place: "one of the creatures most acutely aware of the passing of time is the *fiddler* crab himself" (149; italics added). This information he got, not from Southern lore, but from, he readily acknowledges, the *New York Times,* "which has the animal kingdom ever in mind." White then summarizes the fiddler crab's necessary capacity, ending with a declaration of the necessity of adaptation to inevitable change, this too expressed more or less indirectly—and effectively. Color is precisely the matter.

> Tiny spots on his body enlarge during daytime hours, giving him the same color as the mudbank he explores and thus protecting him from his enemies. At night the spots shrink, his color fades, and he is almost invisible in the light of the moon. These changes are synchronized with the tides, so that each day they occur at a different hour. A scientist who experimented with the crabs to learn more about the phenomenon discovered that even when they are removed from their natural environment

and held in confinement, the rhythm of their bodily change continues uninterrupted, and they mark the passage of time in their laboratory prison, faithful to the tides in their fashion. (149)

The fiddler crabs are, of course, programmed, but humans, too, adapt—as White shows that he did to Southern "customs."

One reason that the ending works so well, I think, is that it is *observation*, rather than reflection: White simply, surely, presents, without (editorial) comment. It is hardly impersonal, of course. Indeed the postscript, in "The Ring of Time" and elsewhere in the *Essays*, is based in observation and so almost exclusively descriptive. "The writing man," he suggested earlier in "The Ring of Time," *is* a "secretary," a steward as well, then, who is inevitably called upon to give testimony. So a "recording secretary" is therefore charged with preserving and keeping alive, or, as he puts it, "charged with the safekeeping of all unexpected items of worldly or unworldly enchantment, as though I might be held personally responsible if even a small one were to be lost." With the postscript to "The Ring of Time" White effectively and successfully discharges his duties to "the oldest of societies"—the *human* race.

"But," said Adam, "I've seen pretty clear, ever since I was a young un, as religion's something else besides notions. It isn't notions sets people doing the right thing—it's feelings." . . . sympathy—the one poor word which includes all our best insight and our best love.
—George Eliot, *Adam Bede*

Her Oyster Knife Sharpened

Control of Tone in Zora Neale Hurston's
"How It Feels to Be Colored Me"

ZORA NEALE HURSTON'S SPLENDID, taut "How It Feels to Be Colored Me" is by no means the only essay to begin slowly, with a lengthy, seemingly disproportionate description. E. B. White's on his teacher-mentor Will Strunk notoriously takes its time getting from a sluggish account of Manhattan and mosquitoes there in summer to the curt advice to "simplify, simplify, simplify" Thoreau brought to the act of composition. I have said elsewhere—in *Tracing the Essay*—that the essay as form is characterized by sneakiness, and perhaps it is that that prompts Hurston to delay her real subject until fully one-third through.

Actually "How It Feels to Be Colored Me" begins slowly only if you exempt the opening one-sentence paragraph and the first sentence of the next: "I am colored but I offer nothing in the way of extenuating circumstances. . . . I remember the very day that I became colored." She thus announces, asserts really, her theme at the outset, but rather than focus on the signal day mentioned, she describes ordinary life "in the little Negro town of Eatonville, Florida." There difference exists only in that "white people . . . rode through town and never lived there." Already Hurston establishes *control* as her subject: control of tone, control of feelings. White people rewarded Zora "generously of their small silver" for her entertaining them, whereas "the colored people gave no dimes. They deplored any joyful tendencies in me." Of course, Hurston leaves unstated that "colored people" had few dimes to give her. The whites, though, celebrated difference—kept as separation. "I belonged to them [the coloreds], to the nearby hotels, to the county—everybody's Zora." Before the age of thirteen, then, "the very day" that Zora became colored, she may have belonged to the colored people, but she was "everybody's Zora" (293).

Culture makes the difference, not nature: Zora Neale Hurston "*became*" colored. The essay's title reflects, embodies actually, this very tension. Pointedly it is not "how it feels to be colored *like* me." The focus is both highly individual and particular, and suggestive of the act of coloring a picture—which, in a way, is what Hurston herself does to the picture she draws of Eatonville in the essay's opening page, one of three in the essay. The discussion of colors—white, red, and yellow—in the final paragraph and the imagination of her face and body in the cabaret as painted red and yellow and blue ensure that the reader recognize that *color matters*; it *is* the matter.

In the fifth and final paragraph of the essay's opening section—extra, white space separates the essay into three parts—Hurston reveals the day that she became colored. She wastes no words, nor sentiment, in sure control of her focus, manifested in the change of pronouns:

> But changes came in the family when I was thirteen, and I was sent to
> school in Jacksonville. I left Eatonville, the town of the oleanders, as
> Zora. When I disembarked from the river-boat at Jacksonville, she was
> no more. It seemed that I had suffered a sea change. I was not Zora of
> Orange County anymore, I was now a little colored girl. I found it out in
> certain ways. In my heart as well as in the mirror, I became a fast brown—
> warranted not to rub nor run. (293–94)

The control appears not least in the wit and humor, here and elsewhere. Hurston declines to detail those "certain ways" in which she found out she was colored because her subject is, rather, how it *feels* "to be colored me," to become colored, to be sketched and rendered as different.

Then, after the first extra space, comes a magnificent paragraph made of Zora's own insistent, although never strident, distinction—in more than one sense, I dare say.

> But I am not tragically colored. There is no great sorrow dammed up in
> my soul, nor lurking behind my eyes. I do not mind at all. I do not belong
> to the sobbing school of Negrohood who hold that nature somehow has
> given them a lowdown dirty deal and whose feelings are all hurt about
> it. Even in the helter-skelter skirmish that is my life, I have seen that the
> world is to the strong regardless of a little pigmentation more or less. No,
> I do not weep at the world—I am too busy sharpening my oyster knife.
> (294)

Unlike James Baldwin, great essayist that he is, who seeks our sympathy, Hurston does not seem to care whether we like her—and that makes us like her all the more! The world is full of opportunity, she insists, "joyful" as she has always been. Her knife is an oyster knife, but knife nevertheless.

There is, she almost laments, always someone "reminding me that I am the granddaughter of slaves. It fails to register depression with me," for "slavery is the price I paid for civilization, and the choice was not with me." The sentence cuts two ways. Still Hurston accentuates the positive: "No one on earth ever had a greater chance for glory. The world to be won and nothing to be lost. It is thrilling to think—to know that for any act of mine, I shall get twice as much praise or twice as much blame" (294). As colored, she is, in this sense, precisely where she was in youth, on stage, although now the stage is "national."

Hurston displays the sympathetic imagination endemic to the essay. At the same time, you cannot but feel anger held in check, controlled by that more powerful capacity: "The position of my white neighbor is much more difficult. No brown specter pulls up a chair beside me when I sit down to eat. No dark ghost thrusts its leg against mine in bed. The game of keeping what one has is never so exciting as the game of getting" (294). The *feeling* is complex, a sensibility not so much refined, perhaps, as earned.

Difference matters. Declaring what she earlier described upon disembarking at Jacksonville, Hurston says: "I feel most colored when I am thrown against a sharp white background." "For instance at Barnard," she adds, quietly making the point that she has successfully employed her oyster knife. And yet she retains her color, declining to allow her "fast brown" "to rub" or to "run." Notice how quickly—abruptly—and deftly she turns from one kind of difference to another, this second sort based in her retained individuality and particularity: "Among the thousand white persons" — *persons* being more personal than "people" — "I am a dark rock surged upon, and overswept, but through it all, I remain myself. When covered by the waters, I am," she adds, echoing the Biblical declaration, "and the ebb but reveals me again" (294).

There follows a brilliant move, a set piece dramatizing racial difference. Nowhere is Hurston's power of sympathetic imagination greater, this capacity for "envisioning the stranger's heart," for *she thinks otherwise*: "Sometimes it is the other way around. A white person set down in our midst, but the contrast is just as sharp for me" — a remarkable admission-declaration, the word "sharp" resonant. The scene is a cabaret in Harlem. There, amidst the "chatting about any little nothing that we have in common," "my color comes." The account is taut, definitive. Hurston prompts me to share, to quote generously: having been seated by "the jazz waiters," Hurston and her white friend, she recounts, chat, listen differently, react even more differently. And so her "color comes":

In the abrupt way that jazz orchestras have, this one plunges into a number. It loses no time in circumlocutions, but gets right down to business. It constricts the thorax and splits the heart with its tempo and narcotic harmonies. This orchestra grows rambunctious, rears on its hind legs and attacks the tonal veil with primitive fury, rending it, clawing it until it breaks through to the jungle beyond. I follow those heathen—follow them exultingly. I dance wildly inside myself; I yell within, I whoop; I shake my assegai above my head, I hurl it true to the mark *yeeeeooww!* I am in the jungle and living in the jungle way. My face is painted red and yellow and my body is painted blue. My pulse is throbbing like a war drum. I want to slaughter something—give pain, give death to what, I do not know. But the piece ends. The men of the orchestra wipe their lips and rest their fingers. I creep back slowly to the veneer we call civilization with the last tone and find the white friend sitting motionless in his chair, smoking calmly. (294–95)

By this point, Hurston's reader understands the slowish opening page as a learned, perhaps "civilized" response: it *tells* in not getting "right down to business," thus becoming thematically significant, after all. Moreover the passage just quoted embodies the capacity of the imagination for sympathy as it effectively contrasts her imagined "painted" flesh with that coloration that had earlier *come*.

And the white friend's response to the animalistic? Already apparent in the last sentence quoted, it is the opposite, controlled to the point of unfeeling. Strong, "pure" feeling is precisely different from the control that civilization entails, and this remarkable essay is about civilization and the difference on which it indubitably rests. Hurston explains the difference that her white friend represents this way:

> The great blobs of purple and red emotion have not touched him. *He has only heard what I felt.* He is far away and I see him but dimly across the ocean and the continent that have fallen between us. He is so pale with his whiteness then and I am *so* colored. (295; first italics added)

These lines plunge—cut?—right to the heart of this essay, not just to its meaning but to its body and soul, its entire being, indeed. Difference distances, creating that control (or obliteration) of wildness that Thoreau, for one, sought to maintain—or recover. Color now appears as "in touch" with the nature that civilization changes. Of course, the irony here, fully exploited, is that civilization, with its difference, colored Zora.

The reader of "How It Feels to Be Colored Me," you and I, regardless of our color, I am emboldened to reckon, can do little more than Hurston's white friend. We only hear what she felt and succeeds in conveying: she dramatizes, and embodies, while we listen, and merely talk. The paragraph I last quoted, however, goes some distance toward making even me *feel*—with its own pulsating rhythms and sensuous evocations.

At times, Hurston then reveals, "I have no race, I am *me*." That lack of difference, its very eclipse, in fact, occurs precisely at the moment when, in his or her enchantment, the reader of "How It Feels to Be Colored Me" comes closest, perhaps, to realizing *his* difference from the author. When she "saunters" down "Seventh Avenue, Harlem City," she says, she transcends race; her "feelings" then are in check, and she *imagines* herself as "Peggy Hopkins Joyce on the Boule Mich [i.e., Boulevard St. Michel, in Paris] with her gorgeous raiment, stately carriage, knees knocking together in a most aristocratic manner." Then "the cosmic Zora emerges. I belong to no race nor time. I am the eternal feminine with its string of beads" (295). *Then* the world has, indeed, opened itself to her oyster knife, transcendence achieved if only in the (powerful) imagination.

Approaching the close, Hurston reports having "no separate feeling about being an American citizen and colored. I am," she asserts, "merely a fragment of the Great Soul that surges within the boundaries. My country, right or wrong" (295). This last sentiment, a strong declaration of patriotism, is inexplicable to many.

In a reflective mood now, Hurston clarifies: "Sometimes, I feel discriminated against, but it does not make me angry. It merely astonishes me." And so her difference from Baldwin. "How *can* any deny themselves the pleasure of my company? It's beyond me" (295). In these magnificent words appear dignity, honesty, our prized self-esteem, affirmativeness, and self-assertion—all, and more, without rancor or bitterness or arrogance. Hurston's question, her control of tone, here and throughout, ensure that we cannot deny ourselves the pleasure of her company. In her company for three pages, we have experienced pleasure.

What then remains is the last paragraph, which I shall quote in its entirety, affording Zora Neale Hurston almost all the last words, returning her to that long-ago time and place when whites "liked to hear me 'speak pieces.'" Whether we also *feel* here is something only you can answer, having perhaps only heard what she has colored for us. The allegory represents human beings, under the aegis of civilization, as a mixed bag—not unlike the form that is the essay (it is evidence of Hurston's art, her control of the composition, that she effortlessly and seamlessly, here and elsewhere, returns us to themes and ideas that play throughout, a master of resonance).

> But in the main, I feel like a brown bag of miscellany propped against a wall. Against a wall in company with other bags, white, red and yellow. Pour out the contents, and there is discovered a jumble of small things priceless and worthless. A first-water diamond, an empty spool, bits of broken glass, lengths of string, a key to a door long since crumbled away, a rusty knife-blade, old shoes saved for a road that never was and never will be, a nail bent under the weight of things too heavy for any nail, a dried flower or two still a little fragrant. In your hand is the brown bag. On the

ground before you is the jumble it held—so much like the jumble in the bags, could they be emptied, that all might be dumped in a single heap and the bags refilled without altering the content of any greatly. A bit of colored glass more or less would not matter. Perhaps that is how the Great Stuffer of Bags filled them in the first place—who knows? (295–96)

Who, indeed? The bag that is this paragraph seems a jumble; certainly the writing, as well as that written about, is mundane and ordinary, undistinguished, if you will—like diverse humanity. If there is not much difference, color, ultimately, in the great scheme of things, matters little. "The only wisdom we can hope to acquire," wrote T. S. Eliot in *East Coker*, the second of *Four Quartets*, "is the wisdom of humility: humility is endless."

Desmond MacCarthy . . . observes that Montaigne "had the gift of natural candour. . . ." It is the basic ingredient.
—E. B. White, foreword, *Essays*

Intuition tells me that our patients had fewer wound infections and made speedier recoveries than those operated upon in the airless sealed boxes where now we strive. Certainly the surgeons were of a gentler stripe. . . . To work in windowless rooms is to live in a jungle where you cannot see the sky. Because there is no sky to see, there is no grand vision of God. . . . [A] man is entitled to the temple of his preference. Mine lies out on a prairie, wondering up at Heaven. Or in a many windowed operating room where, just outside the panes of glass, cows graze, and the stars shine down upon my carpentry.
—Richard Selzer, "An Absence of Windows"

The Basic Ingredient

Candor and Compassion in Nancy Mairs's "On Being a Cripple"

NANCY MAIRS IS A GIFTED AND remarkable writer, none of her considerable body of work more remarkable than her first collection of essays, *Plaintext* (1986). Of the twelve, divided into three groups with the designations "Self," "Life," and "Writing," none is stronger, or more moving, than "On Being a Cripple." Mairs appears incapable of indulging in either conceit or in concealment, "one thing the essayist cannot do," according to E. B. White.

Early in "On Being a Cripple," Mairs addresses her decidedly "un-pc" choice of language to describe her condition, the result of multiple sclerosis. "To be fair to myself," she writes, immediately following the first essay in *Plaintext*, "On Having Adventures," "a certain amount of honesty underlies my choice."

"Cripple" seems to me a clean word, straightforward and precise. It has an honorable history, having made its first appearance in the Lindisfarne

Gospel in the tenth century. As a lover of words, I like the accuracy with which it describes my condition: I have lost the full use of my limbs. "Disabled," by contrast, suggests any incapacity, physical or mental. And I certainly don't like "handicapped," which implies that I have deliberately been put at a disadvantage, by whom I can't imagine (my God is not a Handicapper General), in order to equalize chances in the great race of life. These words seem to me to be moving away from my condition, to be widening the gap between word and reality. Most remote is the recently coined euphemism "differently abled," which partakes of the same semantic hopefulness that transformed countries from "undeveloped" to "underdeveloped," then to "less developed," and finally to "developing" nations. People have continued to starve in those countries during the shift. Some realities do not obey the dictates of language. (9–10)

Mairs's straight talk bears the marks of her teacher at the University of Arizona, Ed Abbey (she, incidentally, holds a PhD in English, having concentrated in the Medieval period). Alongside the candor—possibly inseparable from it—is compassion.

Mairs is not yet done. She proceeds to and with further reflections on words and her "condition." "Whatever you call me," she writes, with such clarity as comes only from thought and expression in sync, and that is now precisely her subject,

. . . I remain crippled. But I don't care what you call me, so long as it isn't "differently abled," which strikes me as pure verbal garbage designed, by its ability to describe anyone, to describe no one. I subscribe to George Orwell's thesis that "the slovenliness of our language makes it easier for us to have foolish thoughts." And I refuse to participate in the degeneration of the language to the extent that I deny that I have lost anything in the course of this calamitous disease; I refuse to pretend that the only differences between you and me are the various ordinary ones that distinguish any one person from another. But call me "disabled" or "handicapped" if you like. I have long since grown accustomed to them; and if they are vague, at least they hint at the truth. Moreover, I use them myself. Society is no readier to accept crippledness than to accept death, war, sex, sweat, or wrinkles. I would never refer to another person as a cripple. It is the word I use to name only myself. (10)

Mairs thus looks squarely, without blinders—beginning with herself. Like her teacher, the aforementioned modern-day Thoreau, Mairs tells the truth, as she grasps it: candid, careless of reputation (or so it seems), and unashamed.

"On Being a Cripple" implicitly (at least) raises critical questions. Mairs's occasionally brutal honesty—or candor—points to the form's grounding in truth. There is, of course, the issue frequently bruited about of nonfiction's commitment to fact, with one side claiming vociferously that there be no violation or even the slightest veering from the literal, the factual, and (in the case of the personal or familiar essay) the autobiographical. The other side, meanwhile, subscribes to the notion espoused by essayists like Edward Hoagland and Sam Pickering: all writing, nonfiction differing only in degree, engages in and is made of shaping—in Hoagland's finely crafted words, in "What I Think, What I Am," "an essayist soon discovers that he doesn't have to tell the whole truth and nothing but the truth; he can shape or shave his memories, as long as the purpose is served of elucidating a truthful point" (692). Of course, Pickering himself got into trouble once when he veered too far from the literal truth, fictionalizing his persona to the degree that readers found unacceptable.

Hoagland indirectly brought up another, related question when he wrote of spanking a girlfriend with a hair brush. That was a *confession*, and for a host of reasons we—nowadays especially—seem to want our essays virtually free of confession while we avidly consume memoirs that confess the most lurid and prurient experiences. The subgenre of the confession has a venerable history, extending at least as far back as Saint Augustine and morphing for a while into spiritual autobiography, a form of the distant past now hardly read or even considered. More striking, certainly, than Pickering's deviation from autobiographical truth, or even Hoagland's admission, is Nancy Mairs's candor. Elsewhere in *Plaintext*, she—unabashedly and without shame—recounts her love affairs, in her husband's face, as it were. George remains long-suffering, at least in my view; I feel no pity for him, however, but I do feel sympathy. Nor do I feel pity for Nancy herself, no more than she does.

This is one of those places where Mairs is most remarkable as a writer, I feel. I do not consider her admissions—and there are others—*confessional*.

She evidently feels no compulsion "to come clean," nor, I think, should she. She reports—without asking her readers to decide. She simply tells—although in so doing, she is not "telling all." The reasons for her telling lie with her art rather than with her sense of morality. This, I think, is no sophistical distinction. Contrary to E. B. White, then, I believe an essayist *can* indulge in deceit or concealment, although not without great risk. On the other hand, the representation—or, better, embodiment—of candor runs few artistic risks. Nancy Mairs is a master of candor.

In this essay, she writes openly of her life without the disease, then its onset, together with her completely unsentimental acceptance of life as "a kind of gift. I accept all gifts," she writes, plainly and simply (11). Then she adds, having described the effects of multiple sclerosis, "lest I begin to sound like Pollyanna . . . let me say that I don't like having MS. I hate it" (12). Mairs thus refuses to simplify—Thoreau's great admonition. She describes what she *can* do and then describes what she cannot, "this lively plenty [having] its bleak complement." Her further description is as engaging as it is moving as she manages to laugh at herself, including that most awkward situation of tripping and falling; the account is remarkably detailed—and unflattering, except for the candor with which Mairs can write about it.

> These two elements, the plenty and the privation, are never pure, nor are the delight and wretchedness that accompany them. Almost every pickle that I get into as a result of my weakness and clumsiness—and I get into plenty—is funny as well as maddening and sometimes painful. I recall one May afternoon when a friend and I were going out for a drink after finishing up at school. As we were climbing into opposite sides of my car, chatting, I tripped and fell, flat and hard, onto the asphalt parking lot, my abrupt departure interrupting him in mid-sentence. "Where'd you go?" he called as he came around the back of the car to find me hauling myself up by the door frame. "Are you all right?" Yes, I told him, I was fine, just a bit rattly, and we drove off to find a shady patio and some beer. When I got home an hour or so later, my daughter greeted me with "What have you done to yourself?" I looked down. One elbow of my white turtleneck with the green froggies, one knee of my white trousers, one white kneesock were blood-soaked. We peeled off the clothes and inspected the damage, which was nasty enough but not alarming. That part wasn't funny: The

abrasions took a long time to heal, and one got a little infected. Even so, when I think of my friend talking earnestly, suddenly, to the hot thin air while I dropped from his view as though through a trap I find the image as silly as something from a Marx Brothers movie. (13)

Exactly—and exactly rendered.

Without bitterness, rancor, or sentimentality, Mairs writes about "the acceptance and the assistance and, sometimes, the amusement of those around" her. She details her ordinary, daily life. Then doubt suddenly enters, breaking the narrative, and producing the reflections at which Mairs is so good. Nothing is ever simple, least of all Mairs's own responses. Notice how being a "cripple"—with all the power with which that word has become invested in the essay—forever returns to the fore.

> Faking. There's the rub. Tugging at the fringes of my consciousness always is the terror that people are kind to me only because I'm a cripple. My mother almost shattered me once, with that instinct mothers have—blind, I think, in this case, but unerring nonetheless—for striking blows along the fault-lines of their children's hearts, by telling me, in an attack on my selfishness, "We all have to make allowances for you, of course, because of the way you are."

Thus enters the matter that comes to occupy a thematic place nearly as prominent as does candor. Mairs continues:

> From the distance of a couple of years, I have to admit that I haven't any idea just what she meant, and I'm not sure that she knew either. She was awfully angry. But at the time, as the words thudded home, I felt my worst fear, suddenly realized. I could bear being called selfish: I am. But I couldn't bear the corroboration that those around me were doing in fact what I'd always suspected them of doing, professing fondness while silently putting up with me because of the way I am. A cripple. I've been a little cracked ever since. (15)

Along with this fear, according to Mairs, comes "a relentless pressure to please," some instances of which she proceeds to record (15).

The self-scrutiny has become intense, but I never feel navel-gazing, nor self-pity, nor a latent plea for special favor. What works against mere self-expression is Mairs's art, the fact that she is writing an essay. Form restrains, and saves.

Form, in fact, saves the writing from indulgence, just as Mairs's family wards off any tendencies or temptations to feel sorry for herself. Humor plays a large role, as is already apparent, in that formal control. Now, Mairs writes, for example, attesting to the self-control necessary in the face of sympathetic urges:

> Fortunately, at home no one much cares whether I'm a good cripple or a bad cripple as long as I make vichyssoise with fair regularity. One evening several years ago, Anne [her daughter] was reading at the dining-room table while I cooked dinner. As I opened a can of tomatoes, the can slipped in my left hand and juice spattered me and the counter with bloody spots. Fatigued and infuriated, I bellowed, "I'm so sick of being crippled!" Anne glanced at me over the top of her book. "There now," she said, "do you feel better?" "Yes," I said, "yes, I do." She went back to her reading. I felt better. That's about all the attention my scurviness ever gets. (15–16)

Mairs proceeds to write that "because I hate being crippled, I sometimes hate myself for being a cripple." She nicely describes "today's ideal woman" (16), something she says that she has never approached, even before MS. She pulls in fact no punches in detailing her appearance before and after, knowing no more of romanticizing than of self-pitying. Her descriptions approach the strength and effectiveness of her mastery of tone. Mairs's candor is matched only by her bravery.

> Like many women I know, I have always had an uneasy relationship with my body. I was not a popular child, largely, I think now, because I was peculiar: intelligent, intense, moody, shy, given to unexpected and inexplicable notions and emotions. But as I entered adolescence, I believed myself unpopular because I was homely: my breasts too flat, my mouth too wide, my hips too narrow, my clothing never quite right in fit or style. I was not, in fact, particularly ugly, old photographs inform me, though I was well off the ideal; but I carried this sense of self-alienation with me into adulthood, where it regenerated in response to the depredations of MS. (16–17)

The second half of this carefully crafted paragraph treats the "after," with perhaps even greater candor, the picture painted certainly unflattering but the painting just as certainly remarkable:

> Even with my brace I walk with a limp so pronounced that, seeing myself on the videotape of a television program on the disabled, I couldn't believe that anything but an inchworm could make progress humping along like that. My shoulders droop and my pelvis thrusts forward as I try to balance myself upright, throwing my frame into a bony S. As a result of contractures, one shoulder is higher than the other and I carry one arm bent in front of me, the fingers curled into a claw. My left arm and leg have wasted into pipe-stems, and I try always to keep them covered. When I think about how my body must look to others, especially to men, to whom I have been trained to display myself, I feel ludicrous, even loathsome. (17)

At her age, forty-three in 1986 when *Plaintext* appeared, Mairs writes, she does not worry much about appearance. After all, she concludes, when dressed up, rested, and made up, "I look fine." Then that "self-loathing I feel is neither physically nor intellectually substantial. What I hate is not me but a disease"—and "I am not a disease," she writes, with a note of (at once) acceptance, defiance, and triumph. MS may early on have seemed destined to determine "who I am," but no more. There is, however, no denying, or forgetting, that the disease is both chronic and incurable. Still: "Are there worse things than dying? I think there may be" (17).

The fact is, then, Nancy Mairs does not know, cannot know, and has had to adjust to that not-knowing, which itself points at once to the situation of the essay and to the human condition in general. For now, she *lives*, a fact that reveals no real heroism, just choice, the kind of choice that, for Søren Kierkegaard, represents freedom. "At the beginning," writes Mairs, evidently without formal religious consolation or the understanding that might have been expected to accompany her wide reading in Medieval literature and thought,

> I thought about having MS almost incessantly. And because of the un-predictable course of the disease, my thoughts were always terrified. Each night I'd get into bed wondering whether I'd get out again the next morning, whether I'd be able to see, to speak, to hold a pen between my fingers.

Knowing that the day might come when I'd be physically incapable of killing myself, I thought perhaps I ought to do it right away, while I still had the strength. Gradually I came to understand that the Nancy who might one day lie inert under a bedsheet, arms and legs paralyzed, unable to feed or bathe herself, unable to reach out for a gun, a bottle of pills, was not the Nancy I was at present, and that I could not presume to make decisions for that future Nancy, who might well not want in the least to die. Now the only provision I've made for the future Nancy is that when the time comes—and it is likely to come in the form of pneumonia, friend to the weak and the old—I am not to be treated with machines and medications. If she is unable to communicate by then, I hope she will be satisfied with these terms. (18)

Able to face the looming prospect of death, Mairs prepares for it the best she can; she is characteristically clear-sighted about what she does not want. Her understanding results in large part, I reckon, from the capacity displayed here to "get out of self" and to look upon "Nancy" with some objectivity.

As soon, though, as she waxes—here—nearly tragic, she pulls back and away, poking fun at that implacable, still-needing self. Thinking about the disease, she allows, "grew tiresome and intrusive, especially in the large and tragic mode in which I was accustomed to considering my plight." Busyness helped ("George and children and snakes and students and poems"), and she no longer had the luxury of indulging thoughts, fears, and anticipation and anxiety. Moreover "the richer my life became, the funnier it seemed, as though there were some connection between largess and laughter" (18–19).

But Mairs clearly knows one thing, no matter how many adjustments are made, and no matter how satisfactory they may seem: there is no final accommodation possible—"one never finishes adjusting to MS." But of course, with the distance of the impersonal for the nonce, "one does not, after all, finish adjusting to life, and MS is simply a fact of my life." Thus "no amount of worry or anticipation," she writes with neither finality nor triumph nor complete acceptance, but at the very least the capacity to say "I," "can prepare me for a new loss. My life is a lesson in losses. I learn one at a time" (19).

Learning requires patience, and patience is precursor to sympathy, also its confrere. Mairs's learned compassion appears, with striking force, as she reveals the capacity to put herself in her doctors' position. Imagine: in the midst of MS, to be able to commiserate with the doctor charged with attending your disease. Hers is that "sympathetic imagination" familiar in essays, as described by James Baldwin, who recounts his overcoming "bitterness" in order to arrive at his considerable capacity, and as incarnate in Richard Selzer, the surgeon whose capacity for compassion appears virtually limitless:

> The absence of a cure often makes MS patients bitter toward their doctors. Doctors are, after all, the priests of modern society, the new shamans, whose business is to heal, and many an MS patient roves from one to another, searching for the "good" doctor who will make him well. Doctors too think of themselves as healers, and for this reason many have trouble dealing with MS patients, whose disease in its intransigence defeats their aims and mocks their skills. Too few doctors, it is true, treat their patients as whole human beings, but the reverse is also true. I have always tried to be gentle with my doctors, who often have more at stake in terms of ego than I do. I may be frustrated, maddened, depressed by the incurability of my disease, but I am not diminished by it, and they are. When I push myself up from my seat in the waiting room and stumble toward them, I incarnate the limitation of their powers. The least I can do is refuse to press on their tenderest spots. (20)

By this point in the essay, Mairs's own powers as writer and as human being seem almost to know no limitations. Comparison reveals reason to be compassionate.

In the essay's penultimate paragraph, Mairs is candid about the compassion of which she is now capable. That candor extends to her not knowing quite how she came to acquire the capacity. She calls it "gentleness" and admits she did not have it before MS; it is, in any case, inseparable from such humility as marks the form in which she is working:

> Perhaps I'd have developed it anyway—how could I know such a thing?—and I wish I had more of it, but I'm glad of what I have. It has opened and enriched my life enormously, this sense that my frailty and need must be mirrored in others, that in searching for and shaping a stable core in a life wrenched by change and loss, change and loss, I must recognize the

same process, under individual conditions, in the lives around me. I do not deprecate such knowledge, however I've come by it. (20)

Hers is thus the classic tale, at once a confirmation of ancient truth and an enrichment by it. You learn through suffering; that we have known since childhood—or at least we have heard the truism. But there is more, of course, notably the truth in the truism, which proceeds from the value of suffering through something. What Mairs affirms is the presence of a process, whereby the sufferer becomes, in Cynthia Ozick's fine phrasing, able "to envision the stranger's heart."

In any case, one last time, Mairs evidently senses becoming too serious, and so she again modulates, never mocking, or deflating, but human, in context via comparison. That human response, represented as ordinary, acquires a quiet sense of victory, if not quite triumph. I afford Nancy Mairs the last words, which, happily, were only her beginnings:

> All the same, if a cure were found, would I take it? In a minute. I may be a cripple, but I'm only occasionally a loony and never a saint. Anyway, in my brand of theology God doesn't give bonus points for a limp. I'd take a cure; I just don't need one. A friend who also has MS startled me once by asking, "Do you ever say to yourself, 'Why me, Lord?' " "No, Michael, I don't," I told him, "because whenever I try, the only response I can think of is 'Why not?' " If I could make a cosmic deal, who would I put in my place? What in my life would I give up in exchange for sound limbs and a thrilling rush of energy? No one. Nothing. I might as well do the job myself. Now that I'm getting the hang of it. (20)

The test of a first-rate intelligence is the ability to hold two opposed ideas in the mind at the same time, and still retain the ability to function. One should, for example, be able to see things that are hopeless and yet be determined to make them otherwise. —F. Scott Fitzgerald, "The Crack-Up"

It began to seem that one would have to hold in the mind forever two ideas which seemed to be in opposition. The first idea was acceptance, the acceptance, totally without rancor, of life as it is, men as they are. . . . the second idea . . . that one must never, in one's own life, accept the injustices as commonplace but must fight them with all one's strength. —James Baldwin, "Notes of a Native Son"

[W]it . . . involves, probably, a recognition, implicit in the expression of every experience, of other kinds of experiences which are possible. —T. S. Eliot, "Andrew Marvell"

The Work of the Sympathetic Imagination

James Baldwin's "Notes of a Native Son"

JAMES BALDWIN'S FIRST, MAGNIFICENT, and highly influential collection of essays *Notes of a Native Son* invites comparison and contrast with Richard Wright's novel *Native Son*. The title essay of that collection, on the other hand, invites comparison with Zora Neale Hurston's much-anthologized essay "How It Feels to Be Colored Me." Baldwin's observation recorded above as one of my epigraphs invites a larger reflection, for his sense of the *sympathetic imagination*—my term, not his, but shared with Hurston nevertheless and worked out in the last few essays of the aforementioned collection—deserves placement and consideration alongside the more recognized observations of Fitzgerald and Eliot, which also stand as epigraphs here. Baldwin is onto something of the very first magnitude—his description calls to mind, for example, the capacious way of the essay, at the making of which he was an undenied master.

"Notes of a Native Son" begins with the links between father and son that will score the account of "Jimmy," along with those between his father's death and the birth of his last son, Jimmy's new brother; it traces, too, the links between these personal facts and events and, a month before the date in question, the awful fact that Detroit experienced "one of the bloodiest race riots of the century." The essayist observes quietly, opening the second paragraph, "The day of my father's funeral had also been my nineteenth birthday" (85). The essayist, in other words, does not put himself directly into the piece, except for the repeated first-person possessives, until the framework, context, and background—indeed, the major subjects—have been well established.

Here is the opening paragraph entire. Note how the personal and the private precede the public and the cultural, two sentences of the former opening onto two of the last, which associate the public and the private. The last sentence of the paragraph literalizes and concretizes the link, making it physical and direct:

> On the 29th of July, in 1943, my father died. On the same day, a few
> hours later, his last child was born. Over a month before this, while all
> our energies were concentrated in waiting for these events, there had been,
> in Detroit, one of the bloodiest race riots of the century. A few hours
> after my father's funeral, while he lay in state in the undertaker's chapel, a
> race riot broke out in Harlem. On the morning of the 3rd of August, we
> drove my father to the graveyard through a wilderness of smashed plate
> glass. (85)

"Notes of a Native Son" is, in fact, an *autobiographical essay*: both essay and autobiography brilliantly worked into one (on this point, see further Lydia Fakundiny's fine discussion in *Encyclopedia of the Essay*).

Reflecting on the day of his father's funeral, his own birthday, Jimmy links the (aftermath of) the violence done in Harlem to the violence his father perpetrated on his large family—the acts of violence, perpetrators and victims mixed together, and mixed up, like the observable chaos on the streets. Jimmy may very well tell about one sort and act of violence by describing the other.

> As we drove him to the graveyard, the spoils of injustice, anarchy, discon-
> tent, and hatred were all around us. It seemed to me that God himself
> had devised, to mark my father's end, the most sustained and brutally

discordant of codas. And it seemed to me, too, that the violence which rose all about us as my father left the world had been devised as a corrective for the pride of his eldest son. I had declined to believe in that apocalypse which had been central to my father's vision; very well, life seemed to be saying, here is something that will certainly pass for an apocalypse until the real thing comes along. I had inclined to be contemptuous of my father for the conditions of his life, for the conditions of our lives. When his life had ended I began to wonder about that life and also, in a new way, to be apprehensive about my own. (85–86)

A magnificent setting of the stage, this paragraph rather dramatically introduces the notion of the apocalyptic and thereby places the past and the ensuing events in the largest of contexts. The religious will count here, somehow, for all of the essayist's declared disbelief in formal Christianity. His narrative will, here, be a kind of *journey toward understanding*, complete with a scene or two of purgation, not on the grand scale, to be sure, of the paradigmatic Odysseus's visit to the Kingdom of the Dead, but nevertheless resonant and telling. Religion figures deeply in this essay, not just because Jimmy's father was a masterful preacher, in whose footsteps the essayist was once expected to follow, but also because "Notes of a Native Son" functions in a manner the literary and secular equivalent perhaps to the sacred understanding of the Incarnation. Jimmy Baldwin, in other words, writes of a journey toward understanding of Incarnation, without the *the*—and he does so because he is, unlike Joyce's Stephen Dedalus, no "priest of the eternal imagination"; that is to say, whereas Stephen in his formal rejection of *his* father and his religion remakes Christianity in his own image, *forging* a new and bastardized path, James Baldwin the essayist writes an analogy to Christian incarnationism.

"I had not known my father very well," writes the gifted, prodigal son. The reason he attributes to their shared "stubborn pride" (86). His father, says Jimmy, "was, I think, very handsome"; he was also "very black": "he knew that he was black but did not know that he was beautiful. He claimed to be proud of his blackness but it had also been the cause of much humiliation and it had fixed bleak boundaries to his life" (87). This last sentence is not characteristic Baldwin, whose sentences are frequently hypotactic, befitting the focus here on mental agility and intellectual and spiritual suppleness. At the beginning of this essay, however, his sentences are often not hypotactic, that style taking over as the essay becomes more and more discriminating and understanding. Blackness and biography also mingle, with increasing power.

Born in New Orleans, the father had become, "of the first generation of free men," a successful preacher of the Gospel (86). In another sentence without hypotaxis, Baldwin writes of his father the preacher: "He could be chilling in the pulpit and indescribably cruel in his personal life and he was certainly the most bitter man I have ever met" (87). This bitterness becomes the thematic center of "Notes of a Native Son." On the personal front, Baldwin admits that his father loved him: "in his outrageously demanding and protective way"; although he tried, he "never to my knowledge with any success" was able "to establish contact with any of us" (ibid.). As a result, "I do not remember, in all those years, that one of his children was ever glad to see him come home" (88)—a tragically sad indictment.

The present scene remains the drive to the graveyard that eventful summer day, and James Baldwin weaves back and forth between determinative past and current recognition.

> There was something in him, therefore, groping and tentative, which was never expressed and which was buried with him. One saw it most clearly when he was facing new people and hoping to impress them. But he never did, not for long. We went from church to smaller and more improbable church, he found himself in less and less demand as a minister, and by the time he died none of his friends had come to see him for a long time. He had lived and died in an intolerable bitterness of spirit and it frightened me, as we drove him to the graveyard through those unquiet, ruined streets, to see how powerful and overflowing this bitterness could be and to realize that this bitterness now was mine. (88)

The elder Baldwin thus becomes a synecdoche of the black situation and condition, indeed of the poison with the power to infect the entire race. In "How It Feels to Be Colored Me," Zora Neale Hurston deals with much the same subject, but shows very little bitterness, which nevertheless lies as coiled and contained anger in her essay. We do not see how she arrived at some understanding, nor is it part of that essay's project to show the process, but with Baldwin we see his working through bitterness and threatened self-destruction toward a sympathy magnificent in its capaciousness.

Away from home for more than a year when his father died, Jimmy had come to significant if partial understanding:

> In that year I had had time to become aware of the meaning of all my father's bitter warnings, had discovered the secret of his proudly pursed lips and rigid carriage: I had discovered the weight of white people in the world. I saw that this had been for my ancestors and now would be for me an awful thing to live with and that the bitterness which had helped to kill my father could also kill me. (88–89)

The recognition is chilling. Its power of representation derives, in part, from the hypotactic style of this last sentence.

Baldwin records a reluctant and difficult journey toward understanding his father, marked first by comprehension and, only over time and with effort, sympathy. His father had been ill for a long time:

> We had not known that he was being eaten up by paranoia and the discovery that his cruelty, to our bodies and our minds, had been one of the symptoms of his illness was not, then, enough to enable us to forgive him. . . . His illness was beyond all hope of healing before anyone realized that he was ill. (89)

The reader soon realizes, as I suggested above, that what Baldwin writes about his father, much of it anyway, applies to the public, cultural situation of race relations in the United States. His father's paranoia, that is, is also the white man's; as Baldwin insisted in his book *The Fire Next Time,* our illness might be "beyond all hope of healing before anyone realized" the fact, the truth, and the extent of that illness. The book *Notes of a Native Son* goes a long way toward revealing both illness and potential cure. As it turns out, poignantly and ironically, when his father "was committed, it was discovered that he had tuberculosis and . . . the disease of his mind allowed the disease of his body to destroy him" (90). His son's subject, in writing this essay, is to identify (in both senses) the disease of the individual body and that of the body politic.

After representing his father distrusting a white, female teacher, who befriended Jimmy at age nine and introduced him to the theater, Baldwin turns to his own story and evolution during the year preceding; that year "had made a great change in my life," for he "had been living in New

Jersey, working in defense plants, working and living among southerners, white and black" (92). Central in Jimmy's growth in understanding was this: "I learned in New Jersey that to be a Negro meant, precisely, that one was never looked at but was simply at the mercy of the reflexes the color of one's skin caused in other people" (93)—not exactly invisibility, *pace* Richard Wright, but *precisely* what Baldwin reveals. Precision is itself precisely the issue in and of "Notes of a Native Son": that is, realizing exactly before it is too late.

That year in New Jersey, moreover, writes James Baldwin, reflecting in something less than tranquility, making the point with far fewer coordinate sentences, and now taking upon himself such disease as was heretofore the affliction of his father,

> lives in my mind as though it were the year during which, having an unsuspected predilection for it, I first contracted some dread, chronic disease, the unfailing symptom of which is a kind of blind fever, a pounding in the skull and fire in the bowels. Once this disease is contracted, one can never be really carefree again, for the fever, without an instant's warning, can recur at any moment. It can wreck more important things than race relations. There is not a Negro alive who does not have this rage in his blood—one has the choice, merely, of living with it consciously or surrendering to it. As for me, this fever has recurred in me, and does, and will until the day I die. (94)

Then comes the essay's pivotal and most vividly realized scene. Baldwin very nearly succumbed. It was his "last night in New Jersey"; he and a white friend went out, in Trenton. After a movie, they chanced to enter "the 'American Diner,'" where Jimmy was denied service. His blood surging, his rage apparent with such ferocity as Zora Neale Hurston describes in the controlled environment of a Harlem cabaret, a striking representation of racial difference, Baldwin starts walking and continues, until he comes upon a "fashionable" restaurant, which he enters, taking a seat, all the while knowing that he will not be served. The waitress already appears frightened, "a note of apology in her voice, and fear": "This made me more murderous than ever," Baldwin mercilessly reveals about himself. "I felt I had to do something with my hands. I wanted her to come close enough for me to get her neck between my hands" (96), his desire anticipating that of the inhabitants of Harlem. Realizing that he "would have to strike from a distance," Baldwin takes hold of a half-full water mug and hurls it at her, with all his might. She ducks, it thus misses, and shatters against the mirror behind the bar. Suddenly, abruptly, his "frozen blood . . . thawed," he could *see* again, and he knew to be frightened himself, not least *of himself* (97). He therefore runs, as his friend told him to do—escaping what was as close as he would come to nothingness, or the heart of darkness.

Believing that he has betrayed that friend, Baldwin replays the events over and over in his mind, until he reaches a significant understanding, expressed now in language honest and plain, its power a product of that happy combination:

> I could not get over two facts, both equally difficult for the imagination
> to grasp, and one was that I could have been murdered. But the other
> was that I had been ready to commit murder. I saw nothing very clearly
> but I did see this: that my life, my *real* life, was in danger, and not from
> anything other people might do but from the hatred I carried in my own
> heart. (97–98)

The mind thus holds two quite different, and perhaps opposite, ideas together, at the same time. Thus ends the first section of "Notes of a Native Son."

The bitterness that had consumed his father James Baldwin feels in the air as he returns home. His account of Harlem then is precise, gripping, and perspicacious. He observes "the strangest combinations":

> large, respectable, churchly matrons standing on the stoops or the corners
> with their hair tied up, together with a girl in sleazy satin whose face
> bore the marks of gin and the razor, or heavy-set, abrupt, no-nonsense
> older men, in company with the most disreputable fanatical "race" men,
> or these same "race" men with the sharpies, or these sharpies with the
> churchly women.

Within the Black "community," difference collapses, and Baldwin struggles to understand:

> Seventh Day Adventists and Methodists and Spiritualists seemed to be
> hobnobbing with Holyrollers and they were all, alike, entangled with
> the most flagrant disbelievers; something heavy in their stance seemed to

indicate that they had all, incredibly, seen a common vision, and on each face there seemed to be the same strange, bitter shadow. (100)

There was, simply, a permeating sense that "everybody felt a directionless, hopeless bitterness" (101).

On July 28—Baldwin believes it was a Wednesday—he visited his father "for the first time during his illness and for the last time of his life." His first glimpse of him brings recognition of why he had so long put off the visit:

> I had told my mother that I did not want to see him because I hated him. But this was not true. It was only that I *had* hated him and I wanted to hold on to this hatred. I did not want to look on him as a ruin: it was not a ruin I had hated. I imagine that one of the reasons people cling to their hates so stubbornly is because they sense, once hate is gone, that they will be forced to deal with pain. (101)

As Baldwin travels to the hospital, alongside his father's older sister, he begins to feel what he understands later, perhaps in the act of writing: "Between pity and guilt and fear I began to feel that there was another me trapped in my skull like a jack-in-the-box who might escape my control at any moment and fill the air with screaming" (102).

In the hospital at last, Baldwin finds, with a mixture, I reckon, of relief and regret, that his father "was not really in that room with us, he had at last really embarked on his journey." His aunt tries to reassure him by telling him "he said he was going to meet Jesus": "I did not hear anything except that whistling in his throat." Appropriately the essayist then relates the ensuing hours without detail. When, the next morning, the telegram came, the house suddenly filled with "relatives, friends, hysteria, and confusion," and Baldwin exits, heading downtown: "By the time I returned, later the same day, my mother had been carried to the hospital and the baby had been born" (103). Thus ends the second section of "Notes of a Native Son."

The day of his father's funeral Baldwin spent in the downtown apartment of a girl he knew, "with whiskey and wondering what to wear that night" (103–4). The funeral seemed "of course . . . very long." The minister who offered the sermon presented "to us a man whom none of us had ever seen—a man thoughtful, patient, and forbearing, a Christian inspiration to all who knew him, and a model for his children." The essayist's reflections, looking back, wondering how others, relatives especially, now felt, what they thought—these perhaps surprise, although, of course, *we* now know the real son of that man:

> This was not the man they had known, but they had scarcely expected to be confronted with *him*; this was, in a sense deeper than questions of fact, the man they had not known, and the man they had not known may have been the real one. The real man, whoever he had been, had suffered and now he was dead: this was all that was sure and all that mattered now. (105)

As remarkable as this passage is, the following is even more so, seemingly bred by reflection on the sermon and deriving from newfound humility and understanding. The passage is stunning in its simple majesty, beginning with the first words here, themselves indicative of an achieved and proper—respectful—distance. But of course, the words are not simply Baldwin's; rather he has incorporated, and interpolated, the minister's, deliberately blurring the distance between himself and the emotional understanding represented by another:

> Every man in the chapel hoped that when his hour came he, too, would be eulogized, which is to say forgiven, and that all of his lapses, greeds, errors, and strayings from the truth would be invested with coherence and looked upon with charity. This was perhaps the last thing human beings could give each other and it was what they demanded, after all, of the Lord. Only the Lord saw the midnight tears, only He was present when one of His children, moaning and wringing hands, paced up and down the room. When one slapped one's child in anger the recoil in the heart reverberated through heaven and became part of the pain of the universe. And when the children were hungry and sullen and distrustful and one watched them, daily, growing wilder, and further away, and running headlong into danger, it was the Lord who knew what the charged heart endured as the strap was laid to the backside; the Lord alone who knew what one *would* have said if one had had, like the Lord, the gift of the living word. It was the Lord who knew of the impossibility every parent in that room faced: how to prepare the child for the day when the child would be despised and how to *create* in the child—by what means?—a stronger antidote to the poison than one had found for oneself. The

avenues, side streets, bars, billiard halls, hospitals, police stations, and even the playgrounds of Harlem—not to mention the houses of correction, the jails, and the morgue—testified to the potency of the poison while remaining silent as to the efficacy of whatever antidote, irresistibly raising the question of whether or not such an antidote existed; raising, which was worse, the question of whether or not an antidote was desirable; perhaps poison should be fought with poison. With these *several schisms in the mind* and with more terrors in the heart than could be named, it was better not to judge the man who had gone down under an impossible burden. It was better to remember: *Thou knowest this man's fall; but thou knowest not his wrassling.* (105–6; penultimate italics added)

Thus Baldwin has taken over, evidently, the minister's sermon—little hypotaxis here—and mixed it in with his own reflections; who is who and which is which are questions, the essayist suggests, little worth asking. In taking over and re-presenting the sermon, Baldwin at once shows his own skills as a preacher and evidently intends to propose his *essay* as a greater, more effective, more precise and perspicacious account than the minister managed, constrained as he was by his genre.

The son continues to reflect "while the preacher talked" (106). "My mind," he now writes, "was busily breaking out with a rash of disconnected impressions. . . . I thought I was going mad; all these impressions suspended, as it were, in the solution of the faint nausea produced in me by the heat and liquor." His father's favorite songs serve to transport him: "abruptly, I was with him, sitting on his knee, in the hot, enormous, crowded church which was the first church we attended": "I had forgotten," writes the son, "in the rage of my growing up, how proud my father had been of me when I was little" (107). A host of other memories flood him, including the fights. Then Jimmy remembers "the one time in all our life together when we had really spoken to each other." "You'd rather write than preach, wouldn't you?" his father had asked.

I was astonished at his question—because it was a real question. I answered, "Yes."

That was all we said. It was awful to remember that that was all we had *ever* said. (108)

A bit later, as the service nears an end, Jimmy is led up by one of the deacons to look into the casket—he had not wanted to go.

> I cannot say that it looked like him at all. His blackness had been equiv-
> ocated by powder and there was no suggestion in that casket of what his
> power had or could have been. He was simply an old man dead, and it
> was hard to believe that he had ever given anyone either joy or pain. Yet,
> his life filled that room. Further up the avenue his wife was holding his
> newborn child. Life and death so close together, and love and hatred,
> and right and wrong, said something to me which I did not want to hear
> concerning man, concerning the life of man. (109)

It is all mixed up, linked, bound together—including black and white, son and father, too.

Rightly, then, Baldwin returns to the larger, public situation. After the fu-
neral, as he was "downtown desperately celebrating my birthday," a Negro soldier had gotten "into a fight with a white policeman over a Negro girl" (109). Rumors were rampant—and wrong. The issue here, for Baldwin, is invention and lack of precision—he, differently, insists on *getting it down right*. Against the sordid rumors, Baldwin calmly and with circumspec-
tion writes—it is a telling indictment, marred only by the gratuitous slam against Southern white girls:

> The facts were somewhat different—for example, the soldier had not been
> shot in the back, and was not dead, and the girl seems to have been as
> dubious a symbol of womanhood as her white counterpart in Georgia
> usually is [sic], but no one was interested in the facts. They preferred the
> invention because this invention expressed and corroborated their hates
> and fears so perfectly.

The effect of the "invention" was like that of "a lit match in a tin of gaso-
line" (110).

In the event, matters turned out to be less devastating than might have been. The resulting devastation, anyway, mainly to white business estab-
lishments, it turned out, "was doing [no]body any good": "It would have been better [not to riot and loot], but it would also have been intolerable, for Harlem had needed something to smash." And "to smash something

is the ghetto's chronic need," prefigured, anticipated, and exemplified in Baldwin's own private experience in the New Jersey restaurant (111).

"Notes of a Native Son" moves to conclusion with a couple of pages of acute cultural analysis and criticism, delivered in the familiar calm tones and hypotactic sentences:

> If ever, indeed, the violence which fills Harlem's churches, pool halls, and bars erupts outward in a more direct fashion, Harlem and its citizens are likely to vanish in an apocalyptic flood. That this is not likely to happen is due to a great many reasons, most hidden and powerful among them the Negro's real relation to the white American. (111–12)

It is always with "the real" that Baldwin is concerned, concerned to defamiliarize and demythologize; the following lines powerfully instance the kind of thinking that Baldwin advocates, his own thinking scrupulous and meticulous with the prized precision:

> This relation prohibits, simply, anything so uncomplicated and satisfactory as pure hatred. In order really to hate white people, one has to blot so much out of the mind—and the heart—that this hatred itself becomes an exhausting and self-destructive pose. But this does not mean, on the other hand, that love comes easily: the white world is too powerful, too complacent, too ready with gratuitous humiliation, and, above all, too ignorant and too innocent for that. One is absolutely forced to make perpetual qualifications and one's own reactions are always canceling each other out. It is this, really, which has driven so many people mad, both white and black. One is always in the position of having to decide between amputation and gangrene. (112)

What remains, are two powerful paragraphs. The last I have used as an epigraph above, a resonant conclusion, indeed, *telling* what the essayist's journey has wrought. Preceding that is a paragraph only slightly less philosophical, though perhaps more imaginative, in any case requiring quotation here: Jimmy Baldwin is a writer, this essay a kind of apologia pro vita sua.

> "But as for me and my house," my father had said, "we will serve the Lord." I wondered, as we drove him to his resting place, what this line had meant for him. I had heard him preach it many times. I had preached it

once myself, proudly giving it an interpretation different from my father's. Now the whole thing came back to me, as though my father and I were on our way to Sunday school and I were memorizing the golden text: *And if it seem evil unto you to serve the Lord, choose you this day whom you will serve; whether the gods which your father served that were on the other side of the flood, or the gods of the Amorites, in whose land ye dwell: but as for me and my house, we will serve the Lord.* I suspected in these familiar lines a meaning which had never been there for me before. (112–13)

Baldwin thus reaches his most profound understanding, in this essay, this journey, at least; there is powerful difference, Jimmy as if empty but also *receptive*, ready perhaps as well to *conceive*.

All of my father's texts and songs, which I had decided were meaningless, were arranged before me at his death like empty bottles, waiting to hold the meaning which life would give them for me. This was his legacy: nothing is ever escaped. That bleakly memorable morning I hated the unbelievable streets and the Negroes and whites who had, equally, made them that way.

A truly remarkable point, this, concerning culture, followed by another, this one concerning the private and the individual. Baldwin has achieved, in the course of the essay, an ability to envision another's heart as his sympathetic imagination allows him to conceive of what truly matters as "the singular details of a single human life" and especially "the affliction of one human being" (Richard Selzer, "A Worm from My Notebook"):

But I knew that it was folly, as my father would have said, this bitterness was folly. It was necessary to hold on to the things that mattered. The dead man mattered, the new life mattered; blackness and whiteness did not matter; to believe that they did was to acquiesce in one's own destruction. Hatred, which could destroy so much, never failed to destroy the man who hated and this was an immutable law. (113)

Difference is, indeed, the issue, and interpretation the key to getting difference right.

The way toward both private and public health lies in that intellectual and spiritual capacity that Baldwin then describes, that I have adduced as epigraph, and that writers as different from James Baldwin as F. Scott

Fitzgerald and T. S. Eliot confirm. For Baldwin it is acceptance without complacency. The fight, and fight there will inevitably and always be, "begins, however, in the heart" (114), the province perhaps fully as much of the writer as of the preacher.

Following the sentences I have adduced as epigraph above, Baldwin ends "Notes of a Native Son" with these moving words about his heart now and the father who rests within it, a relationship he has worked through and, thankfully, shared, a relationship built on the acceptance of responsibility and of the necessity of witness:

> This fight begins, however, in the heart and it now had been laid to my charge to keep my own heart free of hatred and despair. This intimation made my heart heavy and, now that my father was irrecoverable, I wished that he had been beside me so that I could have searched his face for the answers which only the future would give me now. (114)

The book *Notes of a Native Son* does not end here. A third and final section, of four essays, follows, closing with the powerful "Stranger in the Village." This last essay concerns Baldwin's time in a tiny Swiss village, in which, evidently, "no black man had ever set foot" (159). In this essay, Baldwin fully, perhaps melodramatically, exploits black-white differences, his interest again in deconstructing "simplicity" (166) and revealing the "complex of tensions" that, instead, governs our relations. The problem he identifies trenchantly, if by now obviously: it is that tendency, especially in Americans, to deny "the darker forces in human life" and, in so doing, "to paint moral issues in glaring black and white" (174). I think Baldwin here becomes a little too *positive*, now *pushing* for tension, complexity, and non-oppositional thinking, voiding the very thing he seeks. "No road whatever," he writes, "will lead Americans back to the simplicity of this European village where white men still have the luxury of looking on me as a stranger" (175). By no means invisible now, Baldwin may have gone a bit too far, not in his denunciation of racism and injustice certainly, but in, as it were, stepping out of that middle way that *is* the hardest way of all to maintain. The book's very last sentence rings too positive in its embrace of difference that time has undeniably made: "This world is white no longer, and it will never be white again."

But that failure—if failure it be—only points up the significance as well as the necessity of Baldwin's concluding, and patterning, point in his greatest single essay. That greatness, it must be acknowledged, derives in considerable part from Baldwin's participation in what might be called a tradition, adding a black voice to a hitherto-white understanding: acceptance, "totally without rancor, of life as it is, and men as they are," without complacency or submission to injustice. *That* is extremely difficult to manage, no matter how easy it may seem. One must "hold in the mind forever two ideas which seemed to be in opposition" (113).

. . . almost literature and *almost* philosophy . . .

—Eduardo Nicol, quoted in Philip Lopate,
    The Art of the Personal Essay

Some, to whom Heav'n in Wit has been profuse,
Want as much more, to turn it to its use;
For *Wit* and *Judgment* often are at strife,
Tho' meant each other's Aid, like *Man* and *Wife.*
—Alexander Pope, *An Essay on Criticism*

"On a Line Between
Two Sturdy Poles"

Edward Hoagland's "What I Think, What I Am"

IN *THE ART OF THE ESSAY,* Lydia Fakundiny opines that " 'What I Think, What I Am' must be the best short essay in English on what an essay is." That may well be—and not only because most of the considerable number of essays on the essay are long. "Needless to say," Fakundiny adds, Edward Hoagland's essay, from his 1976 collection *The Tugman's Passage,* "*shows* even as it *tells*" (690). It is, in other words, an *essay* about the essay: both an essay and commentary on the essay. An elegant modesty attends and striates the entire *essai.*

Its opening paragraph marks "What I Think, What I Am" as an essay—in style and tone. That opening is also unhurried and indirect, the way essays are. Hoagland makes some essential points, proffers some crucial distinctions:

Our loneliness makes us avid column readers these days. The personalities in the San Francisco *Chronicle*, Chicago *Daily News*, New York *Post* constitute our neighbors now, some of them local characters but also the opinionated national stars. And movie reviewers thrive on our yearning for somebody emotional who is willing to pay attention to us and return week after week, year after year, through all the to-and-fro of other friends, to flatter us by pouring out his/her heart. They are essayists of a type, as Elizabeth Hardwick is, James Baldwin was. (690)

Hoagland's title suggests another such (crucial) distinction.

The essay established as the subject of "What I Think, What I Am," Hoagland next takes up a matter or two of contexts. Here he springs a surprise, his own essay by no means tracking a straight line. Before he is finished, the short story emerges as the fundamental form—not the essay, which Roland Barthes described as "a-generic," the form from which the genres descend. Thus Hoagland, who means what his opening paragraph has more suggested than declared: that all sorts of things march under the umbrella of "essay":

We sometimes hear that essays are an old-fashioned form, that so-and-so is the "last essayist," but the facts of the marketplace argue quite otherwise. Essays of nearly any kind are so much easier than short stories for a writer to sell, so many more see print, it's strange that though two fine anthologies remain that publish the year's best stories, no comparative collection exists for essays. Such changes in the reading public's taste aren't always to the good, needless to say. The art of telling stories predated even cave-painting, surely; and if we ever find ourselves living in caves again, it (with painting and drumming) will be the only art left, after movies, novels, photography, essays, biography, and all the rest have gone down the drain—the art to build from. (690–91)

"What I Think, What I Am" is a particularly effective essay on the essay, in part, because it is neither dogmatic in its claims nor thoroughgoing in its endorsement of and brief for the form ostensibly its subject. In the thirty years since Hoagland penned "What I Think, What I Am," the essay has enjoyed something of a rebirth, owing not a little to his wish come true: since 1985, the annual *Best American Essays*, under the general editorship of Robert Atwan, has appeared and is flourishing. The essay is much more popular now than when Hoagland wrote.

Story is the *site*, the fundamental site, "What I Think, What I Am" claims, and Hoagland focuses on the short story in order to develop the essay's difference. *That* now begins to emerge, this instance of the form taking a wonderfully, beguilingly mazy track (that very few academics would dare).

> One has the sense with the short story as a form that while everything may have been done, nothing has been overdone; it has a permanence. Essays, if a comparison is to be made, although they go back four hundred years to Montaigne, seem a mercurial, new-fangled, sometimes hokey affair that has lent itself to many of the excesses of the age, from spurious autobiography to spurious hallucination, as well as to the shabby careerism of traditional journalism. (691)

Exactly so! Relative to story, the essay as form *is* new, and newfangled, despite predecessors, notably in ancient Rome and long-ago Japan. It is a child of the Renaissance, from which came its empiricism, individualism, self-consciousness, and celebration of personality, along with a sometimes-uncomfortable bedfellow, Protestant inwardness. The form has indeed lent itself to excesses, not least the twentieth-century invention of the *article*. But extremism breeds reaction, often extreme reaction, and so against Montaignian reflection, perpetuated in the Romantic era, the heyday of the essay form, in this country as well as England, another kind of essay arose. That was the Baconian, which is more familiar than personal, and which derives generally from observation rather than reflection.

Befitting this rather new *thing*, with its penchant for excess, Hoagland next calls it, unflatteringly, "a greased pig." He then denigrates it without the heavy irony that attends White's well-known account of the essay as "a second-class citizen." Writes Hoagland, cleverly deflecting responsibility for the opprobrium:

> Essays are associated with the way young writers fashion a name—on plain, crowded newsprint in hybrid vehicles like the *Village Voice*, *Rolling Stone*, the *New York Review of Books*, instead of the thick paper stock and thin readership of *Partisan Review*. (691)

Immediately comes another swerve, Hoagland ostensibly continuing to distinguish, to render the essay's difference almost palpably. I say "ostensibly" because the distinction drawn, that of this essay's title, reveals itself over time as, instead, an essential link. Essays, says Hoagland, "hang somewhere on a line between two sturdy poles: this is what I think, and this is what I am" (691). Indeed, as I have claimed in both the present book and *Tracing the Essay*, these words—at least those before the colon—describe the form precisely: the essay is a *via media* creature, both a middle way and a site *between* literature and philosophy, experience and meaning, fiction and fact, process and product. But when Hoagland proceeds in the same sentence to repeat his own essay's title, we realize something else, *something more*; thinking and being cannot well assume a place alongside the dualities just mentioned. Rather than "between," both/and governs, for Hoagland clearly intends to link thinking and being. Even more, his evident point is that thinking is essential to being. May the way to being lie in, through, and by means of thinking?

Hoagland proceeds to distinguish, beginning, now, with the essay and autobiography. Note, though, that he immediately narrows his focus to *personal* essays, a very different approach from that with which he began, or so it seems. The link between the first sentence here and the previous one that includes repetition of the essay's title is not immediately clear or direct, at least to me; on reflection, I realize that "what I am" goes with autobiography. By the same token, "what I think," then, hearkens back to the beginning moments of the essay: Hoagland has been treating "what I think" in terms of all those kinds of writing indiscriminately lumped together and called essays. Moreover now he confirms and solidifies the link between autobiography and essay. Hoagland is right, therefore, contrary to my early impression, to narrow to personal essays, for in them the link with autobiography is indeed solid. Difference fades before association and similarity—precisely as Hoagland proceeds to make another set of distinctions altogether! "Autobiographies which aren't novels are generally extended essays, indeed," he writes; "a personal essay is like the human voice talking, its order the mind's natural flow, instead of a systematized outline of ideas." Then follows a major point concerning the formal integrity of essays—a plea, I might say, that they be read as *artistic wholes* (which, of course, connects with and establishes their meaningful literary qualities and merits):

> Though more wayward or informal than an article or treatise, somewhere it contains a point which is its real center, even if the point couldn't be uttered in fewer words than the essayist has used. Essays don't usually boil down to a summary, as articles do, and the style of the writer has a "nap" to it, a combination of personality and originality and energetic loose ends that stand up like the nap on a piece of wool and can't be brushed flat. Essays belong to the animal kingdom, with a surface that generates sparks, like a coat of fur, compared with the flat, conventional cotton of the magazine writer, who works in the vegetable kingdom, instead. (691)

These powerful, stunning words are, I think, little short of brilliant, connecting at once with both Annie Dillard's notion of essays as "feral" and Ezra Pound's of significant writing as "charged." Hoagland here captures, perhaps better than anyone before or since, the crucial importance of the essay's "surface"—in other words, the literalness—as he suggests the electrical power of the letter to set off sparks, resonant with what I am calling *lateral* reading.

Having so described the essay, Hoagland now presents the other side, completing the picture. Even if they possess an electric surface that "generates sparks,"

> essays, on the other hand, may have fewer "levels" than fiction, because we are not supposed to argue much about their meaning. In the old distinction between teaching and storytelling, the essayist, however cleverly he camouflages his intentions, is a bit of a teacher or reformer, and an essay is intended to convey the same point to each of us. (691)

In other words—my words—essays do not so much consist of "layers" as embody a lateral resonance. They do not—to think back to Dryden's opposition in his essay-poem *Religio Laici or A Laymans Faith*—require interpretation, or "expounding." Their "meaning" is presumably the same for "each of us."

In the next paragraph, Hoagland returns to stories and offers a further difference from essays. While his focus lies with the latter, his preference remains with the former, or at least (as he would likely say) his estimation of value and importance. Opening the paragraph, his own mind returns to "what I think," as well as to his earlier point concerning the enduring, abiding power of story:

> This emphasis upon mind speaking to mind is what makes essays less universal in their appeal than stories. They are addressed to an educated, perhaps a middle-class, reader, with certain presuppositions, a frame of reference, even a commitment to civility that is shared — not the grand and golden empathy inherent in every man or woman that a storyteller has a chance to tap. (691–92)

Here Hoagland taps into that enduring sense of a community of readers to which the essay supposedly appeals — "the common reader," perhaps. I for one doubt, however, that the essay's appeal is quite so limited as Hoagland's meticulously chosen words suggest — consider its increased, *general* importance just in the years since Hoagland wrote "What I Think, What I Am."

In any case, from this difference from story Hoagland again turns to a significant link between essay and story. In fact, inevitably recalling Richard Selzer's magisterial "A Worm from My Notebook," and directly resonant with it, Hoagland now considers that story is not infrequently *incorporated* in essays. "The artful 'I' of an essay," he thus begins, intent at first on a subtle, valuable distinction — a kind of putting-in-other-words,

> can be as chameleon as any narrator in fiction; and essays do tell a story quite as often as a short story stakes a claim to a particular viewpoint. Mark Twain's piece called "Cornpone Opinions," for example, which is about public opinion, begins with a vignette as vivid as any in *Huckleberry Finn*. (692)

Hoagland now swerves to a story of his own, about Twain himself, telling a story, in an essay, in "Cornpone Opinions," about what he thought; in other words, one, moreover, that resonates with the representation of the essayist that Hoagland has himself made earlier (e.g., "a bit of a teacher or reformer"; see also the opening of Scott Russell Sanders's wonderful essay on the essay "The Singular First Person," which opens with the writer's linking of essaying and declaiming from a soapbox). It is a long quotation and stands out for that very reason in an essay maybe only four or five times its length!

Twain says that when he was a boy of fifteen, he used to hang out a back window and listen to the sermons preached by a neighbor's slave standing on top of a woodpile: "He imitated the pulpit style of the several clergymen of the village, and did it well and with fine passion and energy. To me he was a wonder. I believed he was the greatest orator in the United States and would some day be heard from. But it did not happen; in the distribution of rewards he was overlooked. . . . He interrupted his preaching now and then to saw a stick of wood, but the sawing was a pretense—he did it with his mouth, exactly imitating the sound the bucksaw makes in shrieking its way through the wood. But it served its purpose, it kept his master from coming out to see how the work was getting along." (692; ellipsis in Hoagland)

But one paragraph remains in "What I Think, What I Am." The opening sentence represents a smooth transition from the story just told—or, rather, retold via quotation, itself a staple of essaying, as William H. Gass, among others, has noted. Hoagland here initiates another distinction, but then quickly reverts to the essay's opening focus on the various sins that the term covers. Distinction appears, but—again—soon fades, yielding place and importance before basic similarity, association, and vital link. Here as elsewhere, Hoagland is scrupulously modest about what an essay can and cannot do, what it is and is not—what it *is*, though, Hoagland never quite says. Indeed neither he nor anyone else can, because as he *shows*, the essay is not a thing, so it cannot be defined. You know it indirectly, the essay known precisely through its difference. In that sense, as I have been claiming, the essay lacks positive force (which is, of course, no negative judgment).

A novel would go on and tell us what happened next in the life of the slave—and we miss that. But the extraordinary flexibility of essays is what has enabled them to ride out rough weather and hybridize into forms that suit the times. And just as one of the first things a fiction writer learns is that he needn't actually be writing fiction to write a short story—that he can tell his own history or anybody's else as exactly as he remembers it and it will be "fiction" if it remains primarily a story—an essayist soon discovers that he doesn't have to tell the whole truth and nothing but the truth; he can shape or shave his memories, as long as the purpose is served of elucidating a truthful point. (692)

By now, of course, difference and similarity have met. "Primarily a story" marks the crucial difference between fiction, short or long, and the essay.

And as to that other form he has been using for comparison and contrast, Hoagland returns, appropriately, concluding his own essay, to the form's link with autobiography. I let him have the final word, agreeing with him in the main, yet continuing to think that the essay "hang[s] on a line somewhere between two sturdy poles," and grateful that this master has shared the "tumbling progression" of his mind with us.

> A personal essay is frequently not autobiographical at all, but what it does keep in common with autobiography is that, through its tone and tumbling progression, it conveys the quality of the author's mind. Nothing gets in the way. Because essays are directly concerned with the mind and the mind's idiosyncracy, the very freedom the mind possesses is bestowed on this branch of literature that does honor to it, and the fascination of the mind is the fascination of the essay. (692)

'Tis hard to say, if greater Want of Skill
Appear in *Writing* or in *Judging* ill;
But, of the two, less dang'rous is th' Offence,
To tire our *Patience,* than mis-lead our *Sense:*
Some few in *that,* but Numbers err in *this,*
Ten Censure wrong for one who Writes amiss.
—Alexander Pope, *An Essay on Criticism*

A Note on Writing the Essay

The Issue of Process versus Product

(with an essay by Cara McConnell)

INTRODUCING *The Art of the Personal Essay,* Phillip Lopate rejects the judgment borrowed from the Spanish philosopher Eduardo Nicol
that the essay is "*almost* literature" and "*almost* philosophy." I used these
phrases as an epigraph in my *Tracing the Essay* and have modified and extended them in the present book. While apparently accepting Walter Pater's
description of the essay's "unmethodical method," Lopate, himself an essayist of no mean accomplishment, offers this claim about one of the most
important, and most troubling, issues facing study, use, and incorporation
of the essay: "From my perspective," Lopate harrumphs, "there is no *almost*
about it: good essays are works of literary art. Their supposed formlessness
is more a strategy to disarm the reader with the appearance of unstudied
spontaneity than a reality of composition" (xxxvii–xxxviii). Surely, though,
the essayist engages in a ramble, such as has been brilliantly described by
Lydia Fakundiny, introducing *The Art of the Essay.* The ramble *is* "a reality

of composition" for the essay. But as so often with the essay, there is more to be said.

Even such obvious rambles as Thoreau's "Walking" and Hazlitt's "On Going a Journey" reflect clear and deliberate structure; they may ramble, but they are not random. The spontaneity—which cannot, of course, be both "studied" and itself—that a reader senses is more real than apparent. There is, operating here, in the essay, paradox, a certain mystery of both one thing and another, together, at the same time. As to spontaneity and structure together: the spontaneity, I cannot but surmise, is, finally, incorporated into a *structure discovered.*

I have no idea how either Thoreau or Hazlitt went about the daily work of writing, that "reality of composition" that Lopate rather teasingly mentions, whether either or both had a design in mind in starting. Shorter essays are, of course, more tractable, and even I can keep to plot when penning a four-pager. Writing an essay, Lydia Fakundiny says, you discover your destination in the going. Lopate strongly disagrees. The imaginative can be, and quite often is, more demanding, more challenging than the logical, requiring subtler mental acuity. When students hear "ramble" and "freedom," they frequently equate such with formlessness, license, and permission to write without regard for shape, direction, focus, or form. The results are almost always disastrous.

Take away a certain freedom from the essay, and you are left with something approaching that "awful object, 'the article,'" the essay's "opposite" (as William H. Gass has summarily dismissed it)—back, perhaps, with the ignoble five-paragraph "essay," whose point is spelled out at the end of the first and repeated at the beginning of the fifth, between them occurring the ordered and linear arguments necessary for proof. Essays are not, however, concerned with proof, rather with exploration; they are tentative to the degree that articles are definitive. They are also open, but openness does not automatically equate with or render permissible digressions; it does not, on the other hand, render them out of order, either. All *depends.*

The essay, it is but fair to acknowledge, is difficult to write, a fact that soon becomes woefully obvious to students assuming that "anything goes." Part of the difficulty stems from the essay's very protean nature and that in-betweenness that marks it as form. It both refuses to stay still, to submit to our needs for easy order of a merely logical sort, and functions not as an object but as a site or locus, where conflicting forces come together and often cross. So what to do, faced with a class who usually demand both definitions and clear procedural instruction? Students want, and expect, a formula, such as that which the five-paragraph "essay" makes readily available. They do not, in short, despite the palaver otherwise, want the individual or the particular.

It is not enough, although tempting, to say, Go read, and you will eventually see how to make one. Read enough essays, and it will be clear what you should do! Worse is to acquiesce and allow students to write what Virginia Woolf disparages as mere self-expression. The result will be something closely akin to diary entries. Worse still is to throw in the towel and conclude that you cannot teach the writing of essays, perhaps returning to the safety and ease of the sort of dreadful stuff that our composition classes all too often produce—and pass off as good, "college," "academic" writing. It may be the latter, but it is certainly not of the sort worthy of the word "good."

Faced with twenty or more students, still feeling a bit guilty for teaching creative writing without a license, and imagining that I ought to do more than oversee a good bit of thrashing about and even floundering, I have invoked, as I so often do, the way of compromise. I would tell the students to write a first draft caring not a whit about form or structure or direction or focus. "You can do that," I said, confidently. Is that not free writing, someone usually asks, to which I reply, "Maybe." Then I hasten on, taking away most all that I have given. Once you have completed that first draft, then rewrite from the get-go, I instruct, this time concerned with form and structure and focus and direction. Likely, I assure them, you will have discovered a point worthy of focus in writing that rambling first draft. If the first draft is self-expression, the second is something different, more artful. My method, this compromise, is driven by an idea, a disembodied one, the product of logic.

Over time I came to refine the advice, taking to heart such a savant as Hilaire Belloc. He is one, and Annie Dillard is another, who subscribes to the notion, I reckon, that writing has a will: you perhaps control it less than it controls you, or, rather, as Dillard puts it, responding to the question of who teaches you how to write, the page does. This is, I find, solid advice, and I still think you have to tap into the flow, direction, and will of your writing. "It wants to go somewhere," I tell my students. "Your job involves finding and then submitting to that will." Some students always nod in approval, but seldom have I noticed a light bulb going off over a tilted head.

At some point along the way, I started to reflect on my own experience writing. Experience is an able and capacious teacher, but it takes a savvy reader—as well, I suspect, as grace—to realize her lessons. By then I had learned, egregiously and shamefully late, the greatest lesson so far about writing. It came via a rejection of a collection of my autobiographical essays, the "teacher" a well-known editor: "I found your writing about the lives of your parents and their families particularly interesting, and moving," she kindly wrote. "You slow down a bit when you write of them, allow the details to accumulate weight."

There it was! A difference between the essay and the kind of writing I had so long done, the kind I had been taught to do, and been paid to do as a professor of literature, that is, as a scholar-critic. My details needed *weight*, and they would acquire that—perhaps—if I *slowed down*. The writer of the "article," driven by logic (and some lesser demands), knows where he or she is going and takes the most direct route, digressions the very worst of sin, as Byron's Don Juan opines. The direct route saves time, and the article is in a hurry. The essayist, on the other hand, is notoriously unhurried, time the very air that he breathes and in which she lives, moves, and has his or her being. Take your time, I thus tell my students. The essay is trying to teach you something about how to live your life.

The second best advice, I tell my students, after "slowing down," is *writing in chunks*. No doubt a more graceful way exists of making the point, more elegant phrasing, but I am partial to the colloquial. "Writing in chunks" harbors no pomposity, and I like to think, the alimentary assists the elementary.

Writing goes like this (I am thinking in these pages not so much of the critical essay, about the writing of which I have directed some comments in my introductory chapter, above): In no hurry, you pen, or "process," a sentence, crafting it in your head, or so you imagine. The page soon takes over, and by that inexact point it is collaborating, sometimes more responsible for the sentence than you are—not just for its size and its shape but also for its thought. Truth to tell, you think through writing, in and by means of it. This is exciting, heady; there is no way that you can think so precisely apart from the page, apart from writing down the page.

It is not reflection in which you are engaged, although I feel confident that reflecting is involved at some point. You do take a line out for a walk, allowing it to go where it will, following it, for as Annie Dillard finely says, the sentence is a "probe." So you are exploring, testing, trying out, weighing, and assessing. Essaying is (also) assaying: you mine; then you weigh.

A sentence is dependent upon the previous, on which it builds. Soon you have an edifice. You do not yet know what it is *of.*

Your concern is solely with the next sentence, the next thought, or, rather, the clarification and amplification of the thinking underway. You extend, "fare forward." If you do this part, each part, well enough, the whole will take care of itself. A chunk is manageable—by more or less ordinary writers, who generally lack the amazing capacities of the makers of literature, able, like chess masters, to hold so much in mind at once. This faith that all will work out—"and all shall be well" (Eliot, in *Four Quartets,* a poem that is also an essay—and an essay-poem that is in considerable part about writing)—you finally appreciate, even if you do not quite understand how it happens. I think grace is involved. But you have to be present: you have to slow down, to listen to and heed the words, to mine them for their willed direction. You have to be fully present, for right then, nothing else in the world matters. Sacrifice is necessary, along with commitment, dogged attention, scrupulousness, and submission.

What I am advocating may recall, unfortunately or no, Swift's commentary in his great satire *A Tale of a Tub,* whose speaker is a Modern Hack writer. At the conclusion—in which nothing is really concluded—the Hack writes: "I am now trying an experiment very frequent among modern authors; which is to write upon *Nothing*; when the subject is utterly exhausted, to let the pen still move on; by some called the ghost of wit, delighting to walk after the death of its body" (352). Perhaps you will remember that Hilaire Belloc titled one of his collections of essays *On Nothing.* The essayist, though, particularly the familiar essayist, writes *upon something*—see the titles of Bacon, or Montaigne, or Nancy Mairs, the tiny preposition pointing to a definite subject outside the self. He does not pretend that his treatment of the subject, whatever that may be, is grand or grandiose, humility being his hallmark, this not quite "second-class citizen." Today, of course, if you decline to rant and rave about yourself, à la the boorish self-aggrandizements of professional wrestlers and politicians, who will notice you? The essay keeps an alternative alive.

Hemingway was not an essayist, although he was a great writer, not least of "nonfiction." He also knew a thing or two to pass along, and one of the most helpful is the advice to stop writing while you still have something left to get down. You tire, physically, emotionally, after a while — thus few of us can go at it, with the concentration and intensity, and submission, above all, submission, required for more than two or three hours at a spell. But you also realize, full well, when you have completed a segment, a section — *a chunk*. At that point, you must stop.

Perhaps above all, you must not hurry; take your time. Your work consists of not the whole essay, nor just one sentence, nor one paragraph. Your work, rather, consists of a chunk — only you can tell how long that is, what it consists of, when you are ready to move to another chunk.

Somewhere, I reckon, between this stoppage and sitting to the computer again, in the morning, say, or when you again take up your pen with pleasure and delight, art happens — or something reasonably close to it. The "chunk" has, as it were, a life of its own; it is very nearly self-sufficient, for all practical purposes complete in and of itself, although it most likely would make too little sense to leave it alone. So you rest a bit.

For a long while, a Luddite, I praised the fountain pen as writing instrument, following Belloc's embrace of "an easy pen" and fine paper, much like the later Edmund White. In the past two years I have finally made the switch and now accept that the computer can, and often does, facilitate writing. Among other advantages, it makes easy the fleshing-out of ideas and feelings, the further development of chunks.

I have found that, when I am fully engaged with the writing, my mind starts working again on the writing after a period, of undeterminable duration, of rest. It gets refreshed, somehow. Ideally, relation swims into ken, connection suggests itself with the preceding chunk, and only with the preceding chunk. You have, in other words, a transition; you are ready to move on, begin again, all over again, although not quite.

Never force a point, or a sentence. When you learn to slow down, you can expect to become a bit more patient. Writing does not equate to waiting — you need not stare at the wall, or into open space, for hours, as I once did, in graduate school, trying to write to please a favorite professor.

(I never did learn what he was looking for.) You write, by the way, at least in my judgment, to please neither yourself nor any other person, real or imagined. I am not even sure that you try to please. Pleasure comes as a result of submitting to the will of the writing and then paying homage, or responding, by crafting "comely and muscular" sentences (Cynthia Ozick).

Now you are in the midst of a larger direction, one that, probably, you did not see while entranced in the previous segment. Is this, then, process? Yes. But it is also more, and different, for you are *in the process of crafting product*. It may not be art, but it *is* surely craft. In any case, you still face the same problems as before this larger direction swam into ken; you must repeat the work of writing done in the previous chunk, each requiring the same attention and scrupulosity. Even at essay's close, you are working in chunks, your final paragraph just as demanding as the first or second or twenty-third.

In her magnificent (and sometimes maddening) little book *The Writing Life*, Annie Dillard describes her process of composition as laying parts out along a table, which she ultimately cobbles together. Scott Russell Sanders has said he does something similar. You can see such stitching in both their essays. That is less a negative criticism than a suggestion that gives the lie to writing as organic. (I distinguish my advice here from Dillard's sense of correcting or "perfecting" as you proceed, for I long ago gave up the— debilitating—idea that one sentence, one idea, one paragraph, one chunk had to appear finished before moving on.) I once described writing the essay as like making a quilt, although I would now offer this caveat or at least clarification: the parts of which the text(ile) are made are not them- selves remnants of some previous effort. The metaphor helps, nevertheless, to indicate the cultural, rather than natural, kind of thing we are dealing with—an artifact.

And yet—there *is* a sense of organic growth, at least within the individ- ual chunks. The essay, I cannot but conclude, is both product and process. Product derives from process, obviously, but product is not limited to the whole; properly managed, a chunk is a product, too, one of several—or, many—that must be related. The writing itself cooperates with you in find- ing those relations. You may need only a transitional tag when you return to work, facing a new chunk to be carved out. You may, of course, need much more, including time and space to develop connections, time and space that promote discovery. It may be, too, that you will need to return after the whole is written, and supply then needed connections. Because relations matter here, not differences, which are never absolute between product and process, we can now appreciate that process is never transcended, or left behind, as product emerges. We cannot, then, separate the two completely, despite my former attempts to posit a bipartite structure as involved in the movement from process to product. The implications of this recognition are considerable.

There is always more to be said—and that more often than not in the form of "and yet." Process and product are two of those "things"—and they are Legion—about which you reach judgment by comparing and weighing them with each other, a notion that is key to reading well, reading responsibly.

Here I add, and end the book with, an essay written at the end of a recent semester by a student in my Freshman Honors class. The assignment was open, so long as students wrote, preferably but not necessarily in essay form, about a text, texts, topic(s), or issues treated during our time together. Cara McConnell chose, uniquely in the group of twenty-three, to write about writing, and produced the following *essay* about essaying and "the joy of writing." It was extraordinarily well received in workshop, from a highly critical and sometimes fractious group; it appears here virtually as it was presented there. I offer it here, with permission, as testimony to what can happen when the essay's invitation is accepted and welcomed.

To My Classmates: The Joy (or at Least Bearableness) of Essay Writing

Cara McConnell

When I was in grade school, there were three yearly occurrences I absolutely dreaded.

Right before school started, I would have to go to the doctor for my annual check-up. I would nervously squirm on the cold examination table until the moment the door opened and the fateful question would burst out of my mouth: "do I have to get a shot this time?" Although the mere thought of vaccinations or blood work still makes every muscle in my body tense up, looking back, I have to admit, the whole ordeal really wasn't that painful—from the condemning "yes" to the injection was only about thirty minutes, and the shot itself was never as bad as I feared it would be. There were much worse things in life—even in my own young life—like what awaited me during Christmas break.

After all the season's eatings, from Halloween candy to Christmas cookies, there was the ever-frightful return to the dentist. Perhaps you had the luxury of going to a dentist whose primary clientele weren't constantly shrieking and crying five-to-eight-year olds; I, however, had no such luck. And regardless of how great an effort I had made in the previous twelve months to rid my teeth of plaque, I would always have to get a filling. Combine the lovely mood of my fellow dental detainees with metal contraptions wedging my mouth open for hours on end, and you create the kind of ambiance that would put the average medieval torture chamber to shame. But even then, this ordeal only took up one afternoon a year, and afterwards, while my mouth was still numb from novocaine, my mom would take me for a milkshake at the Baskin Robbins on the way home. So really, even this fearful event was quite short and manageable.

Spring brought the worst torture of all. Starting in third grade the spring research paper became a horrible part of each year. Let me explain. As a child I loved reading, and eventually, as all bookish little kids do, I began to want to write my own stories. My teachers encouraged my desire to write, and would even give me extra creative writing assignments. Papers, however, were a completely different matter. After spring break, I would receive a long, detailed schedule of all the due dates for research and note cards and outlines and drafts until finally, at some point way off in the distance, there'd be a date for the final paper. For a nine-year-old, a two-month writing process is about the most mind-bendingly long and terrifying thing to think about. Two months of researching, of drafting, of red-pen revising, until finally you have to hand in the culmination of what feels like your entire young life's work (on something ridiculous like starfish, no less), was too much for such a short-term-oriented mind to grasp. The whole process was supposed slowly to ease me into junior high and high school "essay" writing, but instead it never stopped being anything but a tedious, torturous ordeal. As the fun little creative writing assignments I loved phased out of the curriculum in favor of more papers, I began to hate writing.

Things really began to bottom out for me writing-wise in seventh grade, when my teacher introduced a familiar little concept known as the eight-point paragraph. In case you've forgotten—or more likely, it's been so ingrained in you it's now second nature—the eight-point consists of a topic sentence, concrete detail, two sentences of analysis, another concrete detail, another pair of analyses, and a concluding statement. This was apparently so crucial to my writing ability that for a while I had to fill out worksheets where I would break down every body paragraph I wrote in a paper into this format. Each time I turned in another paragraph-construction worksheet, I became less creative and more mechanical. I learned how to build a strong analytical paper, but it came at a high price: a price I didn't realize was so dear until recently.

I'm sure you've been taught the same things I have about writing. You know the rules. You've written your fair share of eight-point para-graphs, with topic sentences that support a well-crafted, all-encompassing thesis—and you know exactly where that thesis goes: at the end of the introduction. You've used "one" when you mean "you" and reworked every sentence to eliminate even the mere suggestion of the pronoun "I." And, although it's never explicitly taught, to be truly insightful and to relate truly to your topic is expressly forbidden. Basically, you've learned to remove every glimmer of personality and creativity from your writing in favor of an admittedly strong writing formula.

But essay writing should be anything but formulaic, impersonal, and uncreative.

A lot of colleges call their required English course "University Writing." For a good chunk of the people who take such a class, it is the last English class they will ever have to take. The goal, therefore, is to make them as good, or at least understandable, writers as possible, lest they torture their future professors with comma splices and passive voice for the rest of their collegiate days. Ours, however, is an Honors class—something beyond the bare minimum—and as such, there is a slightly different expectation, that, rather than come out of this class merely comprehensible, we come out of it good academic writers, but more importantly, good *essay* writers.

Towards the beginning of the semester, Professor Atkins gave a lecture he called "The Joy of Writing." If you recall, this was just a few classes after we'd done our first in-class writing. At this point, the joys of writing for an English class were a completely foreign concept for me, and nothing put me less in a mood to be convinced of them than an in-class essay. I was still an adamant adherer to "the rules": the detached, academic voice I used in papers I wrote for English and the more personal voice I used in the post I wrote for my blog and the editorials I wrote for the newspaper absolutely did not mix. To use the same sort of voice and style I used outside of class—even in small doses—seemed unpolished and lacking the sort of seriousness academic writing demands. Likewise, to relate my own personal experiences or theories about life to the thoughts of great authors felt like the mistake of a very cocky youth, who assumes he or she knows the ways of the world despite supposedly having such little experience and wisdom.

Atkins's lecture changed all that for me. In case you missed out, here's a recap of what he said. Atkins first made a clear distinction between papers (or as he termed them, "articles") and essays. Articles are the sorts of detached, academic papers that I had written since grade school. Essays, however, are lively; you can tell an essay is written by a person, not a machine. As such, an essay breaks "the rules": it uses first person, it breaks the eight-point model, it digresses and goes where it must, rather than following some strict and straight path. But most important, essays are personal. They are about the subject, but they are also equally about the author. They are expressions of relation: how the author relates to the subject, how the subject relates to something greater, and how it all relates to the audience.

Maybe I had just been waiting for someone to say something I already subconsciously knew—that writing, at least about literature, should never be so detached. In another paper I wrote this semester, I argued that literature is the study of life, that it's how you gain wisdom about living through the experiences of others. Why, then, if this is the case, should we feel the need to be so detached? We, even as freshmen and sophomores in college, surely have some valid personal perspective on life in general. We can begin to relate our experience to those of Eliot, of Joyce, of Flaubert, and through relating we begin to understand the messages of these authors, and we begin to learn the life knowledge they are trying to impart. Good writing goes beyond good execution of your ideas. To be able to explain and show examples of the *via media* in literature is merely half the battle—in order to grasp the truth within literature you must be able to relate it to your own understanding of yourself and the world.

In *An Essay on Criticism*, Alexander Pope writes,

If, where the *Rules* not far enough extend,
(Since Rules were made but to promote their End)
Some Lucky LICENCE answers to the full
Th' Intent propos'd, *that Licence* is a *Rule*.

Just as the old rules about personal pronouns and eight-point paragraphs were meant merely to direct the development of basic writing skills and not restrict later on, the "new rules" need to be understood as the mere directives they're intended to be. Not every paper—especially outside the realm of the English department—can break the old rules completely. You must know your audience and relate to them on their level, whether it be through more personal writing in an essay in your English class or more professional, polished analyses for a professor.

Writing shouldn't be a pain. Essays shouldn't loom in the future like a dreaded yearly physical or a trip to a torturous dentist's office. The only reason they do loom, besides deadlines and the fact that most of us (myself included) leave them until the last minute, is that the concept of an essay has been so warped and bastardized that it is no longer a creative, free form of expression but something that is heavily restricted by rules and expectations. After we'd workshopped several essays, Atkins said that an essay is a hard thing to define, and rightly so. To define it is to restrict it in a way that is detrimental to the creative process; to define it is to deny that essays are as individual as the people who write them.

So, if it's three a.m. and you've just realized that you've read my paper and can't remember a single word of the last five pages, at least wake up and pay attention to this last part.

I found the joy in writing, and it's really quite simple. There's even a small reminder at the top of every paper you write—your name. Essays are about you. They're about your ideas, your insight, your introspection. So, even if you can't write in first person, clearly be present in your writing. Bring your enthusiasm. Bring your style. Take risks with your writing— take the risk of sharing a part of who you are with your audience. Then you can write something you truly enjoy, something that truly matters.

WORKS CITED

Atkins, G. Douglas. "Art and Anger: Upon Taking Up the Pen Again—On Self(e)-Expression." *JAC* 20 (2000): 414–25.

———. *Estranging the Familiar: Toward a Revitalized Critical Writing.* Athens: U of Georgia P, 1992.

———. "Going against the Grain: Deconstruction and the Scriblerians." *The Scriblerian* 17 (1985): 113–17.

———. "In Other Words: Gardening for Love—The Work of the Essayist." *Kenyon Review* 13 (1991): 56–69 (rpt. *Estranging the Familiar*).

———. "On Writing Well: or, Springing the Genie from the Inkpot—A Modest Proposal." *JAC* 20 (2000): 73–86.

———. "Poetic Strategies in *An Essay on Criticism,* Lines 200–559." *South Atlantic Bulletin* 44 (1979): 43–47.

———. *Tracing the Essay: Through Experience to Meaning.* Athens: U of Georgia P, 2005.

Bacon, Francis. *Francis Bacon,* ed. Brian Vickers. Oxford Authors. Oxford: Oxford UP, 1996.

Baldwin, James. *The Fire Next Time.* New York: Dial, 1963.

———. *Notes of a Native Son.* 1955. Boston: Beacon, 1985.

Belloc, Hilaire. *Hills and the Sea.* 1906. Marlboro VT: Marlboro P, n.d.

———. *On Nothing and Kindred Subjects.* London: Methuen, 1908.

Berry, Wendell. *The Art of the Commonplace: The Agrarian Essays,* ed. Norman Wirzba. Washington DC: Counterpoint, 2002.

Bloom, Harold. *Shakespeare: The Invention of the Human.* New York: Riverhead, 1998.

Browning, Robert. "Fra Lippo Lippi." *Norton Anthology of English Literature* II, 6th ed., ed. M. H. Abrams et al. New York: Norton, 1993.

Carson, Anne. Interview, by Mary Gannon. *Poets & Writers Magazine* 29 (March–April 2001): 26–33.

Chesterton, G. K. "A Piece of Chalk." In Lopate.

Cowley, Abraham. "Of Solitude." *Essays.* London: Cassell and Co., 1901.

Davie, Donald. *These the Companions.* Cambridge: Cambridge UP, 1982.

Davis, Walter A. *The Act of Interpretation: A Critique of Literary Reason.* Chicago: U of Chicago P, 1978.

Dawson, Christopher. *The Spirit of the Oxford Movement*. London: Sheed and Ward, 1933.

Dillard, Annie. *For the Time Being*. New York: Knopf, 1999.

———. Introduction. *The Best American Essays 1988*, ed. Annie Dillard. New York: Ticknor and Fields, 1988.

———. *Teaching a Stone to Talk: Expeditions and Encounters*. New York: Harper and Row, 1983.

———. *The Writing Life*. New York: Harper and Row, 1989.

Dobrée, Bonamy. *English Essayists*. London: Collins, 1946.

Dryden, John. *Of Dramatick Poesie: An Essay. Preceded by a Dialogue on Poetic Drama by T. S. Eliot*. London: Frederick Etchells and Hugh Macdonald, 1928.

———. *Poems and Fables,* ed James Kinsley. Oxford: Oxford UP, 1962.

Eliot, George. *Adam Bede*. 1856. New York: Signet, 1961.

Eliot, T. S. *After Strange Gods*. New York: Harcourt, Brace, 1934.

———. *Collected Poems 1909–1962*. New York: Harcourt, Brace, 1963.

———. *Essays Ancient and Modern*. London: Faber and Faber, 1936.

———. *For Lancelot Andrewes*. London: Faber and Gwyer, 1928.

———. *The Idea of a Christian Society*. New York: Harcourt, Brace, 1940.

———. *Notes Towards the Definition of Culture*. New York: Harcourt, Brace, 1949.

———. *The Sacred Wood*. London: Methuen, 1920.

———. *Selected Essays*, 3rd ed. London: Faber and Faber, 1951.

———. *A Sermon*. Cambridge: Cambridge UP, 1948.

Emerson, Ralph Waldo. *Emerson's Prose and Poetry,* ed. Joel Porte and Saundra Morris. New York: Norton, 2001.

———. *Essays and Lectures,* ed. Joel Porte. New York: Library of America, 1983.

Epstein, Joseph. *A Line Out for a Walk*. New York: Norton, 1991.

———. *Plausible Prejudices*. New York: Norton, 1985.

Fadiman, Anne. *Ex Libris: Confessions of a Common Reader*. New York: Farrar, Straus and Giroux, 1998.

Fakundiny, Lydia, ed. *The Art of the Essay*. Boston: Houghton Mifflin, 1991.

———. "Autobiographical Essay." *Encyclopedia of the Essay,* ed. Tracy Chevalier. London: Fitzroy Dearborn, 1997. 41–43.

———. Email letter to author, May 24, 2006.

Fitzgerald, F. Scott. *The Crack-Up,* ed. Edmund Wilson. New York: New Directions, 1945.

Gass, William H. *Habitations of the Word*. New York: Simon and Schuster, 1985.

Good, Graham. *The Self Observed: Rediscovering the Essay*. London: Routledge, 1988.

Greenblatt, Stephen. *Renaissance Self-Fashioning*. Chicago: U of Chicago P, 1980.

Hartman, Geoffrey H. *Criticism in the Wilderness: The Study of Literature Today*. New Haven CT: Yale UP, 1980.

Hazlitt, William. "On Going a Journey." In Fakundiny.

Hesse, Hermann. *Siddharta,* trans. Hilda Rosner. New York: New Directions, 1951.

Hoagland, Edward. "What I Think, What I Am." In Fakundiny.

Hume, David. *Selected Essays,* ed. Stephen Copley and Andrew Edgar. World's Classics. Oxford: Oxford UP, 1993.

Hurston, Zora Neale. "How It Feels to Be Colored Me." In Fakundiny.

Johnson, Samuel. *Rasselas, Poems, and Selected Prose,* ed. Bertrand H. Bronson. New York: Holt, Rinehart and Winston, 1952.

————. "The Solitude of the Country." In Lopate.

Kenner, Hugh. *Paradox in Chesterton.* London: Sheed and Ward, 1948.

Krutch, Joseph Wood. "No Essays, Please!" *Saturday Review* 4:10 (March 10, 1951): 18–19, 35. Rpt. in *The Dolphin Reader,* ed. Douglas Hunt. Boston: Houghton Mifflin, 1986. 1030–35.

Lewis, C. S. *Reflections on the Psalms.* New York: Harcourt, Brace, 1958.

Lopate, Phillip, ed. *The Art of the Personal Essay.* New York: Anchor-Doubleday, 1994.

Lukács, Georg. *Soul and Form,* trans. Anna Bostock. Cambridge MA: MIT P, 1974.

Lytle, Andrew. *The Hero with the Private Parts.* Baton Rouge: Louisiana State UP, 1966.

Mairs, Nancy. *Plaintext.* Tucson: U of Arizona P, 1986.

Meynell, Alice. *Prose and Poetry.* Centenary Ed., intro. by V. Sackville-West. London: Jonathan Cape, 1947.

Miller, J. Hillis. *Poets of Reality: Six Twentieth-Century Writers.* Cambridge MA: Belknap-Harvard UP, 1965.

Montaigne, Michel de. *Essays,* trans. Donald M. Frame. Stanford CA: Stanford UP, 1954.

Morowitz, David. Introduction. *Trifles Make Perfection: The Selected Essays of Joseph Wechsberg,* ed. David Morowitz. Boston: Godine, 1999.

Oates, Joyce Carol. Introduction. *The Best American Essays 1992,* ed. Joyce Carol Oates. New York: Ticknor and Fields, 1992.

Orwell, George. "Reflections on Gandhi." In Fakundiny.

Ozick, Cynthia. *Metaphor and Memory.* New York: Knopf, 1989.

Park, Clara Claiborne. *Rejoining the Common Reader.* Evanston IL: Northwestern UP, 1991.

Paulin, Tom. *The Day-Star of Liberty: William Hazlitt's Radical Style.* London: Faber and Faber, 1998.

Pickering, Samuel F., Jr. *A Continuing Education.* Hanover NH: UP of New England, 1985.

————. *The Right Distance.* Athens: U of Georgia P, 1987.

Pope, Alexander. *Pastoral Poetry and* An Essay on Criticism, ed. Aubrey L. Williams. Twickenham Ed. I. London: Methuen; New Haven CT: Yale UP, 1961.

Pound, Ezra. *ABC of Reading.* London: Routledge, 1934.

Root, Robert L., Jr. *E. B. White: The Emergence of an Essayist.* Iowa City: U of Iowa P, 1999.

Rosenberg, Beth Carole, and Jeanne Dubino, eds. *Virginia Woolf and the Essay.* London: Palgrave, 1997.

Sanders, Scott Russell. *The Force of Spirit.* Boston: Beacon, 2000.

———. *A Private History of Awe*. New York: Farrar, Straus, and Giroux, 2006.

———. *Secrets of the Universe: Scenes from the Journey Home*. Boston: Beacon, 1991.

Schneidau, Herbert N. *Sacred Discontent: The Bible and Western Tradition*. Baton Rouge: Louisiana State UP, 1976.

Selzer, Richard. "An Absence of Windows." In Fakundiny.

———. "A Worm from My Notebook." In Fakundiny.

Shakespeare, William. *Major Plays and the Sonnets*, ed. G. B. Harrison. New York: Harcourt, Brace, 1948.

Sisson, C. H. *The Avoidance of Literature*, ed. Michael Schmidt. Manchester: Carcanet, 1978.

———. *David Hume*. Edinburgh: Ramsay Head P, 1976.

———. *The Discarnation, or How the Flesh Became Word and Dwelt among Us*. Sevenoaks, Eng.: n.p., 1967.

Smith, Alexander. *Dreamthorp*. London, 1863.

Strunk, William, Jr., and E. B. White. *The Elements of Style*. New York: Macmillan, 1959.

Sutherland, James. *English Satire*. Cambridge: Cambridge UP, 1958.

Swift, Jonathan. Gulliver's Travels *and Other Writings,* ed. Louis A. Landa. Boston: Houghton Mifflin-Riverside, 1960.

Tate, Allen. Foreword. In Lytle.

Thoreau, Henry David. *The Portable Thoreau,* ed. Carl Bode. New York: Penguin, 1947.

West, Andrew C. MA thesis, U of Kansas, 2005.

White, E. B. *Essays*. New York: Harper and Row, 1977.

Woolf, Virginia. *The Common Reader*. New York: Harcourt, Brace, 1925.

———. *The Common Reader,* Second Series. London: Hogarth, 1932.

———. "The Death of the Moth." In Fakundiny.

Wordsworth, William. Preface to *Lyrical Ballads* and *The Prelude. Norton Anthology of English Literature* II, 6th ed., ed. M. H. Abrams et al. New York: Norton, 1993.